A Web of Relationship

A Web of Relationship

Women in the Short Stories
of Mary Wilkins Freeman

MARY R. REICHARDT

University Press of Mississippi
Jackson & London

Copyright © 1992 by University Press of Mississippi
Manufactured in the United States of America

95   94   93   92   4   3   2   1

The paper in this book meets the guidelines for permanence and durability of the
Committee on Publication Guidelines for Book Longevity of the Council on Library
Resources.

Library of Congress Cataloging-in-Publication Data

Reichardt, Mary R.
    A web of relationship : women in the short stories of Mary Wilkins Freeman /
Mary R. Reichardt.
        p.   cm.
    Includes bibliographical references (p.   ) and index.
    ISBN 0-87805-555-X
    1. Freeman, Mary Eleanor Wilkins, 1852–1930—Characters—Women.
    2. Women in literature.   3. Short story.   I. Title.
    PS1713.R45   1992
    813'.4—dc20   91-32352
                                                                CIP

British Library Cataloging-in-Publication data available

to

J. E.

CONTENTS

ACKNOWLEDGMENTS

Parts of the following chapters appeared in earlier forms in journals and collections. The author gratefully acknowledges permission to use this material:

Chapter 3, in *Legacy* 4 (Fall, 1987), reprinted in *Critical Essays on Mary Wilkins Freeman*, ed. Shirley Marchalonis (Boston: G. K. Hall, 1991).

Chapter 4, in *Joinings and Disjoinings: The Significance of Marital Status in Literature*, eds. JoAnna Stephens Mink and Janet Doubler Ward (Bowling Green, Ohio: Popular Press, 1991).

Chapter 6, in *American Literary Realism* 22 (Winter, 1990).

Appendix (list of Freeman's short stories), compiled with Philip Eppard, in *American Literary Realism* 23 (Fall, 1990).

In addition, I would like to express my appreciation to others who have helped bring this project to fruition: the National Endowment for the Humanities, for a travel grant that allowed me to conduct research in Randolph, Massachusetts, and Brattleboro, Vermont; the Interlibrary Loan Department at the University of Wisconsin-Madison, for patient handling of many requests; and the Faculty Development Center and English Department of the University of St. Thomas, for the grant and release-time support requisite to completing this work. I would also like to thank Edna Hesford of Randolph, Massachusetts, and Henry Cooke IV, historian at the Randolph First Congregational Church, for their kind assistance.

INTRODUCTION

In Mary Wilkins Freeman's superb short story "The Revolt of 'Mother,'" mother Sarah Penn, frustrated by her husband's refusal to tell her why he is building yet another barn when he has failed to provide his own family with an adequate home, admonishes her young daughter, "You ain't found out yet we're women-folks, Nanny Penn. . . . You ain't seen enough of men-folks yet to. One of these days you'll find it out, an' then you'll know that we know only what men-folks think we do, so far as any use of it goes, an' how we'd ought to reckon men-folks in with Providence, an' not complain of what they do any more than we do of the weather."[1]

In a sense, Mary Wilkins Freeman spent her entire literary career, a long and prolific one, discovering, exploring, and coming to terms with what it meant in her generation and area of the country, a time and place marked by rapid social and economic change, to be "women-folks." Although an immensely popular writer in her day, Freeman has only recently been rediscovered and reevaluated as a realistic recorder of the status and sensibility of the late nineteenth-century and early twentieth-century New England woman.

Freeman was more than prolific; her writing was voluminous. Author of fourteen novels, nearly 250 short stories, several plays, and numerous poems, children's works, and non-fiction articles, Freeman took to heart William Dean Howells's injunction that literature should "cease to lie about life" and imbued her fiction with the reality she knew best, daily life in the largely impoverished, preindustrial New England village. In locating her work in a particular time and place, and in providing realistic detail and authentic dialogue, Freeman has most often been classified as a local-colorist, of some interest but only minor influence in the development of American literary realism. Freeman's work, however, extends beyond the limits of this category. Rather than merely describing surface detail and fact, Freeman probes deeply and perceptively into the motives, fears, and aspirations of her many characters, thus showing herself not only a local-color realist but an anticipator of modern psychological literature as well. Her themes are not merely confined to a particular time and place but achieve a universality that merits Freeman a permanent position in the literary canon.

In writing of what she knew best, Freeman was most concerned with the inner world of women. The village community into which her women are born, where they live out their entire lives, and where they die is a rigid one in which women's roles are strictly defined. Within this tightly controlled framework, Freeman's women strive for an understanding of the roles and responsibilities assigned to them largely by tradition and religion. They test the limits of their freedom through their relationships with and responses to others; they subsequently learn the moral and personal consequences of their acquiescence to or rejection of the expectations imposed on them by the larger community.

In recent years, certain critics such as Marjorie Pryse, Susan Allen Toth, and Michele Clark have lauded Freeman primarily for her portrayal of women who rebel actively against the patriarchal restrictions imposed on them, drawing on the strength of their own wills to attain some measure of individual freedom. Such frequently anthologized stories as "A New England Nun," "A Village Singer," and "The Revolt of 'Mother,'" each of which has as its protagonist a seemingly strong, rebellious woman, are prominent in Freeman's canon and rightly deserve praise. However, limited exposure to Freeman's entire corpus of work has tended to circumscribe our understanding of her themes and skew our judgment of her intentions as an author. The rebellious woman, in fact, constitutes only one image, although an important one, in Freeman's overall fictional portrait of women and womanhood. Freeman's mind and art are much more comprehensive than an assessment based on only a handful of her stories would suggest. Freeman probes equally as sharply into the lives and personalities of women who accept the Victorian "true womanhood" ideal of mother and wife; women rejected by men who feel their lives are now worthless and their futures bleak; women frustrated with and yet submissive to the confines of marriage; women whose sole means of solidarity with other women is through self-aggrandizing gossip; women struggling to conceal a desperate, encroaching poverty; and women who must deal on a daily basis with the twin hardships of advancing age and loneliness. Despite a wide range of subject matter in her large corpus of work, Freeman's overarching theme is the way in which turn-of-the-century New England women of every type struggled toward selfhood despite straitened circumstances and often repressive familial and community relationships. Freeman's women protagonists, therefore, form the backbone of her fiction and, looked at collectively, give us insight not only into Freeman's art but into her vision of women's experiences in this time and place.

Unlike Huck Finn or other male protagonists in nineteenth-century American fiction, Freeman's women are unable to "light out" to new territories to find fulfillment; they are instead inextricably caught up in, and defined by, a web of relationship. Freeman's strength as a delineator of character lies in her ability to express what has been called a "quiet realism," one that focuses on the subtle, unspoken, and often extremely tenuous bonds that hold people together in this web of relationship. As much as her New England predecessor Hawthorne, with whom she has often been compared, Freeman is concerned with the "magnetic chain of humanity," the vital links between human beings that bind them together in some spiritual—and thus ineffable—way (Hawthorne, 285). Like Hawthorne, too, Freeman often illustrates those connections by use of "negative examples"; that is those people who, whether through pride or circumstance, break from these bonds and are subsequently deformed or perverted in character. Time and again she illustrates the pernicious effects of the strong Puritan will. Barney Thayer in the novel *Pembroke* (1894) represents an extreme example of this phenomenon that is usually expressed in more subtle ways in Freeman's fiction; a young man possessed of a strong, prideful will, Barney rashly breaks off his engagement to a young woman after quarreling with the girl's father. Over the years, as Barney persists in unforgiveness, his back becomes increasingly hunched, an outward symbol of his diseased inner will.

It is in the end Freeman's women characters who show themselves concerned with forming and preserving bonds, taking care of relationships. Their search for identities of their own begins in their relationship with or to other people, other things, or their God, and reaches fruition only through a process of defining themselves through, around, and sometimes despite, those others.

As a result, Freeman's women are often inwardly torn in a double struggle: both a fierce urge to assert their independent natures and satisfy their individual needs and an equally strong desire to build and maintain relationships with others, which for a dutiful woman usually meant self-sacrifice. In Freeman's mind the struggle is a moral one. The arena, the human conscience, appears small, but the fight is every bit as looming and fraught with terror as Ahab's legendary battle with the white whale in *Moby Dick*. Freeman came, after all, from Puritan stock; she had inherited what she herself termed that "troublesome New England conscience," a moral earnestness at once profound and agonizingly insistent. "I . . . [was] born in the very hotbed of Orthodoxy," she once wrote to a friend. "I am . . . tacked fast . . . by the woefully strong tacks of my New England conscience, which holds me in spite of other strains of blood" (Kendrick, 333).

Reviewers of Freeman's work through the years have been quick to point out the pervading spiritual overtone of her work. Perry Westbrook, for example, notes that in 1896 the French reviewer Mme Theresa Blanc found Freeman's work "strange," hardly the type of detached clinical realism she recognized in such writers as Balzac and Zola. "It is this spirit superimposed on a rigid physical realism that strikes the modern, materialistic Frenchwoman as strange," Westbrook concludes (108). He himself saw the recurrent "tragedy" in Freeman's stories as a response to the "hopeless spiritual bankruptcy" of post–Civil War New England life. Edward Foster's 1956 biography *Mary E. Wilkins Freeman* labeled Freeman's characters no less than "undefeated neurotics" in their moral dilemmas and spiritual quests: "Neither code nor church can bring them peace. . . . Necessarily, they are frustrated and neurotic to a degree. Yet the thrust toward love and achievement and a sense of belonging cannot be killed. They are all . . . seeking a wholeness of spirit and a fullness of life almost impossible of attainment in the village as Mrs. Freeman knew it" (191).

Abigail Hamblen's 1966 *The New England Art of Mary E. Wilkins Free-man* calls Freeman's stories stark "records of sin and agony, courage and pride, loss of faith. . . . Nothing is glossed over" (8).

In Freeman's New England villages, where the spirit and fervor of Puritan Christianity had long been on the wane leaving only its "ves-tigial conscience" behind, both men and women find themselves heavily burdened by guilt, often over mere scruples, which seeks to be expiated. Far more often than the men in Freeman's world, it is the women who actively pursue the "thrust toward love and achievement and a sense of belonging," which Foster speaks of, in order to find some degree of inner peace or fulfillment. In doing so, they are "care-ful" in the basic sense of the word; their sense of personal morality is based on their role as caretaker. As Carol Gilligan has found in *In a Different Voice: Psychological Theory and Women's Development,* "women not only define themselves in a context of human relation-ship but also judge themselves in terms of their ability to care. Wom-en's place . . . has been that of nurturer, caretaker, and helpmate, the weaver of those networks of relationships on which she in turn relies" (17). This statement certainly holds true for the majority, if not all, of Freeman's many women characters. In striving to form and main-tain relationships, then, Freeman's women not only search for their own identities but also, conscious of the moral dimensions of such relationships, "work out their salvation in fear and trembling."

In searching for intimacy and connection, Freeman's women are more often than not frustrated. In the end, they often fail to achieve relationship in a community where social proscriptions have labeled and isolated them, where communication has broken down. In con-centrating her work on women's moral, interior battles in a repressive society, Freeman achieves a depth and universality of theme that has often been overlooked. Ultimately, her women stand alone; each must confront her individual soul, standing stripped of all support be-fore her God. In coming to terms with the myriad social and psycho-logical influences and pressures surrounding her, a Freeman woman achieves heroism precisely through her unquenchable struggle toward fulfillment.

A Freeman woman character does not and cannot exist in a vacuum; her sense of self is derived from and dependent upon others around her. Indeed, some critics see this emphasis on relationship as characteristic of women writers in general. As Heather McClave states in her introduction to *Women Writers of the Short Story,* "[Women writers] link personal identity and survival to complicated ties to a place, other people, a shared code of behavior, a history. For them, typically, an escape to some lonely vigil in the wilderness serves to *avoid* responsible endurance instead of teaching or proving it. One comes to know oneself most deeply, and most painfully, in relationship" (4).

Recent psychological and sociological theories of the self have indeed made us increasingly aware of the gender-marked tendency in women to define themselves and be defined by that which is outside themselves, by "the non-I that protects the I" (Bachelard, 5). Such research suggests that the female "self," to a greater degree than the male "self," is formed by an intimate response to bodily and physical surroundings and, in particular, to relationships with others around her. The resulting combination of nature and nurture, of personality and environment, in women's maturation has further led psychologists and philosophers alike to posit a different kind of ethical development for women, one that perhaps makes them more altruistic or affiliative in their choice-making than men.

A few brief citations can serve here to illustrate these points. In her influential monograph, *The Reproduction of Mothering: Psychoanalysis and the Sociology of Gender,* Nancy Chodorow convincingly argues that gender distinctions result from asymmetrical patterns of parenting and affect an individual's interpersonal relationships. Because girls tend to identify much longer with their same-sex parent than do boys, "girls come to experience themselves as less separate than boys, as having more permeable ego boundaries. Girls come to define themselves more in relation to others" (93). Carol Gilligan's *In a Different Voice* extends these observations into the realm of women's moral maturation, arguing that our conception of human personal development has been based largely on patriarchal norms stressing independence, competition, and domination over the more characteristically "female" values of interdependence, affiliation, and connection.

Such theories of the relational aspects of a woman's psychological makeup as postulated by Chodorow, Gilligan, and others are useful to the literary critic in providing a model that locates the unique qualities of a woman's writing not only in her individual psyche but in how that psyche refracts the social experience—the cultural codes and relational networks—available to her. Meaning for a woman author thus can be said to reside in the border between society and the mind, a shadowy area where identity itself, due to constantly shifting circumstances and relationships, remains fluid and unstable. For this reason, literary critics such as Sandra Gilbert and Susan Gubar in *The Madwoman in the Attic: The Woman Writer and the Nineteenth-Century Literary Imagination* have found that a woman artist, especially one writing in an earlier era under the constraints of patriarchal authority, struggles against various forms of "inferiorization"—feelings of loneliness and alienation in pursuing her work in a "male" publishing arena; dread of the "unwomanly" act of calling attention to herself—in order to define and assert herself artistically as both woman and individual. In fact, "the one plot that seems to be concealed in most of the nineteenth-century literature by women . . . is in some sense a story of the woman writer's quest for her own story; it is the story, in other words, of the woman's quest for self-definition" (76). The woman writer, it may be said, tends to use her work whatever its overt sequence of events to create and explore various possible versions of self.

Judith Kegan Gardiner corroborates Gilbert and Gubar's findings, explaining in "On Female Identity and Writing by Women," "[A] female author is engaged in a process of testing and defining various aspects of identity chosen from many imaginative possibilities . . . the woman writer uses her text, particularly one centering on a female hero, as part of a continuing process involving her own self-definition and her emphatic identification with her character. . . . Thus the author may define herself through the text while creating her female hero" (187).

"The hero is her author's daughter," Gardiner posits; a woman writer forms a distinctive, nurturing-like relationship with her female characters. Moreover, she may seek through them vicarious fulfillment of those hopes and dreams left unrealized, perhaps, because of her decision to pursue an artist's career at the expense of a "normal" woman's life of marriage and child rearing. This closeness between author and character, Gardiner continues, "indicates an analogous relationship between woman reader and character," thus accounting for the "personal" closeness women often feel toward literature (179).

As a woman author whose writing career consumed her every waking moment for nearly fifty years, whose imagination produced several hundred women characters of all ages and personalities, Mary Wilkins Freeman used her fiction to explore women's relationships and thereby come closer to an understanding of herself and an acceptance of her lifelong feeling of being "outside the pale" of ordinary women's experience.[2] Freeman's many portraits of different women's lives in relationship to parents, lovers, husbands, and friends, as well as her stories of a woman in solitary relationship with her God, can therefore be seen as the author's creating, testing, and exploring versions of self, some of which she had already lived or was living, some of which she had consciously rejected, and some of which were through circumstance closed to her. Moreover, Freeman's enthusiastic women readers over the years have attested to the attraction they have felt to her stories. Attempting to account for the "mysterious charm" of Freeman's "A New England Nun," British reviewer Sylvia Warner in a 1966 "mood" piece published in the New Yorker stated that

> There was no word of a nun; but from the moment when Louisa Ellis tied on a green apron and went out with a little blue crockery bowl to pick some currants for her tea I lost all wish for nuns and animated lives. I had found something nearer the bone. Though I could not have defined what I had found, I knew it was what I wanted. It was something I had already found in nature and in certain teapots—something akin to the precision with which the green ruff fits the white strawberry blossom, or to the airy spacing of a Worcester sprig. . . . [Freeman's] control of detail gives these stay-at-home stories a riveting authenticity [132, 134].

The purpose of this study of women in Freeman's short stories is threefold. After a brief look at Freeman's life and a consideration of the contexts from which her art derived, the remainder of the text discusses her stories under such headings as "Women as Daughters in the Family," "Women, Men, and Marriage," "Women as Friends and Rivals," and "Women Alone." These chapters classify much of Freeman's large and uneven oeuvre of short fiction, providing a heretofore unavailable paradigm for further study and teaching of this author's primary theme of women's relationships in turn-of-the-century New

England. Secondly, in doing so they introduce and discuss many previously uncollected and/or lesser-known Freeman stories along with those better-known works that have been instrumental in the recent resurgence of her popularity. Necessarily, I analyze the lesser-known works by plot and theme; more popular works such as "The Revolt of 'Mother,'" "A New England Nun," and "A Village Singer" receive fuller thematic attention with emphasis given as well to artistic style and technique.

It should be noted here that this study is limited to Freeman's short fiction written for adults. Of Freeman's short stories, 146 were collected in her lifetime and issued between 1887 and 1927 in fourteen separate volumes.[3] Approximately one hundred stories appearing in magazines and newspapers, however, were until recently never collected and most were never republished after their initial appearance.[4] Stories written specifically for children—and Freeman was an extremely popular children's writer for a portion of her career—are excluded from this study. Likewise, this work is not primarily concerned with Freeman's other artistic ventures, her novels, plays, nonfiction, or poetry, although in appropriate places such works are cited to better illustrate the point under scrutiny. Of her fourteen novels, Freeman has one or two such as *Pembroke* or *The Shoulders of Atlas* that are noteworthy and still readable today; the others, as was often acknowledged in her own day, tend to have unwieldy and often improbable plots, reading like spliced-together short stories. Clearly, her genius lay in short fiction.

Third and finally, if indeed as Gardiner postulates, the "hero is her author's daughter," an examination of Freeman's women characters leads us closer to an understanding of the mind—with all its longings, fears, joys, and hopes—of the author herself. A shy and reticent person all of her life, Freeman reveals herself primarily through her fiction. Nevertheless, this study of Freeman's women in relationship makes use of selected portions of her recently published personal correspondence as well as aspects of her biography in its analysis of that fiction, allowing us the necessary background for and thus deeper insight into its themes and concerns. In attempting to accomplish these ends in the following pages, I hope to contribute to the growing evaluation of and appreciation for a remarkable writer, one who well deserves a closer look.

A Web of Relationship

CHAPTER 1

Backgrounds

Despite her long writing career, Mary Wilkins Freeman seldom spoke of her craft even when pressed by interviewers to reveal her working habits and artistic inspirations. In 1898, however, she contributed a short piece, "Good Wits, Pen and Paper," to a collection entitled *What Women Can Earn: Occupations of Women and Their Compensation*. Addressing young people, Freeman stressed that, given a degree of natural talent to begin with, a potential writer should simply set about telling the truth. She should "sharpen [her] eyes and ears to see and hear everything in the whole creation" and write "only about those subjects which she knows thoroughly, and concerning which she trusts her own convictions" (29). As a recorder of women's experience in late nineteenth- and early twentieth-century New England, Freeman acted on her own advice. The vast panorama of womanhood she presents in her fiction clearly evolved from her own experiences as a daughter in a small and closely knit family, as an unmarried woman with close friends, as a successful author, and as a wife. To this list could be added as well her experiences as an aging woman, for her literary career was brought to a halt only upon her death at the age of seventy-eight. However, even from very early in her career, Freeman

3

evinced a great sensitivity to the particular needs of the elderly, especially those women who were alone, destitute, and outcast from the
community in some way. She had indeed "sharpened her eyes and
ears"; her enormous popularity as a writer for women's magazines such
as *Harper's Bazar, Ladies' Home Journal,* and *Woman's Home Companion* among others attests to her ability to speak to women of all
ages about their day-to-day concerns.

We know surprisingly little about Freeman's life. Edward Foster's
Mary E. Wilkins Freeman remains the most important biographical
account to date. A reworking of his unfinished dissertation of several
decades earlier, Foster's monograph benefits from the author's having
personally interviewed surviving members of Freeman's family and cir-
cle of friends. Abigail Ann Hamblen's *The New England Art of Mary E.
Wilkins Freeman,* a hard-to-find, pamphlet-sized work, deals perceptively with Freeman's life story before turning to brief critical analyses
of a number of her short stories as well as the novel *Pembroke* and the
play *Giles Corey, Yeoman.* Brent L. Kendrick's *The Infant Sphinx: Collected Letters of Mary E. Wilkins Freeman* presents aspects of Freeman's
biography as prefaces to chronological groupings of Freeman's letters,
merging the earlier accounts of her life with material gleaned from the
letters themselves. The most substantial recent work in Freeman criticism, *The Infant Sphinx,* with its carefully annotated and documented
text, serves among other things to correct several misconceptions
about Freeman that have been passed down over the years: the statement, "You are fond of people and I never have been," which Freeman presumably wrote to a friend (she actually wrote, "You are bored
by people, and I never have been"), and the confirmation of Freeman's relative happiness, at least in the early years, in her marriage to
Charles Freeman (145, 261–70). Reading through the 510 letters
printed here, however, one is struck not so much by what Freeman
says as by what is left unsaid. "Myself is an object of such intense,
vital interest to myself," she once wrote to a fellow writer (Kendrick,
57), but she was an intensely private and reticent person, and that
self was, one finds in reading through her usually mundane and un-
failingly practical correspondence, conveyed primarily through the
"safer," more objective medium of fiction. Nevertheless, this collec-

tion of Freeman's personal correspondence allows us invaluable insight into the daily life and routine habits of a disciplined and determined author.

Freeman's most carefully drawn women characters exhibit the qualities that she herself valued highly in life: candor, responsibility, independence, hard work, high-minded seriousness, deep concern for others, and a continual striving for knowledge of what life is about and how it may be lived in happiness. Born Mary Ella (which she later changed to Eleanor in memory of her mother) to Warren Wilkins, a carpenter, and Eleanor Lothrop Wilkins in 1852, Freeman grew up in Randolph, Massachusetts, in a pious Congregationalist home. Except for the death of a younger brother, which must have made a deep impression on the six-year-old Mary, her early years appear to have been uneventful. At age seven she entered the common school at Randolph and, because of her frail, blonde, almost fairylike beauty, knew the early ostracism of her more robust peers who, perceiving her to be teacher's pet, called her "little, dolly-pinky-rosy" (Foster, 9). Indeed, as Kendrick found in editing Freeman's letters, she never really did grow up:

> In many ways she was childlike herself. . . . Throughout the letters, the tone suggests a person many years younger than Freeman's actual age, and the suggestion is particularly strong when she signs herself "Mamie," "Pussy Willow," or "Dolly." It becomes even stronger as the reader realizes that nowhere in the letters can there be detected even a semblance of the myriad masks worn so well and so often by adults. Instead the reader detects a lack of pretense and affectation as well as total candor and complete openness [11].

Kendrick's comments also confirm another striking aspect of Freeman's character, one that was often remarked on by her contemporaries. Her general demeanor, her dress, her surroundings never failed to exhibit an extreme femininity. Attentive to every detail, she closely followed the styles in fashion and delighted in fine, elaborate clothing made of taffetas, satins, and laces. Though possessing a fragile, delicate beauty, she routinely refused to allow photographs of herself to be circulated, convinced that they made her appear unattractive. In

1906, for example, she complained that a picture sent to Harper's "looked as if I headed the Suffrage movement, and besides the sleeves [of my dress] are all out of date" (Kendrick, 316). She similarly took great pains in arranging her immediate environment. Fellow author and acquaintance Hamlin Garland relates this anecdote in *Roadside Meetings* as he recalled an invitation from Miss Wilkins to tea:

> I recall visiting her in a small white Colonial cottage, exactly appropriate to her. Her home might have been used as a typical illustration for her stories, and the supper . . . was equally in character. Its cakes and pies, its hot biscuits and jam were exactly right. I felt large and rude like that man in one of her tales ["A New England Nun"], who came into the well-ordered sitting room of his sweetheart with such clumsy haste that he overturned her workbasket and sat down on the cat. . . . As a student of minute forms of conduct, she had no superior" [34].

Both Freeman's childlike manner and exaggerated femininity warrant further commentary here. The former suggests a woman who, remaining dependent on others through much of her life, never fully achieved a separation from her mother. Eleanor Wilkins was indeed a strong, firm, "managing" woman whose death when Mary was twenty-eight left the young woman virtually helpless. Though her correspondence reveals little about Freeman's relationship with her mother, the semiautobiographical novel *By the Light of the Soul* (1907) records, interestingly, the terrifying death of protagonist Maria Edgham's domineering mother, the frustrating ineffectualness of her weak-willed father, and young Maria's subsequent lifelong search for spiritual consolation and earthly security. Many of Freeman's short stories deal with the mother and daughter relationship as well. Similarly, Freeman's emphasis on extreme femininity in her apparel and personal surroundings points not only to a woman who sought continual reassurance of her attractiveness as she grew older—and she greatly feared aging—but also to one who in the quest for self-definition strove to, perhaps, enact a "female" code of behavior in the largely masculine world of publishing. As Susan Brownmiller states in *Femininity*, "In its mandate to avoid direct confrontation and to smooth over the fissures of conflict, femininity operates as a value system of niceness, a code of thoughtfulness and sensitivity" (17). Freeman's letters to her editors, publishers, and friends corroborate this suggestion; the greater majority of them present a portrait of a woman anxious to please and placate, to "do the right thing."

Freeman was aware of this aspect of her personality. Several of the women characters in her fiction are rejected by potential lovers precisely because they are, in some way, "too" feminine. Young Ellen Brewster in Freeman's "factory" novel *The Portion of Labor* (1901) is mocked by the very words Freeman herself heard from her young school mates in Randolph: "little, dolly-pinky-rosy." Martha Elder in the short story "The Balsam Fir" (1903) is described by the narrator as "very pretty . . . but there may have been something about the very fineness of her femininity and its perfection which made it repellent."

Nevertheless, nearly all of Freeman's women take great delight, as she herself did, in the domestic, "womanly" details of everyday life. Indeed, for many of Freeman's women these details are life itself; their sense of self is established and maintained only through careful manipulation of their personal effects and surroundings. Clothing—a "good" black silk for meeting, a proper bonnet for visiting—becomes all important in securing an adequate and equal standing among one's peers; it likewise often represents the sole means many a Freeman woman has for self-expression and beauty in her colorless life. Houses and household furnishings, described in Freeman's stories with minute precision, give witness to a woman's realm, her sphere of influence and control. Pet animals and flowers also figure largely in a woman's life in Freeman's world.

Feminine and childlike yes, but, paradoxically, the other side of Mary Wilkins Freeman—the responsible and self-supporting businesswoman—had its origins in her early years as well. As a child in Randolph, Freeman watched her father become one of the many victims of the post–Civil War depression that broke the once proud spirit of the New England villages. Many of Freeman's best stories, as well as the novel *The Portion of Labor,* deal poignantly with the human aspects of this decline. With the rise of the new industrial centers at Lowell and Boston, tiny Randolph, a shoe-factory town, could no longer survive, so Warren Wilkins moved his family in 1867 to Brattleboro, Vermont, where he opened, along with a partner, a dry-goods store. For a time, prosperity seemed theirs. Wilkins had invested in a choice lot in a fashionable area of town, and he and his family, while living in a cottage nearby, planned to build a large new house. But six years later, in 1873, Wilkins again found himself in the midst of a business decline that spread across New England. Plans for the new house were abandoned; Wilkins sold his store and returned to carpentry. At age twenty-one, her formal education complete (she had attended Mount Holyoke Female Seminary for one year, leaving because it reduced her to a "nervous wreck" due to a "monotony of diet and too strenuous goadings of conscience" [Kendrick, 324]) and with no plans for marriage, Freeman realized that she must begin to contribute in some way to the family finances.

This urge to contribute went beyond the simple recognition of lack of sufficient money for comfortable day-to-day living. In her orthodox religious household with its Calvinistic interpretation of the Bible, Mary learned that "somehow faith and goodness were related to one's material success in the world. In her house, it was always assumed that the poverty of the poor was punishment for sin" (Foster, 14). In the homogeneous, closely knit village of Brattleboro, the Wilkins family—and Mary in particular—knew the covert, desperate agony of keeping up appearances in order to avoid inevitable gossip and social ostracism.

Shy and sensitive, Mary never forgot her shame over the increasingly shabby homes and parsimonious existence the Wilkins family was reduced to over the years they remained in Brattleboro. Threats of the poorhouse, the ultimate humiliation, haunt much of Freeman's fiction. Though Freeman later in life recalled several of the various homes the Wilkins family occupied in Brattleboro, it is significant that she never spoke of the bungalow at 3 Chase Street where she lived throughout her high school years. Foster speculates that not only did the small, cramped dwelling embarrass Mary but "it was associated with her first glimpses of psychic terror" (26). His comment bears repeating and elaboration here. Indeed, the home's situation would be haunting to any young mind, particularly to one that is sensitive and imaginative. Up the hill and removed by several blocks from Main Street, the home's backyard opened directly onto the expansive grounds of the former Vermont Insane Asylum, now the Brattleboro Retreat. In a small clearing in the midst of a thickly wooded ravine, and just a few yards from the Wilkins's property, Mary could see the asylum's cemetery where paupers, the mentally imbalanced, and other castoffs from society were buried. From her window she could also quietly observe the sad journeys of the mentally ill, impoverished, and homeless as they made their way up the hill to an uncertain future in the asylum. Most importantly, Freeman did not observe these scenes impartially; not only was her heart rent over the plight of the individuals concerned but also her fears were magnified as the Wilkins's financial situation worsened daily. The poorhouse was—literally—at their doorstep. The raw emotional intensity in her many stories involving the subtle tension between poverty and pride and the dual arts of giving and receiving charity with grace comes directly from these formative experiences. She continued throughout her writing career to champion the unsung poor, more often than not describing an older woman who faces her meager daily existence with the stubborn courage born of despair.

For the remainder of her life, Freeman equated possession of a large and lovely home with security, social status, and happiness. The symbol of the house, in fact, pervades much of her fiction. Only after her marriage late in life to Charles Freeman did she achieve what for her represented the height of success and a triumph over her early fears of poverty. Her later letters abound with references to the magnificent, meticulously appointed home she and Charles spent years in building and christened "Freewarren."

As her family grew increasingly destitute, Freeman found herself in her middle-twenties in the peculiar situation of the nineteenth-century single woman in financial need, a situation often portrayed in her stories and one that obviously frightened her. Little employment was available in Brattleboro in the 1870s for a woman with no particular skills. Having no interest in needlework, Freeman briefly attempted schoolteaching, but, Foster explains, "lacking incisiveness and caring little for her pupils," she found herself unsuccessful and left the job within the year (36–37). Foster's comment seems curious, for in other places he mentions Mary's interest in children. Her lifelong delight in writing children's stories and poetry would also seem to attest to her affection for them. Whatever her reasons for resigning the position, the Wilkins family, concerned with both of their daughters' futures, no doubt began to exert pressure on her to either marry or chose a gainful occupation. Warren Wilkins once remarked to a friend that, although his younger daughter Anna was a talented musician, "Mary—she has no talent, and I don't know what she will do to make a living" (Foster, 32).

Freeman briefly considered pursuing her interest in painting to make money but found she could not even afford to supply herself with the requisite initial purchases of brushes and paints. Always a good student and an avid reader, she then turned rather naturally to writing. She began with religious poetry and, receiving some encouragement from a local clergyman, then went on to publish without pay some children's verses in a local magazine. In 1881, at the age of twenty-nine, she received her first monetary reward: ten dollars each for the ballads "The Beggar King" and "The Tithing Man" from *Wide-Awake*, a well-known children's magazine. *Wide-Awake* published several more of her poems that year. In December of the same year, her first short story written for adults, "The Shadow Family," won a fifty-dollar prize from the *Boston Sunday Budget* and was published in a January 1882 edition of the paper. No copies of it remain; years later Freeman called it "quite passable as an imitation of Charles Dickens" ("Mary E. Wilkins," *Maiden Effort*, 265).[1]

In 1883 "Two Old Lovers" was accepted by *Harper's Bazar*, and Freeman's long and profitable association with the Harper's firm began. Editor Mary Louise Booth, a scholarly author and translator herself, was about to reject the story because she assumed from the handwriting that it had been written by a child. Upon reading it, however, she discovered her mistake; enthusiastically, she encouraged Mary Wilkins to continue to submit manuscripts. Booth accepted five more of Freeman's stories for publication in *Harper's Bazar* that year; the following year several also appeared in *Harper's Monthly*, which was edited by Henry Mills Alden. Until her death in 1889, Booth continued to provide the young author with criticism, encouragement, and above all a professional role model as Freeman embarked upon her literary career. Henry Alden also became a close friend; it was at his home in Metuchen, New Jersey, that Freeman years later was introduced to her future husband, Dr. Charles Manning Freeman.

Freeman found, with the success of these early stories, both her means of independence and her special talent. Though "childlike" and "feminine" in many ways and despite her fears of rejection and her eager willingness to revise her work according to her editors' suggestions, she mastered the ways of the writing market and became a shrewd businesswoman, carefully negotiating the market value of her works and alert to discrepancies in publishing or copyrighting terms. For a long period, success followed upon success; at the height of her career, she once expressed astonishment at the "ridiculous prices" magazines were willing to pay for her stories (Kendrick, 321). However, the moral and spiritual consequences of her early poverty never left her. Far more important to her than the small-town fame publication of "Two Old Lovers" afforded her in Brattleboro was the twenty-five-dollar check she received as payment for the work. She never forgot her excitement at receiving such a substantial sum. "Twenty-five dollars! I may not be telling the exact truth when I say that I had visions of endowing a great public charity," she recalled years later ("American Academy," 7). When asked in 1903 what she would do with a million dollars if she had it, Freeman remarked, no doubt recalling her childhood longings, "I should give to the unacknowledged poor . . . [those] who have much mental distress over the prospect of an unprovided-for old age, and who lack the little amenities which redeem life from a sordid grind . . . [those] who are embittered and suffering morally from constant misfortune. . . . I should even like to buy some pretty things for young girls who have to do without them and hunger for them" ("Million Dollars," 10).

Just before her earliest successful publishing ventures, Freeman's life was touched by a series of personal tragedies that, coming as close together as they did, must have affected her deeply. In 1876 her only sister, Anna, died at the age of seventeen of "disease of the mesenteric" (Foster, 40). The following year the Wilkins family moved once again for financial reasons, this time into the home of a prominent Brattleboro family, that of the Reverend Thomas Tyler, where Mrs. Wilkins was to serve as housekeeper. A young woman of twenty-five, Mary Wilkins no doubt found this move particularly humiliating, made all the more so by the fact that she apparently had a crush on Hanson Tyler, one of the three sons of the Reverend Thomas Tyler's first marriage. During the time the Wilkins family occupied the Tyler home, Hanson Tyler was serving as a naval ensign and returned only infrequently to the Brattleboro home when on leave.

Only a few years later, Mrs. Wilkins, a strong and vigorous woman, died suddenly at the age of fifty-three. Three years later, in 1883, the same year "Two Old Lovers" was accepted for publication, Warren Wilkins died in Florida where he had gone to work a construction job. At the age of thirty-one, then, Freeman was suddenly alone.

She threw herself into her work, perhaps the one stabilizing factor in her life at the time. A steady stream of short stories appeared in *Harper's Bazar, Lippincott's, Century,* and other popular magazines over the next few years. After the settlement of her father's estate, Freeman was invited back to Randolph to live with a childhood friend, Mary John Wales, and her family. The Wales's farmhouse was large and comfortable, and Freeman was given several fine rooms—a parlor where she could receive guests and several bedrooms—for her own. In Mary John Wales, Mary Wilkins found a soul mate and life-long companion; a strong and forceful woman, Mary John never married and for many years not only ran the household but "managed" the practical details of Freeman's life, leaving her the leisure to pursue her writing.

Freeman's earliest writings were primarily children's works. *Wide-Awake* continued to accept her poems and stories. In 1883 Mary Wilkins's first book appeared, published by Lothrop: a slender, beautifully illustrated volume of children's poems called *Decorative Placques.* Two volumes of children's stories followed: *The Cow With the Golden Horns and Other Stories* (1884) and *The Adventures of Ann: Stories of Colonial Times* (1886). By 1887 Freeman also had enough adult stories written for both *Harper's Bazar* and *Harper's Monthly* to warrant her first substantial collection, *A Humble Romance and Other Stories.* The twenty-eight stories were enthusiastically received; reviewers lauded her accurate portrayal of New England life, her gift of seeing "the symbolism of homeliness, the sacred pathos of the daily toil of dutiful lives" ("Mary E. Wilkins," 103). Perhaps the most important early recognition came from the master of letters himself, William Dean Howells, who in his September 1887 "Editor's Study" for *Harper's Monthly* called her stories "good through and through, and whoever loves the face of common humanity will find pleasure in them" (640). Gratified and encouraged by such praise, Freeman wrote on.

Four years after the publication of A *Humble Romance*, Harper's brought out her second collection of adult short stories, A *New England Nun and Other Stories*. Reviews for this volume also were overwhelmingly positive; in England, as one reviewer commented, her stories were producing "something like a craze" ("Notes," 101). At this point, however, after the publication of some sixty short stories, Freeman decided to experiment with longer forms of fiction. As early as 1885, she had written to Booth, "I am wishing more than I have done, to undertake some larger work. . . . Lately the conviction grows on me, of heights and heights, and depths, and depths, which I have never dreamed of" (Kendrick, 62–63). She may have very well also been influenced in her decision by the as-yet minor rumble of some critics who were beginning to complain that her stories tended to be repetitive in plot, to sound "too much" alike.

Freeman first tried her hand at drama. In 1893 she won minor success with the publication and subsequent stage production of *Giles Corey, Yeoman*, a historical tale of the Salem witch trials. *Jane Field*, her first novel, appeared the same year. A quick succession of novels followed: *Pembroke* (1894); *Madelon* (1896); and *Jerome, A Poor Man* (1897). In between novels Freeman experimented with two more plays and continued to produce a steady stream of short stories for both adults and children. Once established, her rigorous writing schedule formed a set daily pattern for the rest of her life. Mary John Wales, she once half-jokingly told a visitor, "shuts me in my study each morning and won't let me out till I have written at least fifteen hundred words" (Garland, *Diaries*, 128). Over the next thirty years, between 1898 and 1928, her total volume of writing included ten more novels, twelve more collections of short stories, and many uncollected stories, articles, and poems.

Freeman continued to live with Mary John Wales and her family until her marriage at the age of forty-nine in 1902. It was her friend Kate Upson Clark who arranged for Mary Wilkins and Charles Manning Freeman to meet at the home of Henry Alden sometime in 1892 or 1893. Seven years younger than she, Charles Freeman had received his medical degree from Columbia College and at one time had briefly held the position of medical examiner in the Bureau of Pensions in Washington, D.C. He was dismissed from this post, however, for numerous charges of inappropriate behavior including "reading newspapers and smoking on the job; failure to show proper respect; use of profanity; arriving at work late and intoxicated; and boasting of 'vicious habits and practices'" (Kendrick, 203). Charles Freeman indeed had long had the dubious reputation of a "wild," albeit charming, bachelor-about-town. Returning after his dismissal to his family home in staid and respectable Metuchen, New Jersey, Charles began working for his father's coal and lumber business; he never again practiced medicine. In 1897, several years after their initial meeting and after much agonizing over the prospect of marrying at all, Mary Wilkins announced her engagement to Charles Freeman; the couple, however, much to her reading public's dismay, continued to postpone their wedding date for five more years. Finally, they married quietly on 1 January 1902 and settled in Metuchen.

Freeman at first found support and encouragement in her writing from her new husband. In fact, in their early years together, Charles Freeman proved himself to be an ideal partner. He employed household help to free her from domestic duties, helped her plan her social activities around her work schedule, and read and criticized her stories (Foster, 161–62). Several of Freeman's letters to friends at this time show her contentment with both Charles and her new role as a married woman. Kendrick notes, moreover, a subtle indication of Freeman's happiness in her marriage: her insistence that her full married name—Mary E. Wilkins Freeman—now appear on her work despite the public's familiarity with her well-known maiden name (261–62). She and Charles also took great interest in the several homes they occupied over the ensuing years. They completed "Freewarren," a showplace of considerable beauty and size in Metuchen, in 1907; a year earlier they had held an elaborate groundbreaking ceremony complete with a commemorative poem and house prayer written by Mary in which she asked God to grant them both "years of love, health and peace in this House" (Kendrick, 264). Elegant and tasteful both inside and out, this home must have symbolized for Freeman the pinnacle of her dreams, for at this point in her career she epitomized the American success story.

Freeman's idyll did not last long, however. Always delicate in health, she began to be nagged by various ailments that grew increasingly acute over the years: deafness, headaches, insomnia. Even

worse, Charles Freeman soon returned to the heavy drinking he had
done before his marriage. In 1909, only seven years after they were
married, he was confined a short time in a New York sanitarium; ten
years later, at the end of World War I, his addiction to both alcohol
and veronal, a sedative, had rendered him mentally incompetent.
Fearing for her own safety and that of her servants, Mary had him
committed in 1921 to the New Jersey State Hospital for the Insane at
Trenton. He was released not long afterward, but by then his wife had
obtained a legal separation. Moving into the home of his chauffeur,
Charles Freeman died there suddenly of heart failure in 1923.

At his death, a new will was discovered, drawn up only a few
months earlier and cutting off his wife with one dollar. The bulk of
his large estate was left to his chauffeur, a man who had been in his
employment little more than six months. Both Mary Freeman and
Charles's four sisters, with whom she remained close, successfully con-
tested the will, winning a sizable settlement on the grounds that
Charles had been mentally unfit to draw up a legal document. Because
of the worth of the estate—$225,000—the case became a sensation
throughout the county. One can imagine the effect of this drawn-out
media affair on the reticent and retiring "brown thrush of a woman"
(Garland, *Diaries*, 127). Her health continued to decline daily; her
letters are replete with references to her many ailments. But her sto-
icism in the face of life's troubles remained: "I must have a very tough
streak in me," she wrote to a friend in her declining years. "I did not
look so but time has proved it" (Kendrick, 413). Her comments on
Charles less than two years after his death hint more of calm, albeit
ironically humorous acceptance, than of bitterness: "It is a wonderful
thing to be able to feel that your husband was your unshattered ideal.
I cannot feel badly because I can hardly say that of my husband, for I
doubt very much if I ever had an ideal to shatter anyway, and I reckon
Charles may have thought I smashed his to smithereens. After all my
husband had splendid traits" (Kendrick, 394).

The next few years brought Freeman a great deal of recognition;
ironically, however, at her death from heart-failure in 1930, she was
all but forgotten. She was awarded the first William Dean Howells
Medal for outstanding fiction from the American Academy of Arts
and Letters in 1925 and was elected, along with Edith Wharton,

Margaret Deland, and Agnes Repplier, a member of the Department of Literature, the National Institute of Arts and Letters in 1926. In 1938 ornamental doors installed at the American Academy of Arts and Letters in New York were posthumously dedicated "to the Memory of Mary E. Wilkins Freeman and the Women Writers of America." However, Freeman witnessed in her own lifetime a rapidly growing obscurity. Her own conflicting interests, a tendency to overwork, and the changing literary tastes of the reading public contributed to a decline in the overall quality of her work and a subsequent loss of reputation. By 1930, the year of her death, she was simply no longer read; only nine of her forty-one volumes of works were yet in print.

A few months after she died, John Macy, in an article for *The Bookman* entitled "The Passing of the Yankee," used Freeman's descent into obscurity as a metaphor signaling the end of decades of prominence for New England in general: "In the year when Boston was celebrating three hundred glorious years Mary Wilkins Freeman died. Newspapers and literary journals outside Boston noticed her death but made little of it. All her important work was done thirty years ago; her body had outlived her power and her reputation, and she had passed into literary history as a writer of village tales once admired but no longer read" (617).

"Of late she has dropped out of all our circles," Hamlin Garland commented in his diary around 1925. "No one ever sees her. No one speaks of her. What this means I do not know" (129). Though a virtual recluse in her last few years, Mary Wilkins Freeman's artistic vision never failed her; at her death she was considering both a sequel to *Pembroke* and an autobiography requested by Harper's.

Mary Wilkins Freeman was a woman with a story to tell, a rags-to-riches phenomenon acutely sensitive to the mystery of life's vicissitudes. Dependent and independent, feminine and businesslike, poverty-stricken at one time and wealthy and famous at another, her "double vision" enhanced both her remarkable power of observation and her sympathetic identification with others, enabling her to explore and elucidate women's relationships in turn-of-the-century New England. Daughter, friend, and wife herself, and immersed in the small-town New England life of Randolph, Brattleboro, and Metuchen, Freeman spent her career translating her life experiences and exploring herself as a woman and as an individual in her art. The sketchy details of her biography and the even sketchier content of her laconic personal correspondence provide an incomplete albeit important background to entering the world of her fiction. It is when immersed in that fiction, however, that one senses that Mary Wilkins Freeman is best understood through her careful rendering of women at all stages of life and in all types of life's situations.

CHAPTER 2

Contexts

Possessing a practical Yankee temperament and scarred by her early experiences with poverty, Freeman never denied the fact that her earliest artistic impulses were largely mercenary. As had been the case with many American women writers before her, she seized upon authorship as a source of income in the absence of other available occupation; she had, as noted, already tried her hand unsuccessfully at schoolteaching. After experimenting briefly with poetry in the late 1870s and early 1880s, she turned quickly to penning short stories, aware of their greater lucrative value. "I wrote no more *vers de societe.* No more Cherries in Blossom [the title of an early poem]. My dear Sir, do you remember I wrote you that I had to earn my living?" she remarked somewhat petulantly to Fred Lewis Pattee in 1919 as he questioned her at length regarding her artistic influences and goals (Kendrick, 385). Throughout her career as well, she was conscious that she approached her writing far more as a business, or as she would have put it a "duty," than as art;[1] at times such an admission disconcerted her. "To day I have written a little tale, concluding with a neat allusion to church, for the Congregationalist," she wrote to her editor, Mary Louise Booth, in 1886, expressing dissatisfaction with the hack work she often felt compelled to undertake. "I wouldn't write these if I did not like the money. However it only takes a very little while. But it does not seem to me just right, to write things of that sort on purpose to get money, and please an editor" (Kendrick, 66).

But please an editor Freeman did, especially in her apprentice years as she struggled to understand the criticism offered her works and to revise her stories accordingly. Though she was thirty-three years old at the time, a letter dated February 1885 and also written to Booth suggests a much younger writer in its eagerness to comply with whatever was required to see her fiction in print. Booth had evidently suggested revisions for "A Wayfaring Couple," which appeared first in a May 1885 edition of the *Detriot Free Press* and was later collected by Harper's in *A New England Nun and Other Stories*. Freeman responded, "Why, I went straight to work, and altered every sentence in my Wayfairers [sic], which ended with a preposition, and there were ever so many of them. . . . I have been very careless. . . . I will certainly try to polish my style, as you advise. I shall be very careful in this story, which I am writing now, and you see please, if it has not fewer mistakes" (Kendrick, 60–61). Though undoubtedly Booth and later editors gave her excellent assistance in revising her work for the public, Freeman continued throughout her career to be highly sensitive to criticism, admitting to being "cowardly" about reviews and later refusing to read them altogether. At one point she wryly suggested that critics who ventured "scathing" remarks should "write the stories themselves" (Kendrick, 175).

Achieving early success with the publication of her first two collections, *A Humble Romance* and *A New England Nun,* Freeman was occasionally queried about her artistic aims and sources of inspiration. With a reticence about her writing that soon came to characterize her, she insisted she had no goal but faithfulness to truth, portraying persons and circumstances arising from her own experience. She wrote to Hamlin Garland that being "true" was "the only aim in literature of which I have been really conscious" (Kendrick, 83). Likewise, Freeman insisted that she had followed no models in producing her early work and, in fact, had no real literary influences. "If I had been influenced I should have written very differently because most of my own work, is not really the kind I myself like," she wrote to Pattee. "I want more symbolism, more mysticism. I left that out, because it struck me people did not want it, and I was forced to consider selling qualities" (Kendrick, 382).

Despite her remarks to the contrary, both Freeman's artistic aims and her literary influences clearly derived from her immediate cultural and social milieu as well as her own "bookish" tendencies. Happily for Mary Wilkins, several factors had converged around the year 1880, as she was preparing to send out her first adult short story, that helped ensure her quick acceptance into the burgeoning short fiction market. These factors—the advocacy for a "new" realism in fiction by Howells and other influential editors and critics; the antisentimental impulses of a second and third generation of women writers as they rewrote the plots and changed the endings of the women's fiction they had grown up reading; and the current interest in women's New England regional writing—have been studied in depth elsewhere; yet a brief summary of each is necessary here in order to place Freeman's writing within its appropriate contexts.

"I didn't even know that I'm a realist until they wrote and told me," Freeman once remarked in an often-quoted statement (Smith, 4). Though the comment probably contains an element of truth, Freeman could not have avoided being influenced as a novice author by the currents of literary change swelling around her, specifically those promoting realism in fiction. On the vanguard of such change was the *Atlantic Monthly*, which, especially under the editorship of James Russell Lowell (1857–61) and William Dean Howells (1871–81), began to routinely reject sentimental or romantic fiction in favor of stories that bore more verisimilitude, that used concrete, precise detail and true-to-life characterization and showed Americans to themselves in all of their homely—sometimes humorous, sometimes devastatingly serious—customs, concerns, and foibles. Howells defined realism as "nothing more and nothing less than the truthful treatment of material" (*Criticism*, 73). Even before the Civil War, the *Atlantic* was publishing works leading directly to Howells's and other critics' later definitive statements of this "new" vogue in fiction. Rebecca Harding Davis's surprisingly modern-sounding work of stark critical realism, *Life in the Iron Mills*, for example, appeared in an 1861 edition. The phrase "local color," a term coined to describe realistic fiction con-centrating on regional detail, authentic characterization, and careful transcription of indigenous dialect, was used for the first time in an 1864 *Atlantic* review.

Following the *Atlantic*'s lead, competing magazines were soon established, helping to form standards and set popular taste for literary realism and, in particular, local-color writing: *Lippincott's* (1868) and *Scribner's Monthly* (later the *Century Magazine*) (1870), among others. Such growing outlets for short fiction encouraged young writers from all over the expanding and recently reunited states to try their hand at describing their peculiar locale and its unique inhabitants for an eager eastern market. Magazine readers soon could experience such exotic areas of the country as Hamlin Garland's Wisconsin, Samuel Clemens's and Bret Harte's western mining camps, Mary Murfree's Tennessee, and Kate Chopin's Louisiana. Although regional fiction had its roots in the first travel narratives and historical accounts written in America, widespread fascination with the genre reached its zenith in the 1880s and 1890s, coinciding with Mary Wilkins's earliest publishing efforts.

Equally important in establishing Freeman's literary influences is a consideration of the tradition of women's fiction that she was entering. As a "second-generation" American woman writer and a realist, Freeman wrote much of her work in reaction to the earlier romantic and sentimental/domestic traditions, those works she had grown up reading. Like other realists in general and women writers in particular, she used her fiction as a vehicle to criticize sentimental plots and to rewrite endings in order to make her stories correspond more fully to women's lives as she knew them. Secondly, Freeman was also entering into an already formed group of New England women regionalists, a group that has been described as constituting a coherent tradition.[2] In following the lead of such writers as Harriet Beecher Stowe, Rose Terry Cooke, and Sarah Orne Jewett, Freeman not only gained the impetus for her descriptions of the New England village but also evolved her divergences from them as she faithfully sought to render her unique experiences.

As is now well-established in the study of American literary history, the sentimental/domestic fiction prevalent from approximately 1820 to 1870—that chronicling the "trials and triumphs" of female protag-

onists who must make their own way in life and who usually are re-
warded in their struggles by marriage—was by no means superfluous
or "sappy" material. In many ways neither "sentimental" nor "domestic" at all, it was fiction with a serious feminist purpose, albeit a "limited, or pragmatic feminism" (Baym, 18). Seeking to counteract the
degrading image of women perpetuated by such romantic novels of
seduction as Samuel Richardson's *Clarissa Harlowe* and Susanna Row-
son's *Charlotte Temple,* this fiction laid emphasis on the positive abilities of the female protagonist, advocating such admirable Victorian
values as restraint, discipline, and self-control in a woman's *bildung.*
Often, these women were developed in contrast to the passive, hyper-
emotional, "love-struck," or otherwise superficial "belle," a type uni-
versally scorned by sentimental fictionists. After the chronicle of the
young protagonist's development amidst myriad social and psychological obstacles, all ends are usually "euphorically" resolved in a happy
marriage, one that allows the self-respect of the woman to remain
intact (the marriage is her choice, often achieved after the rejection
of other available suitors) while simultaneously rewarding her life's
struggles and trials. Community is reestablished, and relationships
with others validated as the young woman takes her earned and right-
ful place in society.

Alternatively, if the female protagonist fails to overcome obstacles,
resolve the tension between her self-development and the role of
women in society, and achieve ultimate social harmony through marriage, the only other plausible solution is the heroine's death. As
Rachel DuPlessis has pointed out, when a female protagonist in a
historical and economic system that deprives women of power margin-
alizes herself too fully or in other ways tests the limitations on her
behavior too radically, "death enforces the restrictions on female behavior. . . . [It] is the second line of defense for the containment of
female revolt, revulsion, or risk" (16). Yet, often, compensating for
her death is the protagonist's moral or spiritual triumph as she sym-
bolically rises above the oppression of an inferior and degraded society.
In addition, her death is often the catalyst for and necessary price of
the consequent moral transformation of those around her; her spiritual
legacy, therefore, is ensured. Thus women writers of sentimental fiction used their work didactically, urging their audiences to identify

with their female characters in order to gain conviction of women's self-worth and transforming powers in a society that severely restricted their actions.

Sentimental/domestic novels ending in either the marriage or death of the heroine—Catharine Sedgwick's *A New-England Tale* (1822), Susan Warner's *The Wide, Wide World* (1851), E.D.E.N. Southworth's *The Hidden Hand* (serialized in 1859), and Augusta Evans's *St. Elmo* (1867), to name just a few—dominated the literary market in America before the Civil War and for at least a decade thereafter. Eagerly read by women, they constituted a first-generation of women's writing that directly influenced the second generation, that group of which Freeman was a member.

Although "realism" and "local color" in fiction were increasingly in demand after the Civil War, many authors, of course, had to a greater or lesser degree been writing "realistically" for years. Sarah Hale's *Northwood* (1827), an otherwise sentimental/domestic tale, for example, describes parts of regional New England in faithful detail. Alice Cary's *Clovernook* (1852) is likewise a transitional work, mixing some localized scenery and authentic characterization with a broadly sentimental plot. Many of Hawthorne's romanticized tales and novels are deeply rooted in a sense of place, full of "local color" description and character. Popular humorous and vernacular sketches and tales such as A. B. Longstreet's *Georgia Scenes* (1835) and Frances Whitcher's *Widow Bedott Papers* (serialized in the 1840s) are also early attempts to describe regions of the country and native characters and customs. But it is Bret Harte's 1868 publication of "The Luck of Roaring Camp," a humorous mixture of sentimentality and realism set in the California mining camps, that is generally cited as the touchstone for the beginning of the high period of local-color fiction.

By the time Freeman published her first realistic short story for adults, "Two Old Lovers," in the 31 March 1883 edition of *Harper's Bazar*, women's regional writing was flourishing in New England. Led by Harriet Beecher Stowe's New England novels, *The Minister's Wooing* (1859) and *The Pearl of Orr's Island* (1862), and in particular by her series of New England village sketches *Oldtown Folks* (1869), such writers as Rose Terry Cooke, Celia Thaxter, Helen Hunt Jackson, Elizabeth Stuart Phelps, Alice Brown, and Sarah Orne Jewett had already been experimenting in fiction with the techniques of local-color realism applied to their native New England. Close attention to regional detail, careful rendering of authentic idiom, and a concentration on local characters mark such works as Jewett's *Deephaven* (1877), Thaxter's *Among the Isles of Shoals* (1879), and Cooke's short stories collected in *Somebody's Neighbor's* (1881). Active in approximately the same time period, a number of these writers knew each other and some maintained close friendships; they met regularly in literary circles, reading and discussing each other's works at length.

Engendered in large part in reaction to earlier romantic and sentimental traditions, realistic fiction often overtly criticized the perceived excesses and dishonesty of its predecessors. Howells's mocking of "slop, silly slop" emotionalism in *The Rise of Silas Lapham,* his debunking of romantic notions of war in "Editha," and Clemens's symbolic sinking of the *Walter Scott* in *Huckleberry Finn* are but a few examples of a conscious effort to discredit a sentimental approach to life and validate a more realistic one by contrast. Women's realism of the era followed suit, but with a feminist twist. As first-generation female authors had employed sentimental/domestic fiction to express revulsion for the exploitation of women in seduction novels, so women realists in turn used their fiction to critique the Cinderella script that forms the basis of the majority of sentimental works. While retaining an emphasis on strong, practical, and self-determining female protagonists, women writers in the New England local-color tradition not only began to explore alternative endings to the marriage-and/or death-of-the-heroine story but also tempered the evangelical zeal expressed or otherwise implied in sentimental works with growing doubts about the efficacy and justice of patriarchal New England Calvinism.

Women writers of this second generation demonstrated their reaction against "trials and triumphs" fiction in several ways. Most notably, the institution of marriage as a satisfying or fulfilling conclusion to a woman's self-development was questioned, sometimes in a heavily ironic and biting manner. Single life was postulated as a viable and at times preferable possibility. The humorously caricaturized "spinsters" and dour "old maids" of earlier literature began to achieve dimension as a new seriousness was applied to their case. In fact, single women soon came to dominate the fictional world of women's local-color writing, reflecting in large measure the reality of these writers' experience.[3] Additionally, attention was focused on other nonromantic protagonists: older women, impoverished women, single women with children. When they did write of marriage, local-colorists insisted on dispelling romantic myths, often dwelling instead on the reality of women's dissatisfaction within it. It follows that many of these works portray men as the cause of women's sufferings, as weak and passive, and as largely insignificant to the plot at hand. Or, males may simply be absent from these stories altogether.

Women's realistic fiction also came down heavily on the lingering remnants of the long New England heritage of Calvinism, particularly on those elements oppressive to women. In developing their female protagonists, women writers in the sentimental tradition had already initiated an excoriation of formalized, patriarchal religion, offering in the place of its arbitrary and tyrannical God a gentler "female" code of ethics, one emphasizing charity, generosity, and selflessness. Hence, an emphasis on works rather than on faith as leading to redemption was important to the early feminist tone of this fiction, in keeping with the overall "feminization" of American religion which was taking place throughout the nineteenth century.[4] Nevertheless, female protagonists in such fiction were, in general, deeply devout, never doubting the existence and love of God and relying ultimately on divine strength to enable them to surmount their myriad trials. Faith and piety, in fact, were considered efficacious qualities, helping women endure with self-respect their subordinate role in a male-oriented society.

By the latter part of the nineteenth century, the once-forceful spirit of Calvinism had waned so sharply that the New England local-colorists did not hesitate to expose its hypocrisies and demolish its remaining cultural myths. Unlike sentimental writers who had considered the village minister to be their ally and spiritual guide, these latter authors considered him to represent all that was oppressive in patriarchal religion. The least admirable and often least Christian of men, his decisions are shown to be weak-willed, his actions cowardly. Villagers who blindly adhered to formalistic piety without evincing justice, compassion, and love were likewise condemned. Less religiously didactic than the literature of their predecessors, women's New England local-color fiction took a sharply critical look at the vestiges of the older institutionalized religion. As such, this fiction forges a transition between the evangelical Christianity of sentimental writers and the agnosticism characteristic of the modern age.

An avid reader, Freeman spent her youth and early womanhood absorbing the literature of earlier traditions as well as reading and discussing the newer, recently published works of realism. Her immediate environment did much to foster her innate literary bent. Between the years 1867 and 1884, when Freeman lived there, Brattleboro, Vermont, was not lacking in the literary and cultural influences necessary to nurturing a nascent artistic talent. The town's beauty and its reputation as a health spa and summer resort attracted a steady stream of visitors, including some prominent personalities. Several famous artists had been born or later lived there including Royall Tyler, author of *The Contrast,* and the British writer Rudyard Kipling. Brattleboro, in fact, already had several well-established library and book associations when the Wilkins family arrived in town. The Lyceum Series in the town hall, which the Wilkins's attended, sponsored humorists, journalists, abolitionists, and suffragettes alike. Among others, Mary Wilkins no doubt heard author Thomas Wentworth Higginson, an advocate of realism and moral earnestness in fiction, speak during the 1868–69 series; she would have been approximately sixteen years old at the time. Finally, as Kendrick notes, Brattleboro boasted no fewer than seven publications: three newspapers and four periodicals. The *Vermont Phoenix* in particular must have been eagerly awaited by young Mary; in its pages she found stories and tales by Nathaniel Hawthorne, Bret Harte, Harriet Beecher Stowe, Rose Terry Cooke, and Mark Twain (Kendrick, 47–48). The small town's influence was thus considerable as Freeman's writing began to take shape.

With her Brattleboro friend, Evelyn Severance, young Mary Wilkins read and discussed Greek mythology, Goethe, Tolstoy, Dickens, Thackeray, Poe, Emerson, Thoreau, Hawthorne, and Stowe. Though she later stated that she had not read any of Jewett's works as she commenced her own stories, she had in all probability read the work of other women New England regionalists in addition to Stowe—Cooke, Phelps, and Thaxter. Her interest in the new local-color writing would certainly have been augmented by the attraction to places and characters familiar to her. Once her own published work reaped invitations into literary circles, of course, she met, befriended, and at times corresponded with many prominent writers, among them Howells, Clemens, Jewett, Hamlin Garland, and Alice French, and she occasionally joined them as they read and discussed each other's works. Though she maintained toward the end of her life, "I did . . . stand entirely alone. . . . I read nothing which could be said even remotely to influence me" (Kendrick, 382), Freeman's art was thus clearly derived from both her own imagination and the literary, social, and cultural atmosphere surrounding her.

It is perhaps surprising for us today to consider how "new" realistic and local-color techniques in literature seemed to the reading public in the 1880s. In general, Freeman's early work was lauded for her innovation in and/or refinement of four major areas: (1) the faithfulness with which she recorded elements of New England life, especially in its decline; (2) the inner strength or "spirituality" of her characters that accorded her work a universal rather than merely local appeal; (3) the objective, frank realism of her style and the purity of its compression; and (4) her interest in the Puritan conscience and will, seen as a legacy from Hawthorne.

Critics agreed from early on that Mary Wilkins, one of Howells's many young protégées, was producing stories sympathetic to the major tenets of his literary ideology. "Of the genuine originality of these stories it is hard to speak too strongly," one early reviewer stated, adding that "she makes us exclaim with admiration over the novelty, yet truthfulness, of her portraitures" (Scudder, 848). Another commented that "she paints the village life, the people on farms and in workshops and workhouses . . . she sees those things which are of perennial interest—the pathos and beauty of simple lives" ("Mary E. Wilkins," 102). Yet within these faithful descriptions of simple lives, a deeper, human element could be found. The best local-color writing, in fact, was considered that which went beyond mere superficial description to equate the local with the universal, individual characteristics with human nature in general. "She touches a very deep nature, and opens to view a secret of the human heart which makes us cry out that here is a poet, a seer," exclaims one review (Scudder,

848); and yet another states, "back of all her work is the idea, the sense of the mystery of human life, the question, 'Why is this?' and she gently pushes selected incidents and characters before you, as if filled with the desire to learn . . . the meaning of these problems,— clues doubtless, each one in its degree, to the answer to the Great Problem" (Thompson, 675).

Several early critics also set the stage for more recent appraisals of Freeman's work by touching upon the inner strength, determined will, and frequent spirit of revolt that informs many of her characters and directs their lives. "The center of her art, the beginning and the end of it, is humanity, the individual soul," wrote Pattee in 1922; "her favorite theme is revolt . . . often is it internal. On the surface of the life there is apparent serenity and reserve, but beneath there is an increasing fire" (Pattee, 201, 207).

Freeman's style was also new and exciting at the time. "A singular fascination lies in this style of hers, which is after all rather the absence of style—direct, simple, without a superfluous word," wrote one critic (Wardwell, 27); and another stated that her "short, terse sentences, written in the simplest, homeliest words, had a biting force" (Thompson, 669). A third early commentary on Freeman's style is noteworthy because it establishes the nexus continuing today between Freeman's work and that of Jewett. In 1903 Julia R. Tutwiler called Freeman's art "Gothic" as opposed to Jewett's "Grecian" art, "in the somber rigidity of its moral ideals, and in a union of childlike directness and reticence that embroider economy of phrase with delicate and intricate suggestion. . . . Where Miss Jewett suffuses you with a delightful melancholy, Mary E. Wilkins makes your eyes smart with tears that refuse to fall" (419, 424).

From early on, Freeman was considered a successor of Hawthorne. Paul Elmer More's "Hawthorne: Looking Before and After," written in 1905 on the centennial of Hawthorne's birth, traces a "regular process" of inheritance "from the religious intolerance of Cotton Mather to the imaginative isolation of Hawthorne and from that to the nervous impotence of Mrs. Freeman's men and women" (180). "If I am not mistaken, the real progenitor of Miss Wilkins is Nathaniel Hawthorne," another critic had commented a year earlier. "She is inspired by the same ideals and appears to be capable of similarly delicate and exquisite workmanship" (Courtney, 204). Although Freeman failed in the eyes of many of her critics to live up to this early optimism, she continued to be equated with Hawthorne in her intense probing of the Calvinistic will and the serious moral issues she raised. Moreover, like Hawthorne, she was interested in Puritan history (family lore connected the Wilkins's line with Bray Wilkins, a participator in the Salem witch trials) and set a number of her works (the drama *Giles Corey, Yeoman* and the stories collected in *Silence and Other Stories* among others) in past New England. Hawthorne's influence is seen as well in at least two short stories discussed in later chapters: "The Slip of the Leash" is similar to "Wakefield," and "The Three Old Sisters and the Old Beau" is similar to "The Wedding Knell." Characteristically, however, Freeman denied the romancer's impact on her work: "I do not know if I am 'akin to Hawthorne,'" she told Pattee; "I do not care for him as I care for Tolstoi . . . and Hardy" (Kendrick, 385).

Freeman's truthful recording of the New England character and circumstances, her careful rendering of dialect and spare, objective style, and her Hawthorne-like fascination with the Calvinist mind soon won for her an important position in the rise of the new local-color realism being promoted at the time. Equally as important, Freeman also assumed a place in the development of women's regional New England writing, learning from her reading of such authors as Stowe, Jewett, and Cooke, and establishing for herself a perspective on the New England experience divergent from theirs. Like these writers, Freeman at times used her fiction to critique sentimental and romantic images of women and the institutions oppressive to them in an effort to be faithful to her own life's experiences.

Freeman peopled her stories with the most unromantic of female protagonists: elderly women such as Hetty Fifield in "A Church Mouse" and Lucinda Moss in "An Innocent Gamester"; heavyset, dull-skinned, and awkward young women such as Juliza Peck in "Juliza" and Eunice Fairweather in "A Moral Exigency"; and impoverished single mothers such as Marg'ret Poole in "A Stolen Christmas" and Hannah Dodd in "The Strike of Hannah." Moreover, although love interests often initiate the plot and set the story's primary conflict in motion, Freeman usually upsets conventional expectations by soon displacing or otherwise skewing the outcome of that plot. Though the majority of Freeman's women protagonists wish to marry and many eventually do, marriage is never considered a fulfilling "reward" for or ending to a woman's trials. Rather, the story's main focus remains firmly on the intersection of complex social and psychological factors, the inner and outer forces, that beseige a woman as she struggles to decide whether or not she should marry. Among these many factors are her dutiful sense of filial obedience, the limited choice of suitors in the village, the various roles demarcated by her society for "wife" and "spinster," and her own longings and desires.

A young woman in Freeman's world is under great pressure to marry, not only as a result of social expectations, but to fulfill familial expectations as well. She is aware that any unmarried woman over thirty is not only pitied but expected to don a cap and black gown and fade genteelly into placid old age; she chafes at the role of "spinster" assigned her if she does not wed. Moreover, she is cognizant of the isolation that single life brings in a village where people in general and older women in particular are without a supportive community. Complicating the fear of social stigma, Freeman time and again shows us a young woman harried by her mother's insistence that she wed, generally because the marriage will accord the mother a degree of both material security and social prestige. A young woman must come to terms with the limits of her filial responsibility as she simultaneously seeks to placate her mother's desires.

Though Freeman's women are generally realistic about their prospects of marrying and about the relative satisfaction marriage brings, they also "have their dreams," wishing to marry for love. But there are no romantic male heroes in Freeman's villages, only passive, effeminate, weak, or childish men. When Freeman's women do wed, therefore, they often must compromise their dreams and suppress their desires. Ultimately, they do so of their own volition, carefully weighing what is lost and gained by such a union. Yet in Freeman's several stories that take us beyond the wedding day, we are generally shown that marriage for a woman is replete with tension, coldness, and mental suffering.

In her stories, Freeman often initiates a seemingly traditional love plot only to interrupt that plot and subordinate the romantic concern, focusing attention instead on the internal struggles of the main female character. She often does this by way of contrasting a weak, overly emotional woman—the fair, fainting maid of conventional romance—with a stronger, practical, and self-determining one. In forging this contrast, she gleans a technique used by writers of sentimental fiction, but she explores in far more depth than her predecessors the psychological ramifications of the protagonist's plight.

The broad outline of the situation is usually as follows: the love-crazed, romantic woman succeeds in coming between a pair of lovers, sometimes even hysterically "claiming" the male; the stronger woman, who can probably retain the man if she so chooses, eventually and often after much agonizing "gives" him to the helpless female. The protagonist does not do so from altruistic motives. Indeed, Freeman, in these stories as elsewhere, scorns such total self-sacrifice as destructive for all involved. Rather, the passive, vacillating, and weak male is more the romantic ingenue's equal. On some level, the stronger woman realizes this and understands the limited chances for her own happiness if she should continue to hold him. But once she relinquishes him, the practical and self-possessed woman does not, in Freeman's world, find a counterpart to marry. There are no more suitors on the horizon. Relegating the conventional pair of lovers to the subplot, Freeman now concentrates on the mental trauma of the woman who is left alone. Despite the fact that marriage to such a male would clearly be unsatisfactory to her, so equally is the anomalous position of "old maid" which she must now assume. Some of the stories that ironically twist the conventional love plot in this manner are "Juliza," "A Moral Exigency," "A Tardy Thanksgiving," "A Modern Dragon," "Emmy," "A Taste of Honey," "Amanda and Love," and "The Chance of Araminta."

Though not all of Freeman's unmarried women are lonely—a number, such as Araminta in "The Chance of Araminta" and Maria in "Two Old Lovers," find fulfillment in the traditional female role of charitable works—many more of them carefully maintain an unflappable outward demeanor while inwardly seething with frustration, anger, and rebellion. Envying, yet simultaneously scorning the conventional marriages of their peers, they rage against a Providence that, in denying them any real "choice" at all, has seemingly reneged on the covenanted promise of earthly happiness in exchange for assiduous religious piety. In small ways, they may seek revenge by performing covert "selfish" acts, ostensibly at their neighbors' expense though in actuality aimed at provoking God; they delight in the guilty pleasure of such transgression. Additionally, such women often cling tenaciously to what they *do* have, a possession or talent, and react bitterly when it is threatened.

Repressed for years, such frustration and anger often explode, however. Freeman's elderly women tend to go "on strikes" against Providence and in doing so disobey for the first time in their lives the Sabbath obligation. Such extreme rebellion results not only from an older woman's loneliness and sense of being "cheated" by God but also from the injustice and hypocrisy of a society that observes the outer rituals but fails to practice the spirit of Christianity. Isolated, poverty-stricken, and shorn of self-worth, such a woman's rebellious behavior is both a release of years of pent-up emotion and a desperate outcry for help.

In all cases, when the minister inevitably comes to reprimand a transgressant woman, he is held up as the exemplar of the abuses of the patriarchal religion he represents. The least courageous of the men in Freeman's villages, the minister is utterly helpless when it comes to understanding women or sympathizing with their plight; he is embarrassed by their display of emotion. Moreover, the village community likewise displays its hypocrisy. A religious dissenter is gossiped about and ostracized by males and females alike. In their protests against such injustice, Freeman's older women protagonists strive toward a deeper, truer spirituality, one based on efficacious justice and charity.

Freeman, then, takes a place among New England women writers of regional fiction by critiquing the institutions of marriage and patriarchal Calvinism, going beyond the "limited feminism" of writers in the sentimental/domestic tradition to explore in a more forceful and concrete manner the pernicious effects of both institutions on late-nineteenth- and early-twentieth-century women's lives. Like Stowe in such works as *The Minister's Wooing* and *Oldtown Folks*, Freeman condemns a blind adherence to an antiquated Calvinism; like Cooke in "The Mormon's Wife" and "Mrs. Flint's Married Experience" and like Phelps in *The Story of Avis*, she criticizes a sentimental view of marriage; and like Jewett in *The Country of the Pointed Firs*, hers is a world in which men are largely absent or insignificant. Similar to all of these writers, she uses the changing face of New England—that once-proud, yet declining center of American culture—to express a realistic image of the transitional American woman.

In regarding her work vis-à-vis that of these other New England realists, especially Stowe and Jewett, Freeman has been judged less optimistic about women's lives and the possibility of women surmounting the limitations of their roles. Both Stowe and Jewett had indeed envisioned rural New England as a harmonious matriarchy, one in which women nurture each other and preserve values and traditions for the coming generation. In comparison, Freeman's short stories appear bleak; in her world one finds no lingering matriarchy, no supportive female community.

Yet such a reading, truthful as it is, has the adverse effect of continuing the misconception that Freeman's work is necessarily depressing or reactionary. A number of critics, both in Freeman's lifetime and later in this century, have found her raw portraits of the effects of the stubborn Puritan will on the New England character unsavory. Moreover, from the beginning, some readers have been uncomfortable with Freeman's decidedly unromantic female characters. The "bony figures of aging spinsters" that people her pages were not considered—and still may not be considered by some—interesting or even appropriate subject matter for literature (Brooks, New England, 469).

Although Freeman is intent on chronicling a waning way of life and the "terminal moraine" of the New England village, she does not do so cynically or pessimistically. Her work at times borders on naturalism in its unflinching observation of the harsh realities around her and in its probing of the myriad inner and outer forces that constitute people's lives, but she is not a determinist in her view of human nature. Rather, her work may be best seen as pushing us forward from the more simplistically conceived local-color realism into the advent of modern, psychological literature. No matter what the circumstances of the story's plot, her subject matter remains the same: the continual human striving for connection, relationship, and ultimate meaning amidst the breakdown of community and communication.

It is precisely the point at which she strips her female characters of external support that, to my mind at least, Freeman's stories achieve their greatest power. Struggling for meaning, identity, and union with others, Freeman's women must come to terms with their private consciences, their deepest longings and desires, their society's and religion's prescriptions on their behavior, and the needs and demands of others. Such an interior struggle is, ultimately, a spiritual and a lonely one. It is no more and no less than the human condition. In thus rendering the internal conflicts of women in the turn-of-the-century New England village, Freeman's fiction does not merely portray a "dying" world but uses those stark outer circumstances positively to explore in depth women's valiant responses to them.

Freeman's primary strength as a writer is the universal aspects of her themes, particularly as they apply to women's lives. Her best short stories exhibit a keen dramatic sense as the reader is skillfully led through a series of confrontations between characters, each serving to heighten dramatic tension and underscore the subtleties of the main conflict. As mentioned, this main conflict is always internal and often based on an ironic manipulation of sentimental plots. It is fraught with ambiguity, fear, and urgency. With a single line of seemingly commonplace dialogue, a flat, objective delineation of household items or dress, a laconic description of a quiet, yet deliberate move on the part of the protagonist, Freeman masterfully clues us into the magnitude of that internal conflict, alerting us to the basic and unquenchable drive of the human spirit for dignity and meaning.

Some of Freeman's work, especially that produced in her later years, has been descried for its "lapses" from realism into romantic and sentimental veins. In considering this matter, one does find such sentimental strains throughout the large corpus of her work. As noted, Freeman often makes use of sentimental material in order to twist its content and displace its import. This parody of sentimental fiction, only recently studied in the work of women local-colorists, accounts for much of these apparent "lapses" in Freeman's short stories. Freeman often explores the conflict in a woman's mind between a romantic vision of life and the reality of her situation, but she does so in subtle and suggestive ways. A cursory reading of a story may therefore mislead one into regarding it as pure sentiment.

It is also important, however, to note that Freeman remained greatly attracted to romance throughout her life and, as she achieved a comfortable degree of security along with her success, increasingly experimented with it. Foster mentions that she spent much of her youth "reading, reading, reading. She loved fairy tales, which to her seemed completely real" (15). Her earliest published poems were romantic, fanciful ballads and lyrics as the titles suggest: "The Enchanted Tale of Banbury Cross," "All Hallowe'en," "A Midsummer Song," and "The Fairy Flag," and many of her children's tales are stories of fairyland and fantasy with such titles as "The Cow with the Golden Horns," "The Little Persian Princess," and "Seventoe's Ghost." She continued to produce such poems and children's stories throughout much of her life. Believing correctly that she could capitalize on popular interest, she soon turned to the realistic short story; nevertheless, she continued to wish for "more symbolism, more mysticism" in her work written for adults. In her later years, and especially once she married, her reading consisted of mostly romantic and sentimental fiction. When Joseph Edgar Chamberlin visited her home in 1898, he found to his dismay that her mantel shelves were lined with "Scott's novels, and not another book!"; Freeman confessed to him that she "liked to read them often . . . and also Dickens and Thackeray" (155–56). So as not to let her reading "interfere" with her work, Charles Freeman later insisted she read "only the frothiest books—adventure and crime stories, historical novels . . . the funnies and the murders of *The New York Evening Journal*" (Foster, 161).

In further considering the effects of Freeman's idealistic vein, one can for convenience's sake divide her literary career into approximately three periods. The first encompasses the years 1877 to 1882 and consists of the lyrics, ballads, and children's stories that mark her earliest publications. The second, 1883 to 1895, marks the high period of Freeman's success, that in which she earned a permanent place in the history of American literature. During these prolific years she produced the fifty-two stories collected in *A Humble Romance* and *A New England Nun*, including such important tales as "The Revolt of 'Mother,'" "A Village Singer," "Louisa," and "A Poetess"; many of the stories that would be collected after 1895 (for example, all of those in *Silence and Other Stories*); approximately thirty-one uncollected stories published in newspapers and magazines; the murder mystery "The Long Arm," written in conjunction with Joseph Edgar Chamberlin;

three plays, *Giles Corey, Yeoman* and *Red Robin, A New England Drama* and a play based on her novel *Jane Field;* two novels, *Jane Field* and *Pembroke;* and three collections of children's stories, *The Pot of Gold, Young Lucretia,* and *Comfort Pease and Her Gold Ring.*

The adult stories of this second period are, in general, not only Freeman's most realistic but also her strongest. No collection subsequent to *A Humble Romance* and *A New England Nun* shows the consistency she achieves with objective narration, terse dialogue, dramatic intensity, and subtle ironies. This is not to say that the more than 160 stories produced after 1895 are necessarily inferior in and of themselves; but rather, from this time onward, Freeman's writing, for reasons described below, became much more uneven. Many of the stories of this latter period, in fact, exhibit the same marks of originality and skill as those produced earlier; many others, however, fall short of that standard.

Freeman chose the genre of short story not only because it sold well but also, quite practically, because it was *short.* In response to Pattee's question, "What directed you toward the short story?" Freeman replied, "I think the answer is very simple. The short story did not take so long to write, it was easier, and of course I was not *sure* of my own ability to write even the short story, much less a novel. I do consider the art of the novel as a very different affair from that of the short story" (Kendrick, 382). Thus the short story supplied Freeman with a safe arena for her apprenticeship. It is to her credit that, once she had tested and proven her skill in that genre, Freeman would attempt to develop her genius by undertaking longer works. By 1892 her first novel, *Jane Field,* was already being serialized in *Harper's Monthly.*

Freeman's novels, however, are a disappointment to anyone turning directly to them from her early stories. As is quickly apparent (and in many ways quite natural), she was not able to sustain the salient features of her singular style—compression, unobtrusive narration, laconic dialogue, intense unity of action—in a form that by definition required a degree of diffusion and verbosity. Her early critics were quick to point out her "regrettable" ventures into the longer genre. "Miss Wilkins . . . thinks in the length of the short story. . . . [S]he has never been able to see the larger proportions of the novel in their proper perspective," one aptly stated (Thompson, 672). An often repeated comment was that her novels tended to read as if they were rather hastily spliced together short stories. Each one of her longer works contains a number of deftly rendered passages and moments of sheer dramatic excellence; yet the endings often seem forced as Freeman attempts to gather together the various strains of the plot. The overall effect is, in general, lame.

Although technically unsatisfactory, a number of Freeman's novels remain thematically interesting, especially insofar as they illuminate the repeated concerns of her short fiction. *Jane Field*, a study of the New England conscience, contains many themes one finds in the short stories: a troubled mother-daughter relationship made even more acute by the daughter's impending marriage; poverty resulting from a male's squandering of the family money; and the pernicious effects of village women's gossip. *Pembroke*, considered Freeman's best novel and by some even a minor classic of American realistic literature, once again draws together many characteristic themes, this time in a more structurally unified form. Based on an incident occurring in Freeman's own family, the main plot revolves around lovers separated by the stubbornness of the young man who has quarreled with his fiancée's father. Four subplots run parallel to this primary plot, three of which involve thwarted or otherwise unhealthy love affairs and two of which involve mother-child relationships. In addition, Freeman makes some effective use of symbolism in the novel: the male protagonist's bent back comes to stand for the deformity of his headstrong will. Most importantly, Freeman manages here to achieve what is lacking in her other novels: coherent form, unity of tone and atmosphere, and a satisfactory conclusion.

Although Freeman continued writing short stories after 1895, most of her energy was directed toward the twelve novels, some of them running to more than five hundred pages, she produced between 1896 and 1917. For both practical and personal reasons, she experimented with a variety of themes and styles in these works, hoping to simultaneously appeal to public taste and satisfy her own desire to grow artistically. *Madelon* (1896) and *The Heart's Highway* (1900) are romances; *Jerome, A Poor Man* (1897) and *The Portion of Labor* (1901) are critical studies of the effects of poverty; *The Jamesons* (1899), *The Debtor* (1905), and *The Butterfly House* (1912) are social satires; *"Doc" Gor-*

906) is a melodrama; *By The Light of the Soul* (1907) is a quasi-
biography; *The Shoulders of Atlas* (1908), written in a record two
months for a contest sponsored by the *New York Herald,* is a study of
the New England conscience; and *The Whole Family* (1908) and *An
Alabaster Box* (1917) are cooperative ventures. For the most part improbably structured and weakly concluded, none of these novels—
with the possible exception of *The Shoulders of Atlas,* which marks a
return to New England themes and explores among other issues a disturbing and volatile mother-daughter relationship—contributes greatly
to Freeman's artistic merit.

In seeking in her novel writing the dual aims of satisfying an unpredictable popular market and enriching her personal repertoire, Freeman sacrificed in this latter period the spontaneity and powerful originality that consistently characterized her early short fiction. As she
increasingly abandoned her New England themes and sparse, com-
pressed style, the subsequent loss of realism turned to artificiality; the
terse, direct dialogue became labored, overwritten prose. After re-
sounding praise for *Pembroke,* critics routinely and increasingly dispar-
aged each novel to follow. "Inelegant," "in bad taste," and "clumsy"
were among the adjectives hurled at the prose style of *Madelon* by a
typical reviewer. He concluded his remarks with a statement that may
aptly be applied to all of Freeman's subsequent novels: "the work [is]
a curious study in literary awkwardness and affectation" (Preston, 361).
Accusing her of "selling out" to public demand, novelist and critic
Frank Norris likewise voiced his objection to her experiment with
historical romance, *The Heart's Highway:* "A writer who occupies so
eminent a place as Miss Wilkins, who has become so important . . .
cannot escape the responsibilities of her position. . . . [I]n spite of the
fact that those who believe in the future of our nation's letters look to
such established reputations as hers to keep the faith . . . Miss Wilkins chooses to succumb to the momentary, transitory set of the tide,
and forsaking her own particular work, puts forth, one of a hundred
others, a 'colonial romance.' It is a discrowning" (197–98).

Despite such increasingly negative criticism, Freeman continued to
concentrate her writing primarily on longer works. Nevertheless, after
1895 she somehow managed as well to maintain her usual high output
of short stories. Inevitably, some of that short fiction suffers from the

same unfortunate characteristics as the longer works she was concurrently composing: forced prose, implausible plots, weak endings. Her stories still much in demand, she complied during these years with numerous requests to write for holiday issues of magazines and newspapers, as titles such as "Thanksgiving Crossroads," "A Christmas Lady," "Susan Jane's Valentine," and "Mrs. Sackett's Easter Bonnet" suggest. As can be imagined, many of these pieces have contrived "happy" endings in keeping with the publisher's request for lighthearted seasonal fiction. In addition, as with her novels, Freeman now also began to use some of her stories as vehicles for experimentation in style and theme. She wrote, for example, some purely romantic and sentimental tales at this time along with social satires, ghost stories, and symbolic tales.

Together with a number of stories that harken back to New England themes and approach the same degree of excellence as her earliest tales ("The Tree of Knowledge," "The Prism," "The Strike of Hannah," "Old Woman Magoun," "Friend of My Heart," "The Balking of Christopher," "The Saving of Hiram Sessions," and "Sour Sweetings"), the fiction in the ghost stories and symbolic tales is noteworthy and attests to Freeman's continuing skill. Her volume of ghost stories, *The Wind in the Rose-Bush and Other Stories of the Supernatural* (1903), contains several works, such as "The Lost Ghost" and "Luella Miller," that are well-conceived and haunting in their study of the psychology of fear; these stories, too, return us to the New England village. Moreover, the symbolic nature stories collected in *Understudies* (1901) and *Six Trees* (1903), such as "Arethusa," "The Balsam Fir," and "The Great Pine," express Freeman's desire for "more symbolism, more mysticism" in subtle and even poetic ways. Here, she successfully explores the equation between animals, flowers, and trees, and aspects of human nature. And finally, many of the stories produced after 1895, though at times marred by awkward prose and the author's increasing penchant for the sentimental, continue to contribute to a composite portrait of Freeman's New England women characters.

In the first decade of the twentieth century, Freeman's reputation, as well as that of most of the women local-colorists, was also considerably diminished by larger cultural and literary shifts. Rural New England, "female" subject matter, and the Calvinistic conscience were considered passé—naive—in the mental and moral upheaval of the time. The daring and decidedly masculine fictions of Theodore Dreiser, Stephen Crane, and Frank Norris were new and exciting. In fact, the social climate in general in the period just before and after World War I included a sharp reaction against the legacy of Victorian feminine values. Social Darwinism, Muscular Christianity, and Teddy Roosevelt's "big stick" policy all were influences on or manifestations of a period that Ann Douglas has called a "militant crusade for masculinity" (327). In literature, the new naturalism's emphasis on determinism, force, and free expression of the "baser" human instincts scorned the work of the previous generation of writers as indicative of a weak and overly genteelized America. "Observe the condition in which we now are," Van Wyck Brooks wrote in 1934; "sultry, flaccid, hesitant, not knowing what we want . . . [we] stand in mortal fear of letting loose the spiritual appetites that impede our pursuit of a neat, hygienic and sterile success" (*Three Essays*, 169). Likewise, Malcolm Cowley's 1937 *After the Genteel Tradition* condemned writers in the Howellsian tradition as timid, "false and life-denying" and applauded the current "bold and passionate" young generation of writers that "has untied itself from their stepmotherly apron strings" (13–14). "Flaccid," "sterile," "life-denying": clearly, the verbal metaphors of the times indicate a disdain for, if not downright hostility toward, all things not aggressively "masculine" and therefore by definition weak or "feminine."

A 1919 reviewer's vitriolic attack on *The Copy-Cat and Other Stories* (1914) shows the disfavor Freeman's largely feminine subject matter already evoked less than thirty years after her initial widespread success. After explaining that the content of the collection's title story concerns a young girl's school experiences, the critic fairly seethes, "This in the year of our Lord 1914! This in the year when blood began to flow as it has never flowed before; when free peoples everywhere awoke to the presence of Black Evil on earth; when big, generous America with all her faults was not exactly likely to be thrilled or touched or enlightened by the recital of how a plain little girl finally got up enough gumption to wear pink ribbons instead of blue. . . . But it is wretched stuff, really" (Overton, 200).

Even earlier, Freeman's concentration on women and women's concerns was deemed by some a potential liability to her art. Although in most respects a fair and balanced account of her early work, Thompson's article maintains the typical attitude of some critics of the time toward women's subject matter and the possibilities of its representation in fiction; narrow and restricting, it was simply not particularly exciting. "Had [Miss Wilkins] been a boy," Thompson wrote, "she would have roamed the fields, gone fishing and hunting, had the privilege of sitting in the country store and listening to the talk of the men of evenings; she would have . . . learned to look at life as the men look at it, with the larger and more catholic view which is theirs. . . . As she was a girl, her outlook was confined to the household; her sources of information were the tales of gossiping women, which would naturally relate mostly to the family quarrels and dissensions that are the great tragedies of their lives" (668).

It is a shame, Thompson says in effect, that Mary Wilkins was born a woman and raised among women; necessarily, therefore, she had produced and would continue to produce second-rate art. Though female reviewers tended, on the whole, to be more sympathetic to Freeman's works, several chastised Freeman, not for her use of women characters in general, but for her use of a particular kind of woman, which at the turn of the century was considered outmoded. After briefly commenting on the "sorry" male characters in Freeman's stories, critic Mary E. Wardwell stated in an 1899 review, "The women are still more unfortunate. Patience and endurance, which in the struggling days of the colonies two centuries ago were noble qualities, reappear again and again in forlorn old maids and long-suffering wives." Wardwell criticizes Freeman's failure to acknowledge the advent of the "new woman" whose recent entrance into society, she maintains, is rapidly displacing older values:

> To the remotest nook of farthest Vermont and New Hampshire she [the new woman] will penetrate with her clubs and her fashion-books and her scientific housekeeping. There will be no more old maids in many-times turned gowns, living alone with a cat and a poor little memory of some faithless swain . . . but a busy, cheerful set of women, well-dressed, well-fed, and perfectly happy though single. It would be less

quaint, less picturesque, less to her taste, but most interesting if Miss Wilkins would take us back amongst some of her plain-song people after they have been stirred by the broad and vivifying influences of the time [27–28].

Even within Freeman's lifetime, then, changing popular tastes in literature had supplanted her rural, feminine subject matter, contributing to her loss of reputation in those years as well as throughout the middle decades of this century. Only recently, in fact, have Freeman's stories about women and their concerns been ripe for "rediscovery" in an atmosphere that now regards a woman's world—whether she be married or unmarried, old or young, impoverished or wealthy—as a unique, substantive, and interesting part of reality.

Having unwittingly set for herself a standard for literary excellence in the early part of her career, Freeman strove throughout the remaining years of her life to regain the popular acclaim she was sadly and confusedly aware of having lost. Although she was virtually worshipped by her audience in the late 1880s and early 1890s, she could write only thirty years thereafter to an aspiring young author, "Everything is different since the War. . . . As nearly as I can understand the situation, there is in arts and letters a sort of frantic impulse for something erratic, out of the common. . . . I am none too sure of a market for my own wares. . . . I am about as bewildered by the whole situation as you are" (Kendrick, 401–2).

Freeman's initial success with her realistic stories of rural New England occurred not only because such works were in keeping with the vogue for local-color literary realism at the time but also because they consistently exhibited—and continue to exhibit—a freshness of technique and an intensity and depth of theme unsurpassed by anything else she wrote. After 1895, as she increasingly experimented with other genres and styles, her writing began to have much more of the "air of the marketplace" about it; the sheer quantity of the work itself indicates an inevitable corresponding sacrifice of quality or at least an overall unevenness. Nevertheless, in the latter portion of her career she intermittently produced many well-wrought short stories, so many, in fact, that one cannot simply dismiss this period altogether as lacking in artistic value.

Perhaps, finally, it is the uneasy merging of the two sides of Freeman's nature that paradoxically produced her best work and her worst work. A realist grounded in the harsh realities of the turn-of-the-century New England village, a Calvinist for whom a constant probing of the conscience was second nature, she insisted on truth telling and a moral basis to her art. On the other hand, a romantic who delighted in fantasy and fairy tales, an "idealist in masquerade," she attempted as well through much of her career to fulfill her longing for "more symbolism, more mysticism" in her writing. Her greatest work was written by the unflinching realist with an idealist sensibility; her weakest work was written by the sentimentalist whose strict Puritan background overshadowed romantic flights of imagination. It is significant that, when Freeman was once asked her opinion of what the future novel might be like, she voiced her own life's attempt to merge these two disparate sides of herself: "I imagine the great 'Novel of the Future' will be at once romantic and realistic," she replied, "that in it romance and realism will be combined more equally than they have ever been" (Kendrick, 110). In the study of Freeman's short fiction, we find both the romantic and the realist emerging in her many and various portraits of women's lives.

CHAPTER 3

Women as Daughters in the Family

"The Web of Self-Strangulation"

"The family is the first community we know, and it takes the shape of Mother," Nina Auerbach states in her study of women in fiction, *Communities of Women* (34).[1] For Mary Wilkins Freeman, this truth was indisputable. Although her mother died when Freeman was still a young woman, the specter of "mother" as an authority and power figure continued to haunt her adult life, manifesting itself time and again in her short stories.[2] The pictures she paints of mother and motherhood are scarcely rosy. Far from the warmth and comfort of Louisa May Alcott's Marmee in *Little Women*, for example, a woman who guides and nourishes her loving, closely knit family, Freeman's typical mother is physically and emotionally burdened, her family broken and bereft of intimacy. What strength or fortitude she evinces is born mostly of desperation or necessity, rarely of inner security or confidence. Her relationship with her husband is strained; at best, the two staunchly fulfill the duties of their separate spheres, she in the kitchen and he on the farm, and they make no pretense of conjugal intimacy. More typically, however, a mother in Freeman's world is raising a child or children alone; her husband has either died or deserted the family, many times to "go west." The strain becomes, at times, unbearable. Children growing up in such an atmosphere quickly learn to be "seen and not heard"; lonely and misunderstood, they regard their parents with a fear that often continues into their adult years.

By far the greatest tension between mother and daughter in Freeman's stories occurs over the question of the daughter's marriage when she comes of age. A mother often bitterly resents her child's choice, and the child resents her mother's interference. Should the daughter choose not to marry, roles in the family often become reversed, with the adult child now wielding tyrannical authority over the aged, child-like parent.

Freeman has several stories of the relationship between fathers and daughters, but her largest group of stories explores the emotional ties between mothers and daughters in the family. This all-important relationship forges, in Freeman's world, a woman's sense of self and her role in life. Although Freeman's young women often do remain single, they expect for the most part to become wives and mothers, the "one socially respectable, nondeviant role for women" in earlier centuries and in Freeman's turn-of-the-century New England as well (Smith-Rosenberg, 213). Rarely do any of Freeman's young females consider seeking employment other than occasional schoolteaching for necessity's sake. Yet their experiences with and observations of women's roles in the family show those roles to be replete with trouble and frustration. They see little to emulate in their mothers' lives.

Furthermore, many of Freeman's mother and daughter stories concern problems with separation and differentiation of the self, both mother from daughter and daughter from mother. Freeman's biography, sketchy as it is in details about her early family life, may throw some light on this recurring theme. Her mother Eleanor was a firm, practical, and ambitious woman; her father Warren a sensitive, artistic, decidedly weaker individual by contrast. Both families were from old and genteel New England stock; both could trace their heritages back to seventeenth-century Puritan New England. The traditional "code" of New England life, based, as Foster puts it, on the Puritan ideals of "Work, Thrift, Family, Gentility," required a man to provide for his family, ensuring their comfort (20). Although he possessed considerable talent as a builder and architect, Warren Wilkins's business ventures failed repeatedly, reducing the family through most of

Mary's childhood and teenage years to near-desperate straits. Half way through his life, Wilkins seemed to give up; Foster relates that friends and neighbors in Brattleboro "thought of him as a 'putterer' and as one who was always doing little services for others, partly perhaps to maintain his own dignity" (37).

Eleanor Wilkins bore four children: two died in infancy, and the third child, Anna, a talented, active, and popular young woman— from several accounts her parents' favorite—died suddenly in 1876 at the age of seventeen. Mary Wilkins, the only remaining child, was twenty-four in this year. Only a few years later, in 1880, Eleanor Wilkins died while still in middle-age.

Young Mary Wilkins was evidently a strong-willed yet clinging and dependent child, sensitive and moody like her father. A dreamer and a brooder, she must have sometimes felt her energetic mother's displeasure as she sat at the window doing nothing but looking out for hours on end (Foster, 42). Certainly, she recognized her mother's shame and the tension mounting between her parents as their financial situation worsened daily. When Anna died, the relationship between Mrs. Wilkins and Mary must have necessarily altered; Freeman's story "A Gentle Ghost" suggests that this adjustment served to produce an even greater tension between mother and daughter than had previously existed. Moreover, after Eleanor Wilkins's death, both father and daughter were sorely pressed to manage for themselves. Warren Wilkins died three years later, and Mary spent her adult life under the care of a succession of dominating, motherlike figures, one of whom was Mary John Wales, the friend with whom she lived for much of her adult life. Others with whom she formed a parent-child relationship included editors Mary Louise Booth and Henry Alden of *Harper's*; her husband Charles Freeman; and a string of household maids, one of whom evidently called her "Mrs. Baby" (Kendrick, 12).

Few if any of Freeman's letters refer directly to her childhood, but several reveal her belief that men were immature and insufficient, even superfluous in the family. Women, on the other hand, were the practical ones, those in charge. In 1912, ten years after she married, Freeman wrote to a close woman friend,

> So your husband is off in pursuit of bugs and things again. Well, mine
> goes up once a week to look after business, and the rest of the time,

smokes, and stays here like a real nice happy boy. It pleases me to see him having such a good time. He gets nervous, and used up if he does not have good times. I imagine most men do. Women have, on the whole . . . more back bone under difficulties. Why not? They have had harder training. They or their ancestors have borne and reared the men. . . . Also, women have not . . . enough time to waste on such disgraceful affairs as that Chicago Convention, where all the little boys without their mas handy to spank 'em, fought and rolled in the dust of politics for office [Kendrick, 340].

Freeman's hesitancy to marry may have resulted in part from both her childhood experience of a dominating mother and a weak father and from her continuing childlike need for a mother herself. What we can ascertain from perusing Freeman's substantial group of stories that are focused on the relationship between mothers and daughters at home, however, is that Freeman clearly experienced unresolved conflict with her own mother well into her adult years. Moreover, this conflict not only colored her adult relationships with both men and women but influenced her views of womanhood in general. The looming spectre of "mother" in Freeman's fiction thus is an appropriate beginning point in understanding Freeman's portraits of women in relationships.

Discovering the mother and daughter relationship in Freeman's stories first requires a look at the context in which these relationships are formed, the family structure. Freeman was concerned with family life, and in her nearly fifty years of story writing, she explored nearly every aspect of family relationships. She writes, for example, fantasy stories of "ideal" families; stories of struggling single parents; stories of desertion and divorce; stories of adoption; and stories of the loving bonds between grandparents and children. Conspicuous in their very absence, however, is the type of story we might at first expect from a writer who also succeeded in delighting a generation of children with romantic, sentimental tales and poems, works replete with "happy" endings. Out of all of Freeman's short stories written for adults, scarcely a handful involves a cohesive family unit consisting of father, mother, and one or more children; moreover, among these stories only several show the family working or playing together in domestic harmony. As in Freeman's own life, poverty or the fear thereof usually

poses a continual threat to family stability. The dominant parent in
these stories is nearly always the mother; although she might not assert
her will overtly against her husband's, in nearly all cases she is shown
to be more powerful, more effectual, and above all more practical and
realistic than her weaker-willed and often dully unresponsive husband.

"The Revolt of 'Mother,'" one of Freeman's best-known and finely
crafted works, has much to say about familial relationships. Yet because it is one of her small group of stories concerning a "traditional"
family unit, it by no means represents the author's view of the family
in her works as a whole. As in the majority of Freeman stories, the
bald outline of the plot seems simple enough: Sarah Penn, a "meek"
but "immovable" woman, learns that her husband Adoniram is building yet another barn despite his long-standing promise of a new house
for the family. When her patient yet exacting reminder of his failure
to do his "duty" by her is met only by an "inarticulate" front, Sarah,
trembling yet undaunted, acts with firm decisiveness to justify what
she perceives as a breach of contract between them. Taking advantage
of Adoniram's absence on a business trip, she moves her family into
the new barn. Her desperate action so stuns Adoniram upon his return
that he is emotionally overcome, acquiescing in full to her desires for
room partitions in the structure and even for new furniture.

The simple folktale outlines of the plot allow Freeman the vehicle
to explore at length the matter that interests her most: the internal,
private struggles of a New England woman torn between duty and
justice, between submission and revolt. In carefully detailing Sarah
Penn's responses to her daily working environment as well as the exigency of her removal to the barn, Freeman invites us—the woman
reader especially—to read "between the lines" and participate in
mother's moral dilemma.

Freeman's tone and technique here as in many of her stories are
essentially, as Fred Lewis Pattee once stated, the art of the old ballad
(201). Although avoiding authorial comment and standing apart from
her material, she is never detached from it. A writer primarily of short
magazine fiction, Freeman in 1890, the year "The Revolt of 'Mother'"
first appeared in Harper's Monthly, was already skilled at producing
stories that captured the attention quickly and maintained that attention by immersing the reader swiftly in the central conflict. A favorite

technique was the opening of a story *in medias res* with a single line or several lines of dialogue, often consisting of a confrontational, paradoxical, or otherwise startling statement or question. The reader immediately assumes the delicious role of eavesdropper in a matter that cannot help but elicit the desire to hear more. Eleven of the twenty-four stories in the 1891 collection *A New England Nun* open in just this way. "I never heard of a woman's bein' saxton," begins "A Church Mouse" as we are thrust in the midst of a controversy over Hetty Fifield's outrageous claim that women could do as well as men—even better—in keeping up the local meetinghouse. "I don't see what kind of ideas you've got in your head, for my part," begins "Louisa" as we enter the scene of an on-going and bitter conflict between mother and daughter. In "The Revolt of 'Mother,'" Freeman further couples the opening dialogue with the expectations already set up by a humorously ironic title. Mothers do not revolt, at least not conventionally in Freeman's New England. Moreover, Freeman places "mother" in quotation marks, indicating the word's special emphasis. "Mother," we understand, is not a term of absolute identity but an assumed title; this is the story, then, not so much of the revolt of Sarah Penn the individual, but of Sarah Penn the mother. It is precisely this motherly role that gives Sarah sanction for her audacious action in the course of the story.

Sarah and Adoniram Penn call each other familiarly "mother" and "father," preferring titles that mutually define their primary roles as parents to their children Sammy and Nanny. The story opens with Sarah Penn's reasserting Adoniram's role as such with a single call: "Father!" Three times she calls to him with increasing exasperation, attempting to obtain a straightforward answer: "I want to know what them men are diggin' over there in that field for." In its third repetition, "father" is underlined; Sarah's enunciation of the word now has not only urgency in it but a bitter tone as well. Certainly, Adoniram's "growling" statement, "I wish you'd go into the house, mother, an' 'tend to your own affairs," lays derogatory emphasis on the word "mother" while simultaneously bidding Sarah to remember "mother's" place: the tiny, inadequate, and "box-like" house, a contrast to the "the great barn and a long reach of sheds and out-buildings" that make up father's sphere. To this house Sarah retreats; for forty years she has faithfully performed her duties there as wife and mother, before her husband, her children, and her God. Her record is clean, and she knows it.

Adoniram's record, however, is not so clean; from the moment the story opens, he obviously recalls the promise of a new house made forty years ago to his wife and is consequently shame-faced before her. He has purposely hidden the building of the new barn from Sarah as long as he could. From her first queries, therefore, Adoniram is determined to present a hardened front: "there was a sudden dropping and enlarging of the lower part of the old man's face, as if some heavy weight had settled therein." His passive resistance to her entreaties, while cruel, only serves to underscore his uneasiness. Such a stance allows him to keep emotional distance and maintain control in what he realizes is a potentially explosive and even humiliating situation. "I ain't got nothin' to say," he repeats, making Sarah's attempts to "talk real plain" and at length about his promises to her, her patient toiling through the years, and the present injustice of the situation appear ludicrous by contrast. He succeeds, and his silence renders her "eloquence futile with mocking echoes."

In confronting Adoniram, Sarah is attentive to both the form and content of her message; she has obviously rehearsed many times for this moment. She bids her husband sit down, while she herself "stood before [him] in the humble fashion of a Scripture woman." Her appeal is two-fold, both on behalf of herself and on behalf of her daughter Nanny: "you see this room, father; it's all the one I've had to work in an' eat in an' sit in sence we was married. . . . It's all the room [Nanny'll] have to be married in." In dramatic fashion she illustrates her points by throwing open the doors to the bedroom, the pantry, the upstairs rooms: "there, father"; "here, father"; "there, father," she exclaims as she forces him to confront the facts of the matter. "Now, father," she concludes, reiterating the essential injustice of the situation and pointing out unequivocally Adoniram's hypocrisy: "I want to know if you think you're doin' right an' accordin' to what you profess. . . . You can't say nothin' without ownin' it ain't right, father." Adoniram, of course, need all along "say nothing" to have his way—the barn will be built if he so chooses—but in remaining silent, as Sarah ironically indicates, he succeeds in implicating himself even further.

Sarah's inner agitation is apparent as she returns to her chores. An unwonted "clatter of dishes" emanates from the pantry; she "plunged her hands vigorously" into the dishwater, "scrubbed a dish fiercely," and later, when she emerged from her bedroom after a brief absence, "her eyes were red." Moreover, her turmoil is not merely of a day but rather of an entire season: laboring in her kitchen throughout the spring, she is forced to hear "the halloos and the noises of saws and hammers" as the new barn is erected. Adoniram meanwhile is in his element. An impressive structure in the small village, the barn brings spectators: "men came on pleasant Sundays, in their meeting suits and clean shirt bosoms, and stood around it admiringly." "Mrs. Penn," however, the laconic narrator informs us, "did not speak of it."

Though Sarah's appeal has been both for justice for herself and for her children, especially her daughter Nanny, it is in the end her role as "mother"—and not her needs as an individual—that allows her the extreme action of setting up the household in the new barn. Nanny suggests the possibility, albeit in jest: "We might have [my] wedding in the new barn." Though Sarah is at once bemused at and intrigued by the suggestion, she will not act upon it; it yet needs the sanctioning of Providence, and for that she must wait. Sarah, however, is used to waiting; as has been pointed out, her name recalls the Sarah of Genesis who after years of waiting bore a child in her old age (Gallagher, 1). As she waits for the movement of Providence, her attention is called more and more to the fact that her daughter is not well. In her "plain talk" with Adoniram, Sarah has enjoined him to consider Nanny's health: "if we don't have another house . . . Nanny she can't live with us after she's married. . . . She wa'n't ever strong. . . . [S]he ain't fit to keep house an' do everything herself." Now, she observes Nanny sharply:

> "Have you got that pain in your side this mornin'?" she asked.
> "A little," [Nanny replied].
> Mrs. Penn's face, as she worked, changed, her perplexed forehead smoothed, her eyes were steady, her lips firmly set.

Sarah's wait has not been in vain; the sign from heaven comes at an opportune time. Just before the new barn is completed, Adoniram is called away from home for several days. Mindful of Nanny's failing health, Sarah concludes that "unsolicited opportunities are the guide-

posts of the Lord to the new roads of life. . . . It looks like a providence." She has earlier informed Nanny with barely contained scorn
that women "ought to reckon men-folks in with Providence"; now
Providence itself has provided her with the means to overcome Adoniram's stubborn opposition. Though she is fearful as she moves the
household goods into the new barn, she nevertheless performs the task
with the steady deliberation of one who is convinced that the Lord is
guiding her steps.

Freeman's mastery in "The Revolt of 'Mother'" is the careful, dramatic building up of tension in the several confrontations between
Sarah and Adoniram.[3] Each ends in an impasse; mother withdraws
and father continues his plans on schedule. Nothing in the story prepares us for the comic ending; no one could anticipate, given father's
gruff and cold demeanor throughout the majority of the developing
plot, that he would not only give in to mother but acquiesce emotionally as well. In the end, the narrator relates, he "was like a fortress
whose walls had no active resistance, and went down the instant the
right besieging tools were used." The "right besieging tools" were not
Sarah's words—Adoniram could and did refuse to hear them—but
her desperate action. Returning home Adoniram is once again rendered inarticulate, this time not by guilt but by surprise. "Why,
mother!" he exclaims several times as he gazes in a stupor at the warm
and inviting environment Sarah has created in the barn. He has had,
he confesses, "no idee" that Sarah had meant what she said, "no idee"
that she "was so set on't as all this comes to."

The story's comic reversal is a satisfying one; mother has triumphed
while continuing to maintain her moral superiority. Justice has been
served. "Father" has been a bad father in not caring for the needs of
his children (let alone those of his wife), but he will now attend to
those needs; "mother's" status has increased by her performing, under
God's guidance, the role of a caring and solicitous mother in providing her children with an adequate dwelling. The children meanwhile
have asserted, the narrator tells us, "an inborn confidence in their
mother over their father."

Later in her life, tired of readers and reviewers focusing attention
on this story (Theodore Roosevelt, evidently, added to its popular
acclaim by recommending it to mothers "for its strong moral lesson"

[Williams, 169]), Freeman stated that "The Revolt of 'Mother'" "is not in the least true. . . . There never was in New England a woman like Mother. . . . She simply would have lacked the nerve" ("Mary E. Wilkins Freeman: An Autobiography," 75). The story, however, rings false on another account when compared with Freeman's other stories of family life. Father and mother, though largely unable to comprehend one another, do manage here to come to some sort of mutual understanding or at least compromise. Father "sees" mother's needs for the first time; he has, it seems, not really been a cruel man, but a blind one. Sarah also, while acting to secure justice for herself, has been careful to pay full respect to her husband and to fulfill her duties as a wife. This, in the end, is perhaps Freeman's fullest portrait of love between husband and wife; she rarely again comes this close to suggesting a growth in their affection for or understanding of each other. Rather, married couples in Freeman's world live in mutual tolerance with little communication between them, each one a complete mystery to the other.

More often than not, if a Freeman story presents a traditional family structure, the father of that family is weak, emotionally distanced, or "touched" in some way that renders him incapable of concrete, practical decision or action. Freeman may well have regarded her own father in this way. In a story with obvious autobiographical overtones, "A Gentle Ghost" (1891), Mrs. Dunn, emotionally overwrought and haunted by the recent death of a daughter, turns to her remaining child, Flora, for comfort since her husband is incapable of understanding or responding to her grief. He is "slow-brained, patient, and unimaginative"; he daily sits dozing in his chair while mother and daughter contend with mounting fear. Mrs. Dunn "looked at him, sleeping there, with a bitter feeling. She felt as if set about by an icy wind of loneliness." Here Freeman, in a story no doubt painful to write, remembers back to her mother's sorrow at Anna Wilkins's death, her father's withdrawn silence, her feelings of helplessness in attempting to comfort her mother, and perhaps her own guilt at being the only surviving child in the family. We know that the story's theme personally haunted Freeman until she was able to express it in her writing. In 1889, after sending her the story, Freeman wrote to Sarah Orne Jewett, "You don't know how glad I am that you do like my Gentle

Ghost. . . . [T]hat forlorn little girl had been in my head a matter of a dozen years. . . . I felt that she must be disposed of, so . . . I put her in the Gentle Ghost" (Kendrick, 97).

Loneliness of a different sort besets Susan Rice in "The Cloak Also" (1917). In this story Freeman possibly records her own mother's fright and humiliation as the Wilkins's family funds continued to dwindle and she was forced to take on a menial job. Susan's husband Joel, an impractical and dreaming man, loses first her savings and then the family's in his futile attempt at storekeeping. As a young bride, Susan's trust in her husband had been absolute; later, however, as she silently watches him become more and more obsessed with his schemes, and as sickness and the birth of several children reduce them to poverty, she loses all faith in him. Every time he enters a new business venture, she now has "no doubt of his failure"; he senses her bitterness and growing lack of respect. Doggedly, Joel works on, until finally in a fit of angry passion he rails against the community he feels has failed him and commits suicide. Susan survives and quickly stabilizes the family finances, supporting herself and her children by giving music lessons. She soon settles more or less contentedly, as the narrator tells us, "into that peace of negation which sometimes comes, like a dew of blessing, after a tragedy."

Several other Freeman stories involve a husband who, under the guise of receiving a "call" from religion, loses touch with the real world and leaves his uncomprehending family to shoulder both the physical burden his irresponsibility creates and the burden of humiliation suffered from neighborhood gossip. Hiram Sessions, in "The Saving of Hiram Sessions" (1915), unaccountably "goes forward" at meeting one Sunday, declaring himself a changed man. Mrs. Sessions has no such illusions. "How on earth," she exclaims to herself, "is Hiram going to be a Christian and keep on living?" Hiram's naive attempt to live a totally "honest" life after his conversion results in sheer chaos as he alienates friends and family alike; finally, in despair, he breaks down one day into vehement cursing. "Your father," Sarah dryly informs her children as she goes about her daily routine, "has backslid." The story ends comically as Hiram publicly confesses his foolishness and is reunited with the community.

An earlier story with a similar theme is grim in outcome. "A New

England Prophet" (1898), reminiscent of Hawthorne's tales of the Puritan past, tells of Solomon Lennox, who, also suddenly "getting religion," succeeds in terrorizing both family and neighborhood. A once quiet and unemotional man, "his complete deviation from a former line of life produced among them the horror of the supernatural." In his new-found religious fury, this self-proclaimed prophet of Millerism preaches a steady gospel of God's imminent wrath. He insists on holding prayer meetings three times a day, so that "the housewives' kitchen tables were piled high with unwashed dishes, the hearths were unswept and the fires low, the pantry shelves were bare, and often the children went to bed with only the terrors of the judgment for sustenance." Mrs. Lennox becomes mesmerized with fear of her husband's actions; daughter Melissa's mind nearly becomes unhinged with the strain. Only when Solomon's prediction of the end of the world does not come true on the appointed day is the man chastened. Cold and miserable, the family returns home in the gray dawn after a night of frenzied watching and praying, and Solomon, like "a prophet brooding over the ashes of his own prophetic fire," falls into a lethargic stupor for the rest of his days.

A final story illustrating Freeman's conception of the irresponsible or ineffective husband is also reminiscent of a Hawthorne tale. "The Slip of the Leash" (1904), much like "Wakefield," concerns a man who "went wild" one day and deserts his wife, four children, and comfortable farm. "I was being tore to pieces betwixt them all," he tells himself, "and soon there would have been nothing at all left of me." His flight to the West is short-lived, for he has no ambition short of escaping his home life. He soon finds himself returning. Stopping just short of the settlement, he hides himself for years in the forest surrounding his own farm. Daily he watches his wife and children come and go, "filled . . . with a torture of yearning," yet resenting the "leash" he feels they would tether him on again should he return. Observing their increasing struggle to provide for themselves, he attempts to slip them money anonymously; finally, in a show of concern over the near-desperation of their plight, "he knew that the time was come when he must return to the trammels of love and happiness and anxiety." He does so, and though the reunion is briefly joyful, he knew that "his leash was upon him again."

If a husband or father is present at all in a Freeman story about family life, that husband or father is generally one who, through emotional weakness, lack of responsibility, or oddity of some type, becomes either inconsequential to the family's daily activity or leads them to financial ruin or humiliation through his behavior. Freeman's stories involving male protagonists are few. In several of these stories a father, grandfather, or uncle is the primary parent. Such stories include "A Moral Exigency" (1887) and "The Love of Parson Lord" (1900), in which the parent is a "cold" and "distant" minister; and a few minor tales, such as "Sonny" (1891), "The Butterfly" (1904), and "Daniel and Li'l Dan'l" (1914). In the latter three, the father-figure is old, weak, or overly sensitive. Indeed, Freeman does not depict a strong or effective father at all.

Far more typical in Freeman's canon are stories of single-parent homes dominated either by a mother or a mother-figure—a grandmother, aunt, or older sister. The father's absence is often unexplained. This typical Freeman scene reflects the reality of New England village life as Freeman knew it, for economic depression became widespread over rural New England after the Civil War. Men and young people abandoned the farms in droves, moving to the cities or the new western states to seek employment; old people and women with small children were left behind. A first-hand account of the personal tragedy resulting from this decline can be found in Rollin Hartt's two-part "A New England Hill Town" from the April and May 1899 *Atlantic Monthly.* Hartt records the result of this impoverishment and sense of decay on the remaining villagers. In particular, he stresses the unhealthy isolation that resulted: "Instead of asserting the spirit of neighborliness . . . we shrink from one another. . . . There is want of contact. We have not achieved the relativity of life; instead, we have simply accomplished its reflexivity; the soul is thrown back upon itself. . . . Less extensive, life becomes more intensive. The narrow stream runs deep. It runs too deep. Better were it shallower, if broader" (563).

The strain of raising children in such isolation and poverty reduces the woman to near-desperation; in at least three of Freeman's stories, this desperation turns her against her will to theft or even murder. In "The Strike of Hannah" (1906), Hannah, whose "helpless" and "childlike" husband is dead, rebels against the poverty that will not even allow her to purchase Thanksgiving dinner for her children. In anguish, she "broke into open revolt" against "Providence's oppressions" and steals her rich employer's Thanksgiving feast, not with any intention of eating it, but simply to "set the law of equals right." Similarly, in "A Stolen Christmas" (1891), grandmother Marg'ret, who keeps her dead daughter's children safe by securing them by ropes from the ceiling—ropes long enough to allow them to run about yet to remain under her eye—and who serves them with the good silver so "they'll think more of themselves," finds herself unable to buy them Christmas gifts one year. Justifying that "what cain't be airned . . . ought to be took," she steals toys from the local dry-goods store. Both of these tales center on the enormous battle produced by such unlawful steps in these women's consciences, for they are certain such extreme acts on behalf of their children will merit them eternal punishment.

A third story of a single woman caretaker, "Old Woman Magoun" (1909), is perhaps the most tragic and bitter tale Freeman ever wrote. Alice Glarden Brand, in an article for *New England Quarterly* entitled "Mary Wilkins Freeman: Misanthropy as Propaganda," has used this story as a prime example of what she sees as Freeman's "rage" in her later years against the "degenerate male image." A strong woman in a tiny settlement of unambitious and weak men, Magoun is helpless in protecting her childlike fourteen-year old granddaughter Lily from Lily's father, Nelson, who intends to "sell" the girl in payment for a gambling debt. In her terror, the old woman, coming upon her granddaughter innocently eating poison berries, does not stop her; she sees at this point no alternative but to allow Lily to die. "That sexual plunder threatens the innocence of a young girl is an obscenity for which the only plausible and exquisite option is death," Brand comments. "Lily is sacrificed in full sentimentalist style. Magoun is grotesquely ennobled" (97).

What, then, does it mean to be a mother of small children in Freeman's world? With few exceptions, Freeman portrays motherhood as a constant battle against physical and emotional poverty, often brought on by the death or absence of a male, but also a result of his irresponsibility or ineptitude when present in the family. Childlike and never a mother herself, Freeman generally remains emotionally distanced from the mothers she portrays. Rather, her empathy is with the children who are raised under such a parent's stress, probably reflecting her own early experience in a strained family situation. Although she wrote numerous fanciful children's stories and poems in her career and cherished fairy tales her entire life, Freeman's adult works more often than not portray a childhood of fear and guilt stemming from the—to the child—incomprehensible and often hypocritical adult world.

To be a child in Freeman's world is to be lonely, misunderstood, lost, and even ghostlike for lack of secure identity in the family. In "Little-Girl-Afraid-of-a-Dog" (1909), for example, young Emmeline, charged with delivering eggs to a "degenerate" neighboring family, lives in constant terror of their fierce dog. She is unable to tell her mother or aunt; they would have ridiculed her fear for "they saw in Emmeline only a darling, obedient, sweet little girl . . . not as she really was." Emmeline becomes physically ill in her dread, cannot eat or sleep and, upon waking each morning, feels like "a condemned criminal might have felt on the morning of his execution." Yet for fear of ridicule she never divulges her dark secret. Likewise, the young protagonist in "How Charlotte Ellen Went Visiting" (1897), cautioned by her mother to "give in" to her "dreadful sensitive" aunt when visiting, takes the admonition so much to heart that she forces herself to eat pie she cannot stomach and to sleep in an overheated room with mice in the bed ticking. Finally the little girl becomes sick from guilt (she has thrown a piece of pie out the window) and, when her mother is summoned, breaks down and confesses her misery. The adults, completely unaware of the child's inner agony, can only laugh at her myriad scruples.

Retreating from their parents' scorn, children in Freeman's world often create an imaginary world in which to hide. Two stories with a similar theme, "Honorable Tommy" (1916) and "Josiah's First Christmas" (1909), concern children ridiculed by their Puritan families for hanging up Christmas stockings as they have seen school friends doing. Entranced with their schoolmates' stories of Santa Claus, the children spend days dreaming of such a benevolent, magical being and long to have him appear at their homes also. They are crushed at their parents' refusal. Only long afterwards do the adults understand the emotional scars their mocking words have left on their children and begin to comprehend the "nobility of the trust of childhood and the enormity of its betrayal."

Childhood is also a time of mental anguish brought on by children's cruelty to one another. In several Freeman stories, little girls are humiliated because their dresses mark them as poor or odd among their companions. In "A War-Time Dress" (1898), the youngest of the fifteen Mann children, Caroline, whose lack of identity is so complete she even has an older sister with the same name, grows up continually ashamed of the made-over dresses necessity forces her to wear. "You must learn that dress is of very little consequence," her practical but unsympathetic mother tells her. "When you get old enough to earn a new one for yourself, you can have one, but you must remember that: Pretty is as pretty does." Similarly, in "The Copy-Cat" (1914), a well-meaning but stubborn mother refuses to recognize her daughter Amelia's embarrassment at having to wear out-of-style clothing. Ostracized by her school friends, Amelia learns she must imitate other children in order to be accepted. In both stories it is the grandmother, not the mother, who finally comes to understand and thus sympathize with the child.

Each of the stories cited above, and in general all of Freeman's adult stories involving children protagonists, are not particularly successful stories in her canon. For the most part, their plots are weakly structured, and their sentimental strain too blatant for modern tastes. However, several of Freeman's ghost stories portraying lost or orphaned children, metaphors perhaps for their emotional abandonment in the family, are well-conceived and truly frightening. Most of these involve a mistreated child who returns after death to search for or to haunt the abusive parent. Alfred Bendixen, in a recent reissuing of these stories, perceptively states that "at the heart of Freeman's ghost stories is the loss of a sense of home [and by extension, mother], of all the qualities the idea of home embodies—safety, security, and love. . . . The source of terror . . . is the perversion of the home, the distortion of normal family relationships" (*Wind*, 247). Usually, these "perversions" occur within the mother and daughter relationship. In "The Wind in the Rose-Bush" (1903), the ghost of little Agnes Dent, neglected by her stepmother, returns to haunt the guilty woman until she is horribly tormented by her own conscience. In "The Lost Ghost" (1903), a ghost child, who repeats an endless litany of "I can't find my mother," appears to the two elderly women now occupying the house the child once lived in with her parents. Slowly, they piece the story together; daughter of a beautiful but irresponsible woman and a father who was rarely home, the child was left to starve and freeze to death in a locked room. In her sympathy, one of the women, Mrs. Abby Bird, is finally able to settle the girl's spirit, and she is last seen "walking off over the white snow-path with [the] child holding fast to her hand, nestling close to her as if she had found her own mother."

Freeman's experiences with a father unable to fulfill his expected role as provider for and head of the family, her lack of differentiation from and unresolved emotional conflict with her mother, and her association of family life with childlike fear and helplessness are all written into the themes of her short stories. Perhaps most acute, however, is the pervading sense of individual isolation and loneliness portrayed in Freeman's family relationships. Each of Freeman's family members typically stands alone and fends for him or her self, unable to understand or sympathize with others. Little communication exists between father and mother, or between parent and child. At best, "normal" family relationships involve a mutual, albeit grudging, tolerance. Motherhood, far from glorified, only provides a woman with an increasing emotional and physical burden; childhood is more often than not a time of loneliness and magnified fear.[4] This, then, is Freeman's portrait of the formative experiences of a young girl as she knew it. Moreover, such experiences carry over into a young woman's family relationships while she is still living at home and is dependent upon her parents.

In 1898, at the age of forty-six and as yet unmarried, Mary Wilkins Freeman published a tale in her collection of stories set in the Puritan past, *Silence and Other Stories,* which, bordering as it does on fantasy and reality, brings us closer than perhaps any other story to the problem of a young woman's relationship with her parents. In "The Buckley Lady," Persis Buckley grows up happily in a pious New England family, but at the age of twelve a dramatic event completely changes her life. As she is gathering wood in the forest one day, a splendid coach with a handsome young prince inside appears. Catching sight of the beautiful young girl and falling in love with her, the man strikes a pact with her father: he will return to marry Persis one day; the family meanwhile is to prepare her accordingly. Thereafter, relieved from her usual chores, she is made to dress daily in her finest gown and to sit in the best parlor, stitching daintily on a sampler.

Though the novelty of the situation attracts her at first, Persis soon grows restless and bored; unable to comprehend her parents' orders, "her first conviction of the inconsistency of the human heart was upon [her], and she was dazed." The days and weeks roll on as Persis's entire family deny themselves for this one child who "represented all the faint ambition" of their lives. The finest materials are purchased for her stitching; she is given piano and dancing lessons; and she is allowed to read such formerly forbidden novels as *Clarissa Harlowe*, all in preparation for the great event to befall her. Their staunch Puritan neighbors soon begin to impose "a subtle spiritual bombardment of doubt and envy and disapproval" upon the Buckley family, the preacher even directing a sermon toward them on "the folly of worldly ambition and trust in the vain promises of princes." Persis, meanwhile, "leading the life of a forlorn princess in a fairy tale. . . . waited in her prison, cast about and bound, body and spirit, by the will and ambition of her parents, like steel cobwebs, for the prince who never came."

In an ironic twist to the typical fairy tale ending, Persis, at the age of twenty-five and after nearly thirteen years in her "prison," falls in love with a local boy she has seen from her window. He manages to steal her away from her parents one night, but only by renting a magnificent coach and disguising himself as the handsome prince. His hopes dashed once he learns what has occurred, Persis's father goes to his grave angry and bitter, having carved on his own tombstone a verse condemning his daughter's "ingratitude."

In the story of Persis Buckley, Freeman expresses in fantasy what she explores again and again in her more realistic short stories. A young girl reaching marriageable age suddenly finds her relationship with her parents or parent dramatically changed. With mounting anxiety, she realizes she is now seen more as a commodity to be sold than as a child to be nurtured. As Freeman herself experienced in her many years as a single adult at home, a woman's opportunities for contributing to the family finances were laughably pitiful in a small, impoverished town that scarcely needed a second piano teacher or bonnet maker. An adult daughter at home, therefore, was often a financial burden on the family.

In these stories, Freeman also details how, as a daughter reaches maturity, the complex and highly emotional bonds uniting her to her parents—and especially her mother—are profoundly disrupted. Modern psychological theory has verified Freeman's observations. Chodorow, for example, explains how mothers and daughters experience a period of ambiguity as their roles begin both to merge and to separate: "Mothers feel ambivalent toward their daughters, and react to their daughters' ambivalence toward them. They desire both to keep daughters close and to push them into adulthood. This ambivalence in turn creates more anxiety in their daughters and provokes attempts by these daughters to break away" (135).

Although Freeman's letters reveal nothing about her own mother's desire to see her married, her stories frequently express much anxiety and tension on the part of both mother and daughter over the question of the daughter's marriage. Josephine Donovan's statement in *New England Local Color Literature: A Women's Tradition* that, in Freeman's world, "mothers . . . are trying to keep their daughters 'home,' in a female world" (121) is, when one examines these stories, generally not true. Freeman's mothers for the most part are actively engaged in procuring well-made marriages for their daughters, but rarely for the most laudable of reasons—their daughters' happiness. Perhaps because she herself had a poor or unfulfilling marriage, a mother in Freeman's world often expects her daughter's marriage to confer on her the emotional or financial security or prestige she finds lacking in her own life. She therefore uses every means to push her daughter toward a marriage that will fulfill the mother's own ambition.

If she realizes this duplicity on her mother's part, and Freeman shows that she often does, a daughter feels trapped; her Puritan upbringing has taught her the importance of filial obedience, yet as she experiences her mother's increasing interference, the daughter grows frustrated with and even hostile toward her. As Gardiner has pointed out, such suppressed aggression and anger often take the form of the

"bad mother" in a woman's mind. "This mother-villain is so frightening because she is what the daughter fears to become and what her
infantile identifications predispose her to become" (186, n. 18). The
"bad" or "villain" mother appears frequently in Freeman stories about
marriage, as do several other mother-figures that could be characterized in more general and archetypal terms: the vampire, the witch,
the self-sacrificing mother.[5] The mother and daughter conflict over the
question of marriage is played out in the search for a husband for the
daughter; yet even when and if the daughter marries, the ambivalent
guilt and hostility on the part of both mother and daughter are rarely
expiated.

A daughter in a Freeman story who, for one reason or another,
rejects marriage or her mother's choice of a suitor finds that her
mother grows bitter and petty; the mother, on the other hand, sees
her child's "ingratitude" not only as a personal offense against her but
as an offense against Providence itself. In Freeman's world, the daughter's awaiting of a "handsome Prince" is merely a dream perpetuated
by a mother who often has little else to hope for in life. Usually, he
fails to appear. Freeman's many stories on this subject, some of them
painfully poignant, involve the aftermath of that dream as mother and
child struggle to readjust their relationship in the light of their personal disappointment.

Three of Freeman's early stories can serve to illustrate an ambitious
mother's desire for her daughter to marry a man who has money; such
a marriage confers prestige on that mother, especially among her
women neighbors. Mrs. Joy, in "Up Primrose Hill" (1891), seeing
daughter Annie snub the attentions of wealthy Henry Simpson, confronts her in anger. When Annie confesses she loves poor Frank Rice
instead, her mother mocks her, further instilling guilt by bidding her
remember the result of such "love" in her own life:

> "Oh! Well, I s'pose that's all that's necessary, then," [Mrs. Joy says].
> "I s'pose if you—*love* him, there ain't anything more to be said."
> The manner with which her mother's voice lingered upon *love* made
> it seem at once shameful and ridiculous to the girl. . . .
> "I guess you'll find out that there's something besides *love* . . ." [her
> mother continues]. "When you get settled down there in that little
> cooped-up house with his father and mother and crazy uncle, an' don't

have enough money to buy you a calico dress, you'll find out it ain't all—*love*. . . . You know how I've dug an' scrimped all my life, an' you know how we're situated now; it's jest all we can do to get along. . . . If you marry Frank Rice you'll have to live jest as I've done. . . . You'll have to work an' slave, an' never go anywhere nor have anything. . . . An' if you have Henry Simpson, you'll live over in Lennox, an' have everything nice, an' people will look up to you."

Annie is silenced, yet she is also adamant; she marries Frank against her mother's wishes. Freeman ends this particular story at this point and does not record Mrs. Joy's reaction to the marriage.

In the minor story "In Butterfly Time" (1887), Rebecca Wheat and Adoniram Dill have been kept apart for nearly forty years because of their mothers' bitter rivalry over money. The two old women confront each other one day after a prayer meeting. Mrs. Wheat has insulted Mrs. Dill by referring to her in public prayer as "old and decrepid." Mrs. Wheat digs up the real source of the argument:

"See here, Mis' Dill, s'pose we come to the p'int. . . . You've allers blamed me 'cause you thought I come betwixt my Becca an' your Adoniram. . . ."

"You didn't think Adoniram was good enough for Becca," [Mrs. Dill responds]; "that was the hull on't. . . . You'd jest set your heart on havin' her git that rich Arms feller; you know you had. But she didn't; she didn't get anybody."

At home, Mrs. Wheat considers for the first time that her daughter might have been hurt by her intervention years ago in her plans to marry. "I've kinder been thinkin' on't over lately, an' ef I was kinder sharp . . . an' hindered you an' Adoniram's makin' a match on't, I ain't above sayin' I might hev been a leetle more keerful," she informs Rebecca. Considering that Adoniram, who has just purchased ten acres of land, "must hev been layin' up money" all those years, she suggests Rebecca reconsider his suit; meanwhile, Mrs. Dill has convinced Adoniram that Rebecca would still have him if he asked. The story ends with the sixty-year old lovers finally united.

Lastly, in one of Freeman's most important stories, "Louisa" (1891), a daughter's marriage is not merely a choice but a necessity: without it an aging mother and senile grandfather face starvation. Twenty-four-year-old Louisa, the sole support of the family, has recently lost her eight-year position teaching school. The story opens with mother and daughter confronting each other bitterly. Louisa will not answer her mother's petulant entreaties; she has, evidently, been subjected for months if not years to her mother's wrath. Instead, she returns to her dogged labor in the potato field and garden, working long days in the hot sun to eke out enough food for the family's meager meals. To her mother's dismay, she even rakes hay in the fields with the men to earn a bit of money. Though Louisa is doing her utmost for the family's survival, Mrs. Britton chides her and nags her at every moment.

The primary source of her mother's anger is Louisa's refusal to marry the only eligible young man in the village, Jonathan Nye. Louisa makes it a point to appear as unattractive as possible when he calls. She slouches nearby in the parlor as her mother entertains the embarrassed young man with glowing reports of Louisa's successful school teaching. As soon as Jonathan leaves, Mrs. Britton falls to berating her daughter: "You'd ought to be ashamed of yourself—ashamed of yourself! You've treated him like a—hog! . . . Comin' into the room with that old thing on, an' your hair all in a frowse. I guess he won't want to come again." Louisa, responding only that she "doesn't like him," creeps off to bed, "her mother's scolding voice pursuing her like a wrathful spirit." Poor all her life, Freeman states, Mrs. Britton considers her daughter's marriage to well-off Jonathan "like a royal alliance for the good of the state." Weak with hunger, she envisions the Nye household to be one that daily has plentiful food on the table. "There was no more sense, to her mind, in Louisa's refusing him," the narrator comments, "than there would have been in a princess refusing the fairy prince and spoiling the story."

Louisa remains adamant; she will not marry. She has no other lover in mind, but "she had her dreams." When her mother hears through neighborhood gossip that Jonathan has begun to court another girl, she further humiliates Louisa by suggesting that Louisa chase after him. "'Twouldn't hurt you none to hang back a little after meetin', and kind of edge round his way. 'Twouldn't take more'n a look. . . . Men don't do all the courtin'—not by a long shot." Louisa is shocked.

"I wouldn't do such a thing as that for a man I liked, and I certainly sha'n't for a man I don't like," she retorts. "Then me an' your grandfather'll starve," her mother shoots back.

In desperation, Louisa walks seven miles to beg food from a relative who years before has cut the family off in an angry argument. Uncle Solomon grudgingly gives her the food she asks of him but refuses to help her cart it home. Rather than leaving part of it behind, Louisa carries half of it a short distance, returns for the other half, and continues on in this way until, exhausted and famished, she nearly faints from exertion as she enters her home. Nevertheless, her effort "was like a pilgrimage, and the Mecca at the end of the burning, desertlike road was her own maiden independence."

"Louisa," in all other respects a bleak tale, ends on a note of hope; Louisa discovers upon her return home that she has received her job as schoolteacher again. Furthermore, Mrs. Britton, who meanwhile has been informed by Mrs. Nye that "if Jonathan had . . . [Louisa], he wa'n't goin' to have me an' father hitched on to him," informs Louisa she is now pleased with her refusal to marry such a man. The story ends with Mrs. Britton bustling about joyfully as she prepares the first substantial dinner the family has had in months, while Louisa rests in the peaceful summer twilight.

Like many of Freeman's stories of women in impoverished circumstances, "Louisa" leaves us admiring the solitary courage and stubborn pride evinced by the female protagonist. Despite her desperate situation, Louisa refuses to become bitter. When her senile grandfather pulls up the potatoes she had so arduously planted, she does not reproach the childlike man but returns to do the work again. Louisa's integrity in not marrying a man she does not love for material gain finally reaps her a reward in the end. In maintaining her independence from her mother's dominating will, she is provided with the means of fulfilling her continuing responsibility as the sole provider of the family. Dutifully, she has never sought, nor will she seek, to abdicate that role.

Freeman's mothers, in their frustration over their daughters' lack of obedience in the question of marriage sometimes resort to deception, trickery, or emotional cruelty to exact compliance.[6] In two stories that reveal much about the mother-and-daughter relationship, "Hyacinthus" (1904) and "Mother-Wings" (1921), Freeman's daughters expose their mothers' deceptions and triumph over them morally. Each daughter sees her mother brought to her knees because of her falsehood. In the former story, Mrs. Lynn, angry that daughter Sarah dislikes wealthy but insipid John Mangam and instead prefers the eccentric artist Hyacinthus Ware, reveals her jealousy of Sarah in an emotional outburst: "'You are a good-for-nothin' girl. You ought to be ashamed of yourself. . . . You talk about things you and [Hyacinthus] know that the rest of us can't talk about. You take advantage because your father and me sent you to school where you could learn more than we could'. . . . Then her face upon her daughter's turned malevolent, triumphant, and cruel. 'I wa'n't goin' to tell you what I heard . . . but now I'm goin' to.'"

Mrs. Lynn's "secret" is a deliberate lie. She tells Sarah that Hyacinthus is living with a woman. "Sarah turned ghastly pale. . . . 'You mean he is married?' she said. 'I dun'no whether he is married or not, but there is a woman livin' there,'" her mother replies. Sarah is despondent over this news, for she has long loved and even worshipped the man. She reluctantly decides to marry John Mangam, and "everybody agreed that it was a good match and that Sarah was a lucky girl." However, at the last minute the woman "living" with Hyacinthus appears; she reveals herself to be his half-sister in town for a visit. Guilty at being exposed as a liar, Sarah's mother breaks down before her daughter "with a sob."

Likewise, in the later story "Mother-Wings," Mrs. Bodley, who has "advanced ideas" and ridicules daughter Ann for not keeping up with the "modern" girls in town, indirectly lies by leading her busy-body neighbors to think that Ann plans to wed a wealthy widower. Ann cannot figure out why acquaintances are offering their congratulations, and why Frank, the young man she is interested in, has suddenly stopped visiting. Finally realizing the truth, she angrily confronts her mother:

> . . . [Ann's] little, gentle countenance was fairly terrible. "Mother," she said, almost solemnly, "You have—lied."
>
> Mrs. Bodley cowered before the look and tone. "You tell your own mother—that?" she said, but her voice was a mere whisper.
>
> "Yes, I do. You have been making everybody think I was going to be

married. They congratulated me, and I didn't know why. You made a
fool of me. You have tried and tried to push me into everything else,
and I have submitted. . . . But to try to push me into marriage! To tell
people such a shameful lie when all the time he has never said one
word about marrying me! . . . It was a lie you told, mother, and you a
church member!"

Alone, Mrs. Bodley chastises herself for having caused disaster by
getting "in the path of divine Providence," although it nonetheless
"did not occur to her to acknowledge her sense of her wrong-doing to
Ann." Yet eventually, when Ann's lover Frank returns to her, Mrs.
Bodley acknowledges Ann's honesty and her own guilt. "She will
never tell you her own mother as good as lied," she confesses to Frank.

Strangely ennobled in several Freeman stories is the mother who,
from a perverted sense of "love" for her daughter, sacrifices her very
self in order to see that daughter married. Occasionally the self-sacrificing mother takes the form of a witch. Ann Douglas Wood, in "The
Literature of Impoverishment," has written briefly but perceptively
about the recurring image of witchcraft in women's local-color writing. Wood attributes Freeman's portrayal of the witch to a manifesta-
tion of Freeman's feeling that she was not only different from others,
an "outcast," but that she may also have been in some way responsible
for "sapping" the life of those around her. Wood thus concludes that
"witches were popularly supposed to have the power to blight life, and
this power, Freeman, who had lost a lover, a sister, a mother and a
father within a short space of time in her young womanhood, must
surely have felt was hers" (27). Indeed, two Freeman stories, "The
Soldier Man" (1918) and the ghost story "Luella Miller" (1903), portray vampire women who somehow manage to "sap" the life out of all
who try to love them.

Whether or not Freeman felt personal guilt at these early losses in
her family cannot be fully substantiated. However, evidence from at
least two short stories, "The Witch's Daughter" (1910) and "A Modern Dragon" (1887), indicates that Freeman sometimes associated a
daughter's failure to marry and lead a "normal" woman's life with a
powerful witchlike mother, who must first be annihilated before the
daughter can be united with a man. In the end the daughter's guilt
over wishing her mother dead is expiated by the deifying of this

mother-love; in a parody of the Christian sacrifice, such love becomes understood as nobler and purer than that between the daughter and her male lover. The mother-figure is thus—often grossly—glorified. Although writing of Jane Austen's endings, Nina Auerbach's statement that "in the end, the malevolent power of the mother is ennobled by being transferred to the hero, and the female community . . . is dispersed with relief in the solidity of marriage" also applies to this group of Freeman stories (55).

Set in the New England of the past, "The Witch's Daughter" concerns old Elma Franklin who is feared by and ostracized from the community largely because of her odd appearance. Because of her mother's reputation, Daphne, Elma's beautiful sixteen-year-old daughter, has no suitors. Elma knows she is to blame: "Young men sometimes cast eyes askance at Daphne, but turned away, and old Elma knew the reason why, and she hated them." Daphne falls in love with one young man, Harry Edgelake, who, once his relatives discover the situation, is hurriedly sent away to school. She becomes disconsolate, and Elma grows bitter: "[She] watched and he came not, and old Elma watched the girl watch in vain, and her evil passions grew."

Finally Elma, despairing over the failing health of her daughter, decides that "if she were indeed witch as they said, she would use witchcraft." "Sweetheart, thy mother will compel love for thee," she whispers to Daphne. The honest girl at first refuses. However Elma insists, "There is but one way, sweet daughter of mine. Step thou over thy mother's body . . . and I swear to thee, by the Christ and the Cross and all that the meeting-folk hold sacred, that thou shalt have thy lover." Elma sacrifices herself in order to conjure up Daphne's young lover, Harry. Only as she lies dying is her deed seen by her daughter as a glorious one: "[Elma] sank down slowly . . . and she lay still at the feet of her daughter and the youth, and they stooped over her and they knew that she had been no witch, but a great lover."

An early story, "A Modern Dragon," likewise portrays a self-sacrificing witch-mother who is ennobled finally as the "greatest lover" of all. Mrs. King is known in town for her eccentricity; a proud woman, she wears her hair and skirts too short, ploughs in the fields like a man, and is reputedly a "spiritualist." Mothers warn their sons to avoid her daughter Almira. Almira, however, falls in love with David

Ayres, a naive young man who has dared to court her. When David's mother forbids him to see her again and Almira therefore begins to pine away, Mrs. King lowers her skirts and goes to meeting one Sunday in an attempt to appear respectable. This failing to accomplish its object, she, with "the demeanor of a hunted criminal," takes a drastic step and goes to Mrs. Ayres to beg her to relent. To her utter humiliation, the woman remains immovable. Knowing now that only by her own death can the two lovers be united, Mrs. King falls gravely ill. After securing David's promise to wed her daughter, she dies, at which Almira cries out, "Oh, mother! . . . I love you best! . . . I never will love him as much as I did you."

Freeman's petty and manipulative mothers, her cruel or deceptive mothers, and her self-sacrificing or witchlike mothers all point to profound ambivalence, tension, and perhaps guilt in Freeman's mind over her role as daughter in relation to the question of her own marrying. Many of the mothers she portrays see their daughters largely as extensions of themselves; in striving to influence their daughters' decision in marriage, mothers seek to fulfill, even vicariously, some aspect of life they themselves have been deprived of: financial security, reputation, or, in the case of the self-sacrificing mother, simply a "normal" woman's life in the community. A daughter who cannot or will not comply with a parent's wish, moreover, is made to feel morally culpable. Whether this was indeed Freeman's relationship with her mother, whether Eleanor Wilkins pushed her eldest daughter toward a marriage that would ensure the material security of the impoverished family or would raise the Wilkins's name to its former genteel status, or whether Freeman felt guilty at her mother's death is not known. However, in all of these stories of a mother's oppressive will and a daughter's often rebellious need to "have her own dreams," Freeman clearly shows the lingering power and fearful hold the mother-figure exerted over her adult life.

One way or another, most of Freeman's mothers see that their daughters do marry. An interesting group of stories, however, explores the life of the adult woman who has not married and who has grown to assume the caretaking responsibilities of her parent or aged relative. That daughter, in a reversal of roles, has become a parent to the older person, reducing her former guardian to the fears and strictures of a

child. Lucy Fischer's study of contemporary mother and daughter relationships, *Linked Lives,* has concluded that this phenomenon, usually taking place when the parent has become physically or emotionally infirm, parallels the ambiguity of the relationship between a
teenage girl and her parent: "Just as a parent and adolescent child are
likely to disagree about whether or not the adolescent has achieved
adult status, there may be disagreement across generations about
whether or not the parents should be considered 'postadults'" (163).

In Freeman's stories, this role ambiguity takes the form of the adult
daughter's exerting tyranny over the aged parent by insisting on
absolute order and cleanliness; she considers her parent no more than
a "sloppy" child who needs picking up after. The elderly parent, in
turn, often covertly stages small "rebellions" in an attempt to reassert
his or her disintegrating identity. These stories are interesting in a
study of Freeman's parent and daughter relationships because here
Freeman switches the point of view and hence her sympathies from
daughter to parent. Now it is the daughter who, parentlike, assumes
the aspects of the "cruel" or "cold" mother, considering her elderly
parent no more than an extension of herself. The parent-turned-child
is continually humiliated and guilt-ridden. Freeman's compassion
therefore remains with those, young or old, who experience childlike
powerlessness under domineering and tyrannical "mothers."

Elderly Lucinda Moss in "An Innocent Gamester" (1891), for example, finds her life "revolutionized" when niece Charlotte comes to
live with her: "[Lucinda] had no longer any voice in anything, and
she had come almost to forget what her own original note had been.
She was growing deprecatory and shamefaced about herself." When
Charlotte catches Lucinda hiding a packet of playing cards under the
Bible, she is "pitiless" in humiliating the woman, her voice expressing
a "calm contempt" and "dignified scorn." In the name of doing what
is "good" for her aunt, out of a sense of duty toward her kin, Charlotte
completely disrupts the older woman's comfortable though disordered
existence. With a firm and unrelenting hand, she maintains the once
messy home in perfect cleanliness and denies her aunt her favorite
foods, succeeding thereby in convincing Lucinda that "her own tastes
were not to be considered when they interfered with her own good."
Only after Lucinda disappears for several days does Charlotte, "tor-

tured by remorse," relent: "I've been setting myself up, because I thought I knew more. . . . I've been taking the self out of her." In this story at least, unlike the two following, the daughter is finally able to acknowledge the older woman's right to a separate identity.

One of Freeman's few stories concerning a male protagonist, "Emancipation" (1915), concerns the similar disruption in Old Billy Thomas's life when his daughter Esther takes charge of the household after the death of his wife. Like Charlotte's tyranny in the previous story, Esther's comes from her sense of "duty" and takes the form of insistence on order and neatness. Old Billy, who wishes his daughter were "as easy-goin' as her ma," rebels by crumpling and stamping on the newspaper and purposely disordering the immaculate room when Esther is away. Upon her return, Esther sees her father sitting quietly with the religious newspaper on his lap, just as she has left him. "Esther surveyed the disorder of the room. Old Billy felt her eyes turn toward him. He made no sign. He knew from past experience that she would not exclaim nor question. Esther straightened carefully 'The Landing of the Pilgrim Fathers,' the vases on the shelf, the pile of books on the table. . . . Billy never raised his eyes."

Billy succeeds in "enjoying himself immensely" at Esther's expense; his small acts of rebellion are his only means of asserting his will against that of his daughter. Esther in turn is convinced that her poor father is becoming senile. Her self-imposed sense of "duty" toward the old man has kept her from marrying her suitor Willard Comstock, who remains at home caring for his aged mother. Finally, Billy's crony Sam, seeing the old man's misery, intervenes: "So both of you, Willard and Esther, have been thinkin' you were doin' your duty and feelin' real miserable over it when you wasn't neither one of you doin' your duty at all. What you haven't neither one of you sensed is that enough sight oftener than folks realize doin' their duty is havin' their own way and lettin' other folks have theirs." Billy regains his freedom and happiness when Esther leaves the household.

Lastly, in the tragic tale "A Village Lear" (1891), two cruel and abusive daughters regard their aged and senile father Barney as no more than "some venerable cricket . . . which for some obscure religious reasons they were bound to harbor." They persuade the old man to divide his property between them, and Malvina, with whom he is to live, uses part of the inheritance to redecorate her house: "[She had] every room . . . newly painted and papered; then she stood before them like a vigilant watch-dog. She had been neat before, but with her new paint and paper and a few new carpets, her neatness became almost a monomania." Disheveled and untidy, Barney is made to feel unwelcome in her home; he takes to living out back in his old shoe shop. To his dismay, Malvina even refuses to allow him to attend his granddaughter's wedding ceremony: she admonishes him to "keep away from the door. . . . Such a spectacle as you are, an' the folks beginnin' to come!" A few weeks later, hearing that Malvina is now bent on tearing down his ancient but comforting shoe shop, Barney dies of utter grief and loneliness.

Freeman's portrayal of family life—the complex ties between husband and wife, and between parent and child—culminates in her portrayal of the mother and daughter relationship. As a child's "first community," the family in Freeman's New England asserts the primacy of the strong mother or mother-figure over the weaker father; this matriarchy, however, born of necessity, is rarely a gentle or nurturing one. Despite the hardship and deprivation they see in their mother's lives, young women in Freeman's world grow up desiring to marry if only to escape their mothers' emotional domination; however, they assert their freedom by insisting on marrying their own choice of a suitor. Freeman's stories show us the conflict, ambiguity, guilt, and reversals that the relationship between mother and daughter involves, possibly a continual exploration in fiction of Freeman's own experience as a child and later as an unmarried adult in the family. What Freeman tells us, ultimately, in her many pictures of the mother and daughter bond is that young women in her time and place entered their adult lives and relationships often lacking the fundamental security and assurance of the efficacy and value of both motherhood and womanhood. If indeed a female writer uses her text and female heroes to explore facets of her own personality, then it is with these unresolved tensions between daughter and mother that Freeman herself embarked upon her adult years.

CHAPTER 4

Women, Men, and Marriage

"Reckoning Them in with Providence"

Growing up in Freeman's rural New England, a young woman found herself beset with contradictory messages about both marriage and men.[1] Her observation of her mother's daily struggle for emotional and physical survival had certainly instilled in her an image of marriage as—for a woman at least—repressive and replete with frustration. Despite this image, however, Freeman's women usually both expect and desire to marry. Indeed, marriage is on the minds of nearly all of Freeman's female protagonists for several reasons. It not only seems to promise them a type of freedom, however illusory, from the confines of family and the tyranny of mother, but it was in the New England village as Freeman knew it still a social and practical necessity; unmarried women, as Freeman shows us over and over, are pitied for having missed or, even worse, lacked "chances." Marriage also seems to promise women some degree of financial security; unskilled and often uneducated, they are hard pressed to support themselves. Freeman's unmarried women, therefore, often fear both the poorhouse and the social stigma their single state accords.

Freeman's women, however, also want to marry for love. Despite the deprivation they see in their mothers' lives, and despite their anxi-

eties over remaining single, they struggle against their mothers' coerc-
ing them into a marriage for material or emotional security alone. Like
Louisa in the story by the same name, they "have their dreams," but
in maintaining the integrity of these dreams, they find their choice of
marriageable men considerably diminished. The fact of the matter was
that the post-Civil War New England village in which the majority of
Freeman's stories are based simply held few able men of any age. Many
had been killed in the war. Many more, finding increasingly that their
small-time farming or craft work could not compete in the new national grain market or factory system, had deserted the village for
brighter prospects in the city or the West.

In Freeman's fictional world, those men remaining in the villages
were more often than not weak-willed and weak-minded, stubborn
and eccentric. Indeed, Freeman's men often leave much to be desired.
Alice Glarden Brand does not exaggerate excessively in describing
them as "the nadir of humanity. Their ignorance is exceeded only by
their bestiality. If they choose to assert, they are aggressive. If they
choose to withdraw, they are foolish" (84). Brand reads Freeman's
work as primarily "an exposé of contempt for men's impotence, in-
competence, and aggression and for women's passivity, dependence,
and rage" (83). Though several of Freeman's stories such as "Old
Woman Magoun" clearly support Brand's reading, the severity of this
stance is in general unwarranted. Though Freeman rarely shows us a
strong or sympathetic male, several *are* present in her works: they are,
however, never the heads of families and are more often than not
products of sentimental fiction, idealized and implausible, too good to
be true. Examples of these men—noble, faithful, and courageous to
the point of caricaturization—occur in a few stories, "The Christmas
Sing in Our Village" (1898); "Joy" (1904); "The Underling" (1907);
and "The Coronation" (1914). Freeman's overall intent in her short
fiction, however, was neither to express a "contempt" for men nor to
idealize them but to question and probe, in a characteristically introspective manner, the life, the roles, and the relationships in which a
woman found herself immersed in the turn-of-the-century New England village.

Evidence from her letters and facts gleaned from her biography indicate that Freeman at times disliked her many years of singleness and

wished to marry if only to settle her life-long feeling that she was "different" from normal women. At the same time, she delayed marriage out of fear that its demands of caring for husband and household might force her to reduce her high literary output and even annihilate or, as she put it, "swallow" her personality. Few details of Freeman's early romances, if any, are known; Foster's biography tells us that young Mary "could not imagine herself falling in love with any of the boys who came her way in Brattleboro; they seemed to her dull, clumsy, self-conscious, and appallingly young" (32). As noted previously, she was commonly assumed to be smitten in her early twenties with the young navy lieutenant and family friend, Hanson Tyler; Mrs. Wilkins was "virtually certain" that the two would marry (36). Her love for Tyler appears to have gone unrequited, but indications are that Freeman corresponded with him regularly well into her thirties. In November 1886, she wrote Mary Louise Booth that she would be unable to accept an invitation for a Sunday outing if Tyler's ship had not yet set sail, for "Sunday might be his last day in the country and, in that case, he would be hurt, if he were not to see me" (Kendrick, 74). Two months later she told Booth of a "long letter" recently received from him, adding that "my friend writes very interesting letters, he has so many funny stories to tell in them" (Kendrick, 77). None of Freeman's correspondence with Tyler, however, survives. Though little evidence exists that Hanson Tyler returned Freeman's affection, he evidently occupied a place in Freeman's romantic imagination for the rest of her life. In her last years, she wore his naval uniform buttons on her own clothing and once remarked to a friend, "[I]f there is an afterlife, he [Tyler] is the one person I should like to see" (Foster, 194).

Once Freeman became immersed in her writing career, she considered marriage only a remote possibility, believing it would interfere with her work. In a letter written to a close woman friend when she was thirty-seven, Freeman stated, "I do not see any reason to apprehend that I ever shall be married. I simply cannot support a family yet. . . . If I had to see to a man's collars and stockings, besides the drama [she was working on *Giles Corey, Yeoman* at the time] and the story and Christmas and the new dress, in the next three weeks, I should be crazy" (Kendrick, 100). Of interest here is that Freeman not only assumes marriage consists largely of "taking care" of a man but also that it will be her responsibility and not her husband's to "support"—financially, no doubt—the family. This indeed appears to be what she experienced in her own family life and what she had come to expect was a woman's lot once married. Subsequent letters also voice the anxiety that she would not or could not be able to accomplish this without a major, and disconcerting, alteration in her life and habits.

Later, when she met Charles Freeman, she continued to delay their imminent marriage for a number of years. Several remarks in her letters during this time reveal both her apprehension of fulfilling a wife's role and her dread of the unknown territory she was about to compass. "I am wondering if I will make a good wife and my husband will be happy," she confessed to a friend soon before her marriage in 1902. "I shall try, but it is dealing with unknown quantities and sometimes I feel afraid" (Kendrick, 256). But more importantly, Freeman had real fears that marriage violated the essential "self." In a telling letter written to a friend who was herself about to marry, Freeman expressed the concern that marriage might "swallow" a woman up, absorbing her identity completely: "I am to be married myself before long," she wrote. "If *you* don't see the old *me*, I shall run and run until I find her. And as for you, no man shall ever swallow you up entirely" (Kendrick, 243). The oddly insistent and serious tone of this letter indicates that Freeman truly feared an annihilation or abdication of her entire personality in marriage. Several of her stories about marriage, including "The Prism" and "Arethusa," deal directly with such fears.

Freeman's view of men as "childish" and her questioning of the desirability or efficacy of marriage are expressed in her many stories concerning a woman's decision to marry. In her afterword to *"The Revolt of 'Mother'" and Other Stories*, Michele Clark asserts that "[Freeman's] young women consent to marry only if they are assured that their personal integrity will not be tarnished or confined" (198). When one considers Freeman's women in the bulk of her stories, however, this statement requires some qualification. Although a Freeman woman often struggles against her mother's will in order to secure her wish to marry for love, she is, for the most part, realistic in her views of men and marriage. She longs for an ideal: maintaining self-respect and integrity in a happy marriage. Yet she knows fully well that this ideal must often be compromised. Freeman's stories about marriage most often record the inner battle a woman undergoes as she ponders her choices—for she does have choices, albeit limited ones—and comes to a decision in a matter that will determine much of her future. Above all, Freeman contemplates the mystery of choice-making coupled with immutable circumstance in women's relationships with men.

As always, Freeman considers the matter from every angle. Many of her strongest stories involve practical and decidedly unromantic young women who are weighing the strengths and shortcomings of their young men and then making a decision to marry or to remain single for a time. In some cases, women refuse to marry until they have met an unpaid debt or until they are certain that life holds no better option. Misunderstandings sometimes keep lovers apart for years, each one stubbornly bent on "winning" the argument. In other stories, young women are "given the mitten," Freeman's homespun term for being rejected, and pine away physically as well as emotionally for lost lovers. Still others consider women's lives after marriage and the often painful adjustments they must make to new relationships with both husbands and mothers-in-law. Finally, a small but significant group of stories presents the romantic ideal of a woman "saving" a man; her generous care and concern raise a dejected man's spirits and self-confidence.

"[M]ost young men in Wilkinston make brief appearances in a world where the decisive relationships are those that women have with each other. Typically, a young man's physical appearance and economic status are briefly delineated. He comes courting, stands at the door, sits in the parlor on a haircloth sofa, or is seen working his fields. But it is as if we see him always in half-light, shadowed. Men may cause the commotion, but they never get the center of the stage" (Clark, 197).

Men are indeed "backstage" in the majority of Freeman's works; she apparently had little power of sympathetic identification with the male mind. Nor, it appears, did she strive to have any. Freeman knew herself to be a woman writing primarily but not exclusively for a female audience, and she was nearly always content with relying on her female viewpoint to make sense of her world. The richness of that viewpoint, although undeniably one-sided, was an essential part of her realism; she was committed to recording only what she knew or had experienced firsthand. Her rare attempts at delineating the inner life of a male generally do not have an authentic ring; her male protagonists usually seem like women in male attire. As in the stories "A Kitchen Colonel" (1891) and "The Butterfly" (1904), they are often "househusbands," in a day when such a role was far less acceptable than today. Freeman wrote of what she knew; she wrote of men through the eyes, heart, and mind of women.

In Freeman's stories, young women view men in several ways. If the woman is simple, meek, and generous to a fault, she may find a simple and good man to marry; these "happily ever after" stories represent Freeman's occasional lapses into sentimentality and are among her weakest in theme and probability. As will be noted by the dates of these stories, Freeman continued to produce some sentimental fiction throughout her career and in increasing amounts in her later years. Such stories include "A Humble Romance" (1887), "A Wayfaring Couple" (1891), "The Umbrella Man" (1914), and "The Bright Side" (1923). Increasingly attacked by her critics, such stories contributed in part to her decline in popularity after the turn of the century.

More frequently, the loving and giving woman is also intensely practical, fully aware that the men who court her may be "only after a pretty face" or that they are weak-willed or vain. She may thus be rejected for her lack of passion, or she may herself slowly come to the conclusion that such a man, however initially attractive, would not be a wise choice. A more independent or fiery young woman, on the other hand, often finds herself scorning a young man for his stubbornness, slowness, or irresponsibility. She may go through a process of learning to compromise with him; she may overtly refuse his attentions; or she may lock horns with him in a battle of wills that may carry on much of her adult life.

"A Humble Romance," one of Freeman's earliest popular stories (the title story for her first collection and later issued in London separately in a small volume), is one that, dripping as it does with Victorian saccharin, most likely holds little appeal for modern readers.

Poor, homely Sally, an overworked servant girl, is "rescued" from her plight by a passing tin peddlar. Jake promises to be good to her if she will consent to marry him. Sally's only objection is her lack of a proper wedding dress; to her credit, she insists on purchasing one herself. At her concern, the "peddlar stared at her, half in consternation, half in admiration. 'Well,' said he, 'I guess you've got a little will o' your own, arter all, little un, an' I'm glad on't. A woman'd orter hev a little will to back her sweetness; it's all too soft an' slushy otherways.' " Sally gets her dress, the two marry, and then journey together, "two simple pilgrims, with all the beauty and grace in either of them turned only towards each other." When the peddlar disappears one day and is gone for years on end, Sally "bears up" faithfully as he has bid her; even when learning of his bigamy (he has had a wife living in a distant town all those years), she forgives him without remonstrance and agrees to resume her life with him upon the death of the former wife. The story ends with Sally's exclaiming over the prospect of wearing her wedding dress again as the two are remarried: "Oh, Jake, my blue silk dress an' the white bonnet is in the trunk . . . jest the same, an' I can git 'em out . . . an' wear 'em to be married in!"

Fortunately, such blatant sentimentality is not found in the majority of Freeman's stories. Those that most appeal to modern sensibilities are the ones in which a woman does indeed "hev a little will"—certainly more of it in her relationship with a man than Sally has in the story above. Freeman is not lacking in portraits of strong and practical women.

"Juliza" (1892) is one such story. Juliza Peck is a young woman who, overweight and not particularly attractive, has few friends among her peers, but she is intelligent, loyal, and extremely talented as an orator. She is called upon at every social or church event to recite a poem or some other piece and always greatly moves her audience. From childhood on, Juliza has expected to marry Frank Williams; though he has not proposed outright, he has consistently courted her in the proper manner, walking her home from church and paying his weekly parlor call. One day, however, he is unusually aloof. Discovering that his aged mother, with whom he lives, is ill, Juliza quickly proposes a solution: "There ain't but one thing to do," she tells him. "I'll get married to you right away, and come over to your house. That'll settle it.

I'm a good cook and a good housekeeper: mother says I am." When Frank seems to hesitate, she is surprised. "You don't mean you don't want me to marry you, Frank Williams," she queries. "I hadn't a thought but you wanted me to. I don't see what you'll do if I don't marry you."

Frank remains silent. Practical and blunt of speech, Juliza has done the unthinkable in broaching the subject of marriage before her lover has. She, however, is not embarrassed and sees no need for apology: "I haven't done anything I'm ashamed of; if anybody has, it's you. I supposed you took it for granted I was goin' to marry you, an' I don't think you show much common-sense about it," she tells him. Frank, however, can only reply shamefacedly, "there's something to be considered besides common-sense, sometimes." At home too, when Juliza's mother derides her for making a "laughin' stock" of herself, she adamantly insists, "I don't see why it's any worse for a girl to speak than 'tis for a man. I always supposed he wanted me to marry him, I've never wanted to marry anybody else, an' I knew his mother was so miserable. . . . I don't think he's shown common-sense."

Several days thereafter, Juliza confronts a "sulky" Frank in an effort to discover the truth. After much hesitation, he confesses "like a bashful child, blushing, and half-smiling" that he is enamored of another girl. Juliza is astonished but remains firmly in control; in the end she even offers to care for Frank's mother while he goes to court his new love. Frank soon marries; on his wedding day, Juliza, called on to recite, "spoke as she had never done before. Her gestures were full of fire; every line of her form and face seemed to conform to the exigencies of the situation; her voice rang out with a truth that was deeper than her own personality. Everybody listened. The bridal couple were forgotten."

A lengthy and beautifully constructed story, "Juliza" is an as-yet undiscovered gem among Freeman's works. Published in an obscure late nineteenth-century magazine, *Two Tales*, it has only recently been reprinted. A number of important themes concerning Freeman's conception of a woman's relationship with a man are seen here. Juliza, like Freeman herself was, is artistically talented and feels isolated from her "normal" women peers. She is, moreover, secure in the knowledge of her own talent and independent strength of mind. Although she wishes to marry, she does not depend solely on marriage for assurance of her self-worth. A practical and level-headed woman, Juliza is also unromantic; for this reason, she is rejected by a decidedly more childish and weaker male, one she would have had to take care of should they indeed have married. Here, as she does in many stories, Freeman interrupts and displaces a seemingly conventional love plot in order to focus attention on the inner dilemma of the unconventional woman, the woman who does not "win" the man. More importantly, "Juliza" makes a strong statement about artistic sublimation as well, one which is much akin to that made in Freeman's popular "A Village Singer." Juliza triumphs in her ability to hold the wedding party so spellbound with her recital that they virtually "forget" the center of attention, the bridal couple itself, yet her art is of necessity compensatory, as well as being a means of channeling her feelings into acceptable forms. Juliza's art consists of repeating what others have written, just as her life is bound up by what others decide. She does resist, however, and does so successfully, within the limits of her options.

Freeman continued to explore several of these themes in a later story, "The Chance of Araminta" (1904). Araminta, like Juliza, looks to her own abilities and not to marriage for happiness and fulfillment. Unlike Juliza, she forcibly terminates her engagement when finding her lover unfaithful. Still beautiful though in middle-age, Araminta, people agree, is "the happiest-looking mortal" they have ever seen. Her joy lies in her generosity; she can always be relied upon to help those in need. Araminta's happiness, we discover as the story unfolds through the gossip of two garrulous old women, lies in the fact that she had a "chance" to marry as a younger woman but decided to give up that chance. "She's seemed a good deal happier ever since," Sarah tells Martha. Araminta had loved a handsome yet unstable young lawyer, Daniel Rodgers. "We thought Daniel Rodgers was a young man who had an eye for something besides a pretty face, that he could see the true worth as well," Sarah relates, recalling as well that "there was a good deal more to Araminta than a pretty face." However, Araminta soon discovers Daniel's unfaithfulness: he had courted, then deserted, a girl in a neighboring town. That young girl comes to plead frantically with Araminta one day. "You don't know, you don't know . . . how terrible it has all been," she mourns. "I've watched and watched for him to come." After calming the younger girl, Araminta takes her home. With firm decision, she immediately breaks off her engagement and refuses to speak of the incident thereafter. Elderly Sarah tells Martha that she tried to reason with Araminta to no avail:

> "Well, I've always thought it was the right way for a woman to be married, if she could, and I wanted her to be happy. But she wouldn't listen to anything I said. She just laughed, and said she was bound to be happy anyway. . . ."
> "Well, marriage ain't everything," said [Martha].
> "No," said Sarah; "it isn't so much as giving it up and behaving yourself, if the Lord shows He hasn't planned to have you married. . . . [T]hat's what Araminta did."

As noted earlier Freeman has a number of such works setting up a rivalry between a weaker, more conventional woman and a stronger, independent woman over the matter of a lover. As the story continues, Freeman relegates the conventional woman to the subplot while probing deeply into the stronger woman's inner world. In addition to "Juliza" and "The Chance of Araminta," this list includes the stories "A Moral Exigency" (1887), "Emmy" (1891), and "The Parrot" (1901), and several relationships in the novels *Pembroke* (1894), *By the Light of the Soul* (1907), and *The Shoulders of Atlas* (1908). In these works, Freeman generally admires the strong woman but does not disdain the weaker one. The weaker woman, often the blond, helpless female from sentimental fiction, usually "wins" the man who—weak, dependent, or "flawed" in some way himself—is more her match. The stronger woman, Freeman implies, is often better off alone than with such a man. Yet the fact is that such a woman does remain alone— and consequently may suffer not only loneliness but social ostracism as well. After Eunice Fairweather relinquishes her lover Burr Mason (a "terribly vacillating," boyish man) to Ada Harris in "A Moral Exigency," for example, Eunice despairingly hugs Ada—they are old school friends—and sobs, "Love me all you can, Ada . . . I want— something." "Plain" and "getting older," Eunice will, we are informed, probably have no more opportunities for marriage.

Freeman's protagonists Juliza and Araminta learn, not without some pain, that "marriage ain't everything." Straightforward, practical, and

open in nature, both find that they cannot accept a man who will not
be honest with them, and both learn, ultimately, that it is their own
abilities that will bring them whatever contentment there is to be
found in life. Two other Freeman stories revolve around this theme,
but with a major difference. Whereas Juliza and Araminta are firm,
yet gentle and unassuming women, Lydia Hersey of "Lydia Hersey
of East Bridgewater" (1898) and Catherine Gould of "The Secret"
(1907) are fiery and passionate. They simply will not tolerate any foolishness from their prospective lovers and are quick to make it known
that their intentions will not be thwarted.

"Lydia Hersey" takes place in Puritan New England. A beautiful
and regal woman, Lydia scorns the childish antics of her fiancé, Freelove Keith, as he and his friends prepare to "crash" a wedding party.
She shames him in front of them; he angrily retorts, "If you thought
I'd be ordered back by you before them all, like a whipped puppy, you
were mightily mistaken." A few days later, when the minister visits to
remind her it has been a full ten months since her wedding banns
were posted, Lydia insists she will not marry Freelove because of his
immature and irresponsible behavior. "Either Freelove Keith has got
to do as I say or I have got to do as he says before we are married, if
the banns have been cried a thousand years," she retorts to the minister. He leaves, condemning her sinful "frowardness."

Lydia refuses to see Freelove thereafter, but when a college youth,
Abel Perkins, begins to court her, she "wickedly" decides to use his
affection to make Freelove jealous. Inviting him in and tying an apron
on him, she bids him do her housework and tend her garden. Love-
struck Abel "never rebelled against her rule." One day, however,
suddenly overcome with frustration, Lydia orders him away. "I am
ashamed for you," she tells him. "No man can make a woman like
him by doing everything she tells him to; she only despises him for
it." When Freelove then returns to her, Lydia decides, finally, to
marry him. He has not changed, but she has learned that his stubborn
willfulness, much like her own, is the basis of her attraction to him.

Similarly, "The Secret," a well-developed and forcefully written
story, involves a "beautiful and confident" young woman, Catherine
Gould, who, refusing to tolerate what she sees as the "childishness" of
her fiancé, John, must eventually weigh the consequences of choosing
such a man with those of remaining single. Arriving home late on an

evening when Catherine knows John has been waiting for her, she refuses to answer his petulant inquiry concerning her whereabouts. In anger, John dashes the box of candy he has brought her to the floor and leaves; Catherine coolly picks up each piece and throws it after him. Her aunt and mother scold her:

> "Why wouldn't you tell him where you'd been?" the aunt asked. . . .
> "Because he asked," replied Catherine.
> "Because he—asked?" repeated Mrs. Gould.
> Catherine turned a set face upon her. "Mother," said she, "let us have no more talk about this. . . . John suspected me of going somewhere or doing something I should not. He questioned me like a slave-owner. If he does so before I am married, what will he do after? My life would be a hell. If I see that a door leads into hell, I don't propose to enter it if I can keep out."

When Catherine subsequently asks her mother if she ever "regretted" marrying, "[her] mother blushed. . . . 'Marriage is a divine institution,' said she, and closed her lips tightly." At this, Catherine unleashes her full scorn. "Oh, nonsense! Tell the truth, mother, and let the divine institution go. I know father was a fretful invalid two-thirds of the time."

Though in the following weeks Catherine misses John, "her pride and her innate joy in existence itself . . . sustained her like a sort of spiritual backbone. . . . [S]he knew herself to be strong enough for anything." Two years go by; Catherine hears of John only through rumor, but one day he returns, apologizing. He refuses now to listen to the "secret" that has kept them apart all this time. "Catherine," he explains, "Don't you know, that if you do tell, you must always suspect me of suspecting, and that if you don't tell, you will know I don't?" When he proposes marriage, Catherine considers carefully; finally, she accepts, for "she realized dimly that if she were to say 'No' . . . in spite of her triumphant philosophy of obtaining whatever she could from the minor joys of existence . . . she would miss the best and sweetest of food for her heart. There was nothing of the nun about her. She was religious, but she was not ascetic."

Whereas Juliza in "Juliza" and Araminta in "The Chance of Araminta," intelligent, self-sustaining and practical women, make a decision *not* to pursue or accept a childish or dishonest lover, Lydia of "Lydia Hersey" and Catherine of "The Secret," equally intelligent and strong women, finally decide to compromise their dream of a stronger or more mature husband with the consequences of remaining single; both choose, ultimately, to marry the lovers they have. Yet they do so only when their young men capitulate. In all of these cases, Freeman implies, the women ultimately "win"; in deciding either for or against marriage, they demonstrate and maintain the integrity of their own wills. Married or single, they have few illusions of what the future holds for them, but they are prepared to face it with courage.

Nina Auerbach has described the novels of Jane Austen, and by extension other romantic fiction of courtship, as works about "waiting": "waiting for the door to open and a Pygmalion to bring life into limbo defines the female world" (38–39). Many of Freeman's stories about the relationship between the sexes also concern women's "waiting" but, as so often in her writings, parody the sentimental convention. While women in these stories do wait for men to court them, they do not do so resignedly or passively. Rather, Freeman highlights their frustration at men's seemingly intolerable stubbornness and slowness, and she emphasizes such women's insistence on living a fulfilling life despite their wait. In Freeman's world in which it was yet considered socially reprehensible for a woman to make the first move in courtship or marriage, an unresponsive, passive, or slow man must have literally driven a more active or energetic woman, as Freeman was herself, crazy. At times Freeman's stories, especially her early ones, fairly seethe with what must have been for her a personal frustration.

"A Conflict Ended," "Two Old Lovers," and "A Patient Waiter," all published in Freeman's first volume, A Humble Romance (1887), are three such stories about a woman's "waiting." In the first, Esther Barney has waited nearly a decade for hard-headed Marcus Woodman, her one-time fiancé, to "come to his senses." Ten years earlier, Marcus, having quarreled with the town's minister, swore he would never again enter the church doors. Every Sunday since that time, he has obdurately sat outside on the church steps during the service. As a consequence, Esther has refused to marry him: "Do you s'pose I was going to marry a man who made a laughing-stock of himself that way?" she confides to her young relative Margy. Esther admits she has barely managed to suppress her anger these long years: "I've got over it a good deal, though sometimes it makes me jest as mad as ever. . . .

But I try to be reconciled, and I get along jest as well, mebbe, as if I'd had him—I don't know."

Significantly, it takes the death of Marcus's mother, with whom he has lived, for the two to finally marry; this death allows Esther the freedom to make the conciliatory first move. As Marjorie Pryse explains, "had [the mother] lived, Esther realizes, she could not have called on Marcus" ("Afterword," 325); now, however, Esther can assume a socially acceptable "motherly" role toward Marcus. In doing so, she shows not only that her love for him is predominantly maternal, which is often the case in Freeman's male and female relationships, but also reveals Marcus's inherent childishness. He gives up his quarrel easily; like a stubborn child, he has simply been waiting for an excuse to do so.

In "Two Old Lovers," Maria Brewster has waited more than twenty-five years for David Emmons to ask her to marry him. Maria's feeling for David, like Esther's for Marcus, is "eminently practical" and "rather mother-like than lover-like." A much stronger person than he, she, though alone, lives a full and cheerful life whereas his is lonely, narrow, and miserable. Although "she never doubted for an instant that he loved her," he simply "had never reely come to the p'int"; decorum, of course, will not allow Maria herself to suggest they wed. Maria pities David as she watches him grow old and feeble. Only on his deathbed does David mournfully confess, 'I allers meant to— have asked you—to—marry me." As Pryse perceptively comments, even here David cannot assert himself and ask; he can only "mean to have asked" ("Afterword," 316).

Perhaps the ultimate "waiting" story in Freeman's canon is "A Patient Waiter." Reminiscent of Dickens's Miss Havisham in *Great Expectations*, protagonist Fidelia Almy, true to her name, has based her existence on faithful waiting for the lover who, having deserted her over thirty years before, never returns. A nervous and obsessed woman, Fidelia walks several miles twice daily to the post office hoping for his letter; she keeps her house in immaculate order and her fine clothes and linen unused in anticipation of his momentary arrival. Her waiting extends to her death; her final words are full of "triumphant resolution": *"I ain't goin' to give it up yet."* Unlike that of "A Conflict Ended" and "Two Old Lovers," however, Freeman tells this story of a woman's waiting with tragic pathos. Fidelia, holding on to her romantic delusions and refusing to accept the reality of her situation, clearly represents one of Freeman's many portraits of imbalanced characters, both male and female, whose stubborn and intractable wills have completely distorted their lives.

Freeman's women characters, then, must often wait for or otherwise tolerate men who, stubborn and passive, "never reely come to the p'int." However, Freeman also has several interesting stories in which a young woman, her overweening pride chastened, learns to accept a man's inadequacy precisely because she is able for the first time to see her own. In these stories, perhaps, Freeman is recording the pride that kept her during her lifetime from associating with "common" men and women: though she always maintained several close friendships, she had the reputation in both Randolph and later in Metuchen of being cold and aloof.

In "Humble Pie" (1904), Maria Gorham, a school teacher in her thirties, lives "quietly poised . . . in her own self esteem"; confident of her good looks, fashionable clothing, and above average wit, she particularly scorns the faithful, kind, yet, to her, dull attentions of her long-time suitor, Dexter Ray. Feeling the need to get away from the "common" folk, Maria decides to vacation for a month at a mountain hotel. She refuses Dexter's offer of a ride to the train station, not wanting to be seen in his company. Once at the hotel, she checks into her room; dresses carefully in her new "sacque," a dress she has made especially for the trip; and descends to dinner. However, much to her consternation, Maria realizes upon entering the room that the other women are wearing evening gowns and not sacques; she has, in other words, committed an egregious social error among the very company she had expected to dazzle with her fine taste.[2] "She saw them looking askance . . . she heard furtive chuckles," but Maria, trying hard to appear composed, finishes her dinner and retires to her room. The next morning, she proudly dons her new "wrapper" for breakfast but in horror discovers that in this company it too is hopelessly out-of-style. When a "kindly" woman makes a stumbling attempt to inform her of her error, Maria "suffered tortures. Ridicule was the hardest thing in the world for one of her kind to endure." No one else bothers to converse with her during her two-week stay, and during this time Maria, "thought a good deal about Dexter Ray. She thought how if she had a husband with her like many of the other women she would not have felt so defenseless and isolated in her wrapper. . . . She remembered how very plain Dexter Ray was, and how clumsy . . . and [these] seemed to her like the wrapper and the cambric sacque, something for people who had not love and appreciation in their hearts to make fun of, but nothing of any consequence to those who could see what was underneath; the honesty, and the affection, and the faithfulness." Maria returns home to Dexter, having eaten her slice of "humble pie."

Similarly, a story within a story, "The Horn of Plenty" (1911), concerns a proud, young, single woman who learns enough humility, this time through vicarious experience, to appreciate the man she has previously scorned to marry. Sensing that her half-sister Lucilla, who has just returned from a visit to New York, is depressed, Mrs. Abby Armstrong questions her. Lucilla only responds, "I am over thirty." Abby surmises the real problem. "You are a young woman . . . and you have all your wits and plenty to live on," she reminds her. "You can do about as you are a mind to—travel or stay at home . . . and here you are eating nothing and looking glum just because you think you haven't quite all that ought to come to you." Abby then relates the story of a haughty young woman, Rebecca Reddy, who refused to marry her long-time suitor because she thought him not good enough for her. Finally, with all of her other suitors having married and her father down on his luck, she is forced for the first time to scrimp for a living and even to accept charity. In her new-found humility, Rebecca accepts her patient lover; she, interjects Abby, "was looking too high, and missed the flower at her feet for the sake of straining after the star in the sky."

> "Maybe I am like Rebecca Reddy," [Lucilla admits as Abby finishes the story].
> "I don't know what you mean now," [Abby responds.]
> Lucilla's blush deepened. "I mean Sammy Lane. . . . I got accustomed to thinking he was just Sammy, and he has always been at my feet, and when I went to New York I saw men who were not just Sammy, and had not always been at my feet, and though I didn't really want them, I got more unsettled. . . . I'll look no higher than Sammy for the rest of my life."

Freeman, then, shows us women of various ages and in different situations who temper their ideals with both the shortcomings of their own personalities and their very real and limited options in life; they learn that forming and maintaining relationships with the—in their point of view—often weak, passive, or inadequate men around them usually requires some form of compromise. Their decisions, Freeman tells us, are nevertheless always conscious, and herein Freeman's female protagonists reveal not only their inner strength but at times their heroism.

Freeman's stories of a woman considering marriage or adjusting to her new life once married usually picture that woman as both submissive to and independent of a man. Reading her stories today, we tend to be uncomfortable with this ambiguity and perhaps long "to rewrite beginnings and reshape endings of her stories or to manipulate details to fit [our] notion of a feminist model" (Glasser, "She Is the One," 188). Understandably, the resurgence of interest in Freeman's fiction today focuses on her tales of "rebellious" women or women who refuse to marry. Yet only a fraction of this latter group—one or two stories really—concern a woman who says, and means, "no." More typically, a young woman in Freeman's world merely delays marriage because she yet dreams of a better partner, because she feels it is her duty to care for an aged parent, or because she wants to provide herself with a suitable "dowry" so as not to enter her husband's family in need. Two early stories with these latter themes are "Robins and Hammers" (1887), in which a young girl puts off her marriage until she can earn enough money to provide herself with "at least two silk dresses," and "Old Lady Pingree" (1887), in which an impoverished girl refuses to marry in order to provide for her sickly mother. Once these conditions are met—and given a suitor of their choice—these young women marry willingly.

Two well-known Freeman stories collected in *A New England Nun and Other Stories* (1891), "Louisa" and "A New England Nun," have received considerable attention because of the protagonists' apparent rejection of marriage. Yet neither story presents us with a heroine who determinedly chooses a single life over the married state. Louisa in the first story simply does "not like" her suitor Jonathan Nye. Freeman makes it clear that Louisa's choice stems not necessarily from the qualities of the man himself—although "tall and clumsy, long-featured and long-necked," Jonathan appears to be an acceptable partner—nor from an outright rejection of marriage, but rather from Louisa's own implacable self-will and stubborn pride. Intent on her own dreams, Louisa above all insists on opposing the materialistic wishes of her nagging mother.

It is a tribute to the artistry of "A New England Nun" that various interpretations of the work have evolved over the years. The story, quite simply, is a masterpiece of ambiguity. Louisa Ellis's breaking of her fourteen-year engagement to Joe Dagget and settling back into her peaceful routine has been read as a triumph of womanly order, domesticity, and stability over masculine chaos and flight; Louisa herself has been called an "artist" and a "visionary," "heroic, active, wise, ambitious, and even transcendent" (Pryse, "Uncloistered," 289). On the other hand, "A New England Nun" has been seen as a study in obsession and sexual repression, a "rejection of life" (Hirsch, 135) in which Louisa "for self-protection . . . builds cloistered walls behind which she buries her sexuality" (Glasser, "She Is the One," 193).

The ambiguity resulting in these differing points of view is certainly intentional; in this story Freeman carefully weighs the personality of the protagonist against the prospect of what she stands to gain and to lose should she marry. It is important to note that Freeman does not scorn, but neither does she admire, Louisa, who, finding her faithful fiancé in love with another woman, merely releases him from his commitment to her. Her subsequent peace, her "prayerfully numbering her days, like an uncloistered nun" is, given the tone of the work and the equivocal language used throughout, scarcely a triumph of womanly spirit or independence; neither, however, can Louisa's solitary existence be seen as an unhealthy "martyrdom" resulting from her fear of sexuality. Rather, Freeman lays emphasis on the fact that Louisa is, above all, a methodical and unimaginative person who has merely bowed to circumstance. Though she could have held honest Joe Dagget to his promise and would have certainly married him had she not overheard his covert conversation with Lily Dyer, she is relieved to find him in love with the other girl. When she has the opportunity to speak with him, she tells him the truth: "she simply said that . . . she had lived so long in one way that she shrank from making a change."

At several points in the story, we are made aware of Louisa's "shrinking" from change and her lifelong subsequent lack of concrete decision. She may or may not ever have been in love with Joe; it is her mother, we discover, who talked her into accepting him: "Fifteen years ago she had been in love with him—at least she considered herself to be. Just at that time, gently acquiescing with and falling into the natural drift of girlhood, she had seen marriage ahead as a reasonable feature and a probable desirability of life. She had listened with calm docility to her mother's views on the subject. . . . [Her mother] talked wisely to her daughter when Joe Dagget presented himself, and Louisa accepted him with no hesitation."

Just as the "natural drift of girlhood" led Louisa to become engaged to Joe, so did the "natural drift" allow her to wait for him "patiently and unquestioningly" all those years, "never dreaming of the possibility of marrying anyone else." Louisa Ellis, so unlike Louisa Britton of "Louisa," has few dreams. Her only wish is for a continuation of the "pleasant peace" she has created for herself by meticulously controlling every aspect of her immediate environment, so much so that any change in habit or routine, or any visitor, becomes an unpleasant intrusion. Her routine scarcely varies; she tends her garden, sews her linen, and makes her tea with perfect regularity. In going about her tasks, she "had almost the enthusiasm of an artist over the mere order and cleanliness of her solitary home"—almost. For Louisa is not an artist—unless one insists on stretching to preposterous limits the meaning of "art"—and Freeman makes this fact more than plain. Far from creative, Louisa's impulse is toward "mere order and cleanliness." When Joe leaves after his customary twice-weekly courting visit, Louisa necessarily hastens to sweep away his tracks and arrange the books he has carelessly handled. Necessarily must she also keep the unpredictable old dog Caesar chained and the fluttering canary caged. Having in the seven years since her mother and brother died limited, ordered, and controlled her life in such a way as to provide for no disturbances to her placid, methodical sensibility, Louisa is constitutionally unable to accept into her life anything that would now upset the "natural drift" of her existence.

The reader is satisfied when Louisa breaks her engagement to Joe. Clearly, the two are unsuited for each other. The changes Louisa would have to make in adjusting to marriage are far too great. She would be forced as well to put up with his "rigorous and feeble old mother," an unsavory prospect at best. Louisa deserves the "peace" she has carefully constructed; "serenity and placid narrowness had become to her as the birthright itself." In the final analysis, "A New England Nun" has little to do with a woman's choosing between marriage or remaining single. Rather, Louisa, "a veritable guest to her own self" is alone and will remain alone whether married or single because of her mental confines.

Freeman suggests further that the "peace" Louisa seeks at all costs is hardly peace at all, but a mere facade of it. In the ambiguous wording of the following sentence, we are alerted to the tension underlying Louisa's careful manipulation of her surroundings, tension that may easily erupt on another day unlike the "calm, serene" one of the present: "Louisa's feet had turned into a path, *smooth maybe under a calm, serene sky,* but so straight and unswerving that it could only meet a check at her grave, and so narrow that there was no room for any one at her side" (emphasis mine). Although Freeman's stronger protagonists make concrete choices among their limited options, Louisa Ellis is yet another illustration of Freeman's frequent portraits of the effects of generations of the narrow and dogged Puritan will on the New England character. Moreover, Louisa invites comparison with other Freeman characters who, in their compulsion for immaculate households, only succeed in tormenting those who live with them: Charlotte in "An Innocent Gamester," Esther in "Emancipation," and Malvina in "A Village Lear." In all three of these situations, Freeman's sympathies clearly lie not with the perpetrator but with the victim of such domestic tyranny.

"A New England Nun" was evidently written somewhere between April 1886 and May 1887, when it first appeared in *Harper's Bazar.* Freeman mentions the "germ" of the story in a letter written to Mary Louise Booth on 28 April 1886: "Monday afternoon, I went a-hunting material too: We went to an old lady's birthday-party. But all I saw worth writing about there was a poor old dog, who had been chained thirteen years, because he bit a man once, in his puppy-hood. I have felt like crying every time I have thought of him. He wagged his tail, and looked so pitiful, he is half blind too" (Kendrick, 69).

Although Freeman initially found little "worth writing about" at the birthday party, her sympathy for the chained dog and her desire to release it were eventually worked into the character of Joe Dagget, who tells Louisa "quite forcibly at intervals," "There ain't a better-natured dog in town . . . and it's down-right cruel to keep him tied up there. Some day I'm going to take him out."[3] In having Joe voice her own concerns and in having Louisa oppose them, Freeman further indicates her disapproval of Louisa. Also, she lays to rest the tendency of some of her contemporaries to equate her too closely with her protagonist Louisa Ellis, a comparison that she heartily scorned.[4]

Freeman was in her mid-thirties when she wrote "A New England Nun," "Emmy," "A Patient Waiter," "Louisa," and a number of other stories that consider from several points of view the desirability of marriage; she continued throughout her writing career and her marriage to explore these themes. As noted earlier, remarks in her personal correspondence at times evince the fear that marriage might not only limit her disciplined writing schedule but also suppress or significantly alter her unique talents. "The Prism" (1901) and "Arethusa" (1900), both published close to the time of her wedding to Charles Freeman, show in their similar themes Freeman's apprehension about the loss of individuality or artistic ability that marriage might exact from a woman. Yet in each of these stories, the woman chooses to abdicate or suppress her creativity to conform to her husband's will.

An odd story in Freeman's canon because of its allegorical overtones, "The Prism" concerns a lonely, introspective girl, Diantha Fielding, who finds reflected in a glass "drop" that she has stolen from her step-mother's parlor lamp a world of fairies and beauty lacking in her own mundane existence. Later, as a young woman about to marry, she attempts to share the well-guarded secret of her prism with her lover, only to find herself ridiculed. "What a child you are, dear!" he impatiently answers when she asks him what he sees in the cut glass. "See? Why, I see the prismatic colors, of course. What else should I see? . . . Don't talk such nonsense. I thought you were a sensible girl." Questioning, because of this episode, her suitability as a wife, he decides to reject her, and Diantha, in despair, buries the prism. "I have put it away," she cries to him. "I saw nothing; it was only my imagination." Relieved, he exhorts her to remember that "this is a plain, common world, and [such fancies] won't do." Diantha marries him. At the end of the story, the narrator, while conceding that Diantha now enjoys a certain "earthly bliss," ironically questions whether or not she had in truth "sold her birthright": "People said how much Diantha had improved since her marriage, what a fine housekeeper she was, how much common sense she had, how she was such a fitting mate for her husband. . . . [However] sometimes Diantha . . . would remember that key of a lost radiance and a lost belief of her own life, which was buried beside it. Then she would go happily and prepare her husband's supper."

Published in *Understudies*, a collection of symbolic tales exploring resemblances between animals, flowers, and human beings, "Arethusa" likewise concerns an imaginative and isolated girl, Lucy Greenleaf, who renounces her rich inner world in order to be accepted by her well-meaning but "practical" husband. Lucy's single joy in life is her yearly pilgrimage to the marsh to sight the "rarest and most beautiful" spring flower, the arethusa. Her mother (who, the narrator informs us, "had been insensibly trained by all her circumstances of life to regard a husband like rain in its season, or war, or a full harvest, or an epidemic, something to be accepted without question if offered, whether good or bad, as sent by the will of the Lord") insists that Lucy acknowledge the advances of young Edson Abbot who has ardently courted her. Lucy, however, hesitates; although she likes the man, "she was made to feel always his firm, unrelaxing will towards her, and his demand for her obedience." Finally, as a result of her mother's coercion, she agrees to marry Edson: "'I will,' she said, tremulously; 'I will, Edson. Mother says I ought to, and I will.'"

That very day, Lucy has discovered the arethusa in bloom. However, when Edson promises to pick it for her, she is, to his surprise, appalled. "If—if you do that, if you pick that flower, I—I will never marry you," she stammers excitedly; consequently, the narrator tells us, "a doubt as to the actual normal mental state of the girl came into his mind." Despite his misgivings, however, Edson continues with plans for the marriage, but on their wedding day, Lucy cannot be found. "Enraged," and barely restraining "a fierce impulse to bend forcibly this other will which had come into contact with his own," Edson breaks a path to the swamp. There he finds Lucy; though he expects her resistance, she docilely returns with him and is married. Thereafter, although "she filled her place as wife and mother well to all appearances," she also quickly learns that she must keep her dreams and her love of beauty to herself in order to preserve them: "while forever his, even in his embrace, she was forever her own."

In these two stories, Freeman voices her concern that marriage is potentially damaging to a woman's individuality; a woman finds she may have to suppress or compromise her dreams or talents in order to fulfill dutifully the role of wife. Moreover, Freeman alters her usual pattern of male and female relationships; in these stories, it is the male who is more "practical" than the female, yet his practicality, in its demand that a woman conform to the traditional role of a wife, allows no room for a woman's creative vision. Both Diantha in "The Prism" and Lucy in "Arethusa" ultimately choose this "normal" life, this "earthly bliss," over free expression of a rich inner world. Freeman's honesty in telling what she knew of women's relationships to men in marriage is evident in these sensitively drawn portraits. Self-sufficient and talented as she might be, a woman in Freeman's world sometimes finds a "normal" woman's role of wife and mother preferable to the independent and creative, yet often isolated and isolating, life lived in the mind.

Several of Freeman's more candid stories also take a hard look at life for a young woman after marriage, although her less realistic stories at times conveniently rely on the "happy" ending. Apparently, for the first several years of her own married life, Freeman was contented; her apprehensions, especially those of falling behind in her writing schedule, were not borne out. Yet just before and just after her marriage, she composed several works that depict a young woman emotionally alienated and even tortured by her husband's cruelty.

"A Tragedy from the Trivial" (1901) explores the emotions of a young orphaned working girl as she enters into marriage and attempts to please her new husband. Unfortunately, Charlotte May has married a tight-fisted, selfish young man; at his command, though willingly enough, she gives up "all her little tricks of style and fashion," which he deems "devoid of sense." But she fails miserably in managing their household budget to his satisfaction. While basically kind, he soon begins to regard her every action with "steady disapproval." Charlotte's resultant guilt at her failure to please him makes her, three years after her marriage, a "sad anomaly—a creature at cross purposes with itself. She was completely under the sway of her husband's will, as regarded her own, yet she was unable to accomplish perfect obedience to its mandate." Still, the narrator maintains, "she was not unhappy, being as fond of her husband as a spaniel, but was more or less anxious and bewildered."

As her husband's disapproval grows, Charlotte despairs and runs away. She returns to her job as a department-store clerk, where, despite others advising her to seek a divorce, she strives to save enough money to repay her husband for what she considers her years of "wasting" his property. Over many weeks, she succeeds in saving a small sum but becomes deathly ill from worry and exhaustion. She finally returns to her husband but dies soon thereafter; in biting irony, the narrator bitterly concludes that "at the last she had learned her little lesson of obedience and thrift against all her instincts, and all her waste of life was over." "A tragedy from the trivial" indeed.

Freeman continued to write stories about the emotional cruelty married life can bring to women after her own marriage. By 1918, the year "Sour Sweetings" was published in *Edgewater People*, she had good reason to be bitter and cynical about marriage, for her own marriage to Charles Freeman was rapidly eroding. Totally dependent on alcohol and drugs by this time, Charles Freeman "would stay on a spree for three and four weeks at a time. . . . He was plagued by hallucinations, and at times his actions bordered on being violent" (Kendrick, 362). Although ending on a false sentimental note, "Sour Sweetings" is perhaps as devoid of romance as any story Freeman wrote.

Julius Caesar Whittemore, a wealthy, handsome, and spoiled young man, marries Nelly Dunn, and the couple move into the palatial family home with his aged mother. Only a week after returning from the wedding journey, however, Nelly consciously "disobeys" her new husband in what she considers a trite matter; she wears a dress less formal than her satin wedding gown to a party given in their honor. Neither Julius nor his mother broaches the matter, but instantly Nelly is cognizant of the enormity of her mistake. That evening Julius, without a word, moves himself into a separate bedroom at the far end of the house, and Nelly thereafter spends sleepless nights alone. Both mother and son continue to refuse to speak with her about the incident; disarmingly kind and respectful, they torture her with cold cordiality. Returning home at regular intervals, Nelly confesses to her mother, "I never say one word any more than the Whittemores do. And I am perfectly pleasant. The worst of it is I know they don't like that. They want me to ask questions and complain and cry, and I am afraid that in the end this ridiculous playing at being enemies will come true. I am afraid Julius won't care so much for me, but I can't give up when I know I am not in the wrong." "I am married," Nelly continues when her mother bids her consider her wedding vows, "and I know that . . . marriage vows are sacred, but married love can be cruel in ways that other love would never dream of."

Finally, the small jabs of "cold politeness" accrue to the point of rendering Nelly physically and emotionally ill; she flees home to her parents. As she leaves, Julius states angrily that "when that sweet-apple-tree has sour apples under it, then I will ask you to come back"—clearly, an impossibility. A year passes as the small town "hummed with gossip" about the affair. One early fall day, Nelly observes Julius furtively working beneath the apple tree. He removes the fallen sweet apples, replacing them with sour ones; as he had hoped, Nelly comes over to taste one, and to her "it seemed to . . . have the sweetness of the whole world, and life itself, typifying, as it did, the surrender of a human soul to love." She returns to her husband—dressed in the white satin wedding gown. Nelly's capitulation here has taken place only in response to Julius's act. Nevertheless, the story's ending remains unsatisfactory as the "love" Nelly apparently continues to experience for Julius is never made plausible; despite his final conciliatory act, Julius is consistently rendered throughout the tale as an egotistic, emotionally immature, and even brutal man.

Although Freeman revealed her distrust for and apprehension of married life in a number of stories throughout her career, she also retained a lifelong romantic ideal of a weak, broken, or lonely man's being somehow "saved" by the loving fidelity of a strong woman. In her minor holiday story for *Everybody's*, "An Easter-Card" (1901), she equates this salvific power with the Resurrection itself. Shabby, run-down Lawrence Brooks, deserted as a young man by the girl he is to marry, is literally kept alive by a yearly anonymous Easter card; he spends weeks waiting for it, and weeks after receiving it, he basks in the "infinite preciousness of being unforgotten." Late in life he discovers that the sender is his former fiancée's cousin who has secretly loved him all those years. When he confronts her, she boldly states, "I will never forgive her [the fiancée] one minute of suffering she caused you. . . . I thought you might feel that somebody thought of you, that it might keep up your courage. . . . You don't love me, you never did, you never will; but I love you with all my soul, and shall as long as I live, and love is worth something even if you don't love back." "You must be different for the sake of the love, Lawrence Brooks," she pleads, and thereupon "he seemed to see his own better-self at [her] side . . . and to see also in her strangely new yet familiar guise the ideal of his life."

Likewise, the sentimental "A Discovered Pearl" (1891) chronicles the story of Gilman Marlow who, by his own admission, has "slumped through" life, ending up in late middle age a physical and emotional wreck. Returning to his hometown, he is astonished to find that his sweetheart of years before, whom he has virtually forgotten, has kept up the mortgage payments on his home in anticipation of his return. Marlow is equally astounded when Lucy shyly admits she has been faithful to his memory and even then would consider marrying him. "Good Lord! to think of me havin' *you!*" he exclaims. "I ain't worth this." In Lucy's care, he recognizes for the first time his worth as a human being; consequently, he is able to appreciate Lucy, who, he acknowledges, has become for him "a pearl caught in some sea-weeds."

"Saving" women such as those rendered in the stories above may be best seen as representing, albeit in sentimentalized fashion, Free-man's conception of the "ideal" female. In these stories, Freeman not only conceives of this ideal woman as one strong in belief, honesty, humility, practicality, and faithfulness but who also shows the efficacy and worth of her self-integrity. All of this leads eventually to the regeneration of a man's life and the reconnection of severed human bonds. Other stories in this vein include "A Pot of Gold" (1891), "The Underling" (1907) and "A Slayer of Serpents" (1910).

Carol Gilligan, in attempting to document and describe the disparate life experiences and differing "voices" or language of men and women, has postulated the thesis that the greatest psychological and developmental conflict in a woman's life is that between her need for autonomy and self-integrity as a separate and unique human being and her equally powerful need to form and maintain intense and meaningful bonds with other human beings. Gilligan states that the decisions a woman must make in light of this conflict are often extremely difficult because they are intimately equated in her mind with her moral being and thus her conception of self. Quite often, these decisions are compromises, for a woman's psychological makeup necessitates that she simultaneously retain a sense of herself as an individual and give herself to another in a relationship. Thus Gilligan speaks of a woman's desire for freedom and autonomy as essentially a human trait, but her fear that "freedom . . . will lead to an abandonment of responsibility in relationships" is seen as a unique characteristic of a woman's, as opposed to a man's, moral and psychological makeup (130).

Freeman's stories concerning women, men, and marriage show us portraits of women involved in many different aspects of this dual inner struggle. Although they more often than not grow up with an image of marriage as repressive for women, and although their experiences with men both before and after marriage may confirm this opinion, women in Freeman's world often choose to compromise some part of themselves in order to form and maintain a relationship with a man in marriage.

Important to Freeman's themes is the idea of free will, of choice making. Although Freeman at times shows us dependent, narrow-minded, and neurotic women, those of whom Freeman approves—practical, intelligent, full of integrity, and sometimes quite creative—are aware of their ability to exist emotionally (though perhaps not always financially) independent of a man. In many cases, they realize that little chance exists of finding a man whom they can respect as an equal. Furthermore, they understand that the "duties" imposed by marriage may well limit their creative abilities and desires. Freeman's women weigh these matters carefully and usually choose marriage over remaining single. They do so for a variety of reasons: to attempt to follow the "normal" course of a woman's life; to avoid the loneliness and social stigma of spinsterhood; to pursue a lingering dream of fulfillment; to give themselves unselfishly to another. As always, Freeman probes the mind and heart of women as they struggle to make this decision in the face of myriad social and psychological pressures.

CHAPTER 5

Women as Friends and Rivals

"Friend of My Heart"

"What particularly distinguishes the women of Wilkinston . . . is that theirs is a world in which women's primary relationships are to each other rather than to men. Wilkins's women . . . are dependent on each other economically as well as emotionally. This dependence, of course, leads to hostility as well as affection. These women fight, envy, disagree, compete, bicker, and manipulate. But underlying the hostility are loyalty and intense involvement with each other, phenomena unique in fiction" (Clark, 195).

Although many of Freeman's stories concern women's experiences with men and marriage, women's relationships to other women also figure prominently in her themes and constitute, in fact, one of the more interesting elements of her fiction. Men are important to Freeman's women: women strive to understand and accept them, and, as we have repeatedly seen, they may choose to compromise their hopes and desires in order to marry. Yet Freeman consistently shows us that in her world women's relationships with other women are at once more fundamental, substantial, and tenacious than women's relationships with men.

102

In and of itself, perhaps, this statement is not surprising. Recent scholars of women's history have made us aware of the importance and necessity of women's mutual bonds, especially in an earlier era. Lillian Faderman's study of women's relationships throughout history, *Surpassing the Love of Men*, explains that previous generations were far more content than our own to regard males and females as largely inexplicable to one another, as "virtually separate species." Moreover, the nineteenth-century concept of separate spheres, Faderman continues, dictated such disparate work and leisure activities for men and women that "outside of the practical necessities of raising a family there was little that tied the sexes together. But with other females a woman . . . could be entirely trusting and unrestrained" (159). Carroll Smith-Rosenberg's *Disorderly Conduct* also speaks of nineteenth-century women forming "supportive networks" full of "emotional richness and complexity" in the face of "severe social restrictions on intimacy between young men and women" (60). Nancy Chodorow's *Mothering* has argued that, because women have not traditionally been "cared for" by men in the way they themselves extend care to men and children, they have learned to "support themselves emotionally by supporting and reconstituting *one another*" (36).

A study of Freeman's stories, however, only partially corroborates these findings. Often estranged emotionally or physically from fathers, husbands, or lovers, Freeman's women form an intricate social network with each other on which they depend for emotional interaction. These female-female relationships are fundamental and enduring; women strive to initiate, develop, and maintain contact with each other on a daily basis. Moreover, a Freeman woman understands her women friends' needs and concerns in a way she can never hope to understand those of men.

Because of these apparent positive aspects reflected in the close bonds between women portrayed in Freeman's works, some critics have considered Freeman to be a protofeminist writer. Such intimate and fulfilling bonds, they maintain, indicate Freeman's women characters—and by extension the author herself, perhaps—were triumphantly independent of men. Marjorie Pryse speaks of a "sisterhood" of common "vision" among Freeman's female protagonists and concludes that "women in Freeman's fiction have available to them . . . a community [of other women] that sustains their spirit and validates their vision" ("Afterword," 335).

Much as modern readers might wish to see her stories comply with such positive models for female-female relationships, however, evidence for such a conclusion is lacking from Freeman's canon. Only a few of her tales depict women who, on an equal status in class, wealth, or intellect, can truly qualify as friends. No Freeman story, therefore, illustrates the celebrated nineteenth-century "Boston marriage" that typically involved cultural and intellectual exchange between "new women," those financially or emotionally independent from men. Women's friendships in Freeman's stories rarely even approach the level of mutual exploration of ideas or sympathetic sharing of feelings and concerns.

Rather, the emotional and mutually dependent bonds women form with other women in Freeman's New England more often than not take on a disturbingly threatening or ominous tone. Freeman consistently portrays relationships between women as unequal in some way. Many of her stories are based on a rivalry or power struggle—over a man, a possession, a reputation—between a dominant or strong woman and a much weaker one. Although intimate to a degree, these unequal relationships usually require both women involved to protect themselves from their "friend's" emotional abuse or scorn. Thus these relationships are in no way honest or open but cautious and restrained. Many of these stories therefore turn on themes of cheating, theft, or false identity, all "sins" committed by a woman to achieve acceptance or to raise her level of esteem in her rival's eyes. Freeman's frequent depiction of the bond between sisters, an especially close and inseparable one, often carries with it a similarly threatening note; one sister's tyranny over or jealous domination of the other lurks just beneath the surface if not overtly forming the events of the plot.

Just as Freeman usually empathizes with the child in writing of mother and daughter relationships, thereby expressing apprehension concerning the mother's control or domination, so also she often writes from the viewpoint of the weaker or more childlike woman when portraying relationships between female friends or rivals. As noted earlier, facts from Freeman's biography indicate that, after both

her mother and her only sister Anna died, she depended on "managing" women her entire life to care for her daily needs as well as to
provide critical help with her writing. Her relationship with Mary
John Wales, the childhood friend with whom she lived nearly twenty
years, was apparently both a close yet unequal one, much the same as
those portrayed in her stories. "As children it had always been 'strong,
vital [and] maternal' Mary Wales who stepped in to protect her
'timid . . . clinging [and] sensitive' friend whenever she was frightened by other youngsters," Kendrick tells us (51), quoting Edward
Foster's unpublished Harvard dissertation ("Mary E. Wilkins Freeman: A Bibliographical and Critical Study," 1934, p. 14).

Foster's published biography of Freeman indicates that Wales played
much the same role in their adult years together: "In Mary Wales
[Freeman] had a mother and sister, who misunderstood her at times
but always accepted her moods of petulance and rebellion," he writes
(Foster, 133). Yet Foster also suggests that Freeman at times rebelled
against such domination. He writes of at least one period in her life
when, "feeling the need to think her own thoughts free from the pressure of Miss Wales' strong personality, she devised a scheme for having
a few days alone" (141). Freeman mentions Wales briefly but affec-
tionately in several letters to others and no doubt corresponded with
her on her frequent trips away from the Wales home and again after
her marriage. Unfortunately, however, none of this latter correspondence exists today.

Freeman maintained several other close friendships with women all
her life, most notably that with Evelyn Sawyer Severance, a friend
from her early days in Brattleboro. When Evelyn married in 1875 and
moved away from Brattleboro, Foster relates that her move was a "severe blow" to Mary Wilkins: "there was no one to take the place of
the adored Evie" (38). No doubt Freeman also wrote to this friend
frequently over the ensuing years; it is disappointing, again, that only
a handful of these letters exists.

Much of our first-hand information concerning Freeman's involvement with other women comes from the epistolary relationships she
formed with writers and editors—Kate Upson Clark, Mary Louise
Booth, Eliza Farman Pratt, and Sarah Orne Jewett. Freeman evidently
cherished such professional and personal contact. "I begin to see that

there is one beautiful thing which comes from this kind of work, and the thing I have the most need of, I think," she wrote to Booth in 1885. "One is going to find friends because of it; and when one has no one of their very own, one does need a good many of these, who come next" (Kendrick, 62). Her letters, often signed with a nickname such as "Pussy Willow" or "Dolly," indicate that these were close and affectionate friendships. Effusive in greetings, apologies for wrongs done, excuses for work she considered inadequate, or requests for advice, these letters further suggest that, despite her steadily increasing popularity and success over the years, Freeman never completely felt that she was these women's equal. Rather, in many ways, these women apparently played a more maternal than friendly role in Freeman's adult life.

Freeman turned to other women to provide her with emotional, practical, and artistic support, yet she perhaps feared and resented such stronger women for their control of or domination over her life. This conclusion can be drawn primarily from her many tales involving women friends who, unequal in social status, talent, or wealth, assume a relationship in which one woman, stronger and more maternal, controls or otherwise dominates a more dependent or childlike woman. Eventually the weaker woman rebels, and the stronger woman, made to "see" her error, is humbled and (usually) relents. In general, this theme emerges as a pattern in Freeman's depiction of women in mutual relationship; in some way and with many variations, a domineering or proud woman is rejected or humbled, and a meeker and more dependent woman quietly triumphs.

"The tenderness of one woman for another is farther reaching in detail than that of a man, because it is given with a fuller understanding of needs." So Freeman's narrator comments on the relationship between two women in the short story "The Tree of Knowledge" (1900). Women in Freeman's stories understand each other's needs well; they may respond kindly and generously, but they are also quite capable, in jealousy or envy, of using those needs to hurt a rival. In other words, women's knowledge of each other allows them a great degree of both power and vulnerability in the relationship, far more, Freeman indicates, than that in the relationship between a woman and man.

Very few of Freeman's women can be said to be "friends" in the sense that they relate to each other on an equal basis, mutually sharing concern or sympathy. One of the stories in which women appear to have an affectionate bond is "Criss-Cross" (1914), a delightful tale in which two elderly neighborhood women, cheated out of their vacation by an unscrupulous third woman, agree to switch households merely to alter their usual routine. For a week they wear each other's clothes, care for each other's houses, and assume each other's habits, returning home refreshed from the very act of sympathetic identification with each other, but their friendship is far from one based on an exchange of intimacies, feelings, or ideas.

Much more commonly, Freeman portrays the relationship between women friends as unequal and thus competitive. One of the women is the other's superior in strength, beauty, wealth, or even moral rectitude; the other woman, often envious, strives to imitate her. Although they may continue for years as "best" friends, these women keep their inner lives secret; they know little about each other's true thoughts or desires. Three stories will serve to illustrate this point. In "Sweet-Flowering Perennial" (1915), an odd story with a "fountain of youth" theme, middle-aged and impoverished Clara envies yet is mystified by her school friend Selma's continuing youthfulness and energy. Though Selma has taken Clara into her wealthy home when Clara's boarding house is temporarily placed under quarantine, Clara insists on spying on her friend in an attempt to learn her "secret." She never does discover Selma's "power of perennial bloom." [1]

In "The Amethyst Comb" (1914), Jane Carew believes that her best friend, Viola Longstreet, has stolen jewelry from her; she remains coldly suspicious of Viola yet silent about the matter for years, although at one point she invites Viola to live with her when that friend falls upon hard times. Only much later is it revealed that a young man whom Viola had once fancied she loved was the culprit. In "Friend of My Heart" (1913), two maiden ladies, both courted in their youth by the same man, find their lives disturbed and their friendship disrupted when he returns, unmarried, to town. Though Catherine, the stronger and more secure woman, knows in her heart that he has come back for her and not Elvira, she reluctantly "gives up" the vacillating Lucius to her weaker, unstable, and unhappy friend. "The women who need men to take care of them are the women who make men able to take care of them," Catherine silently concludes. Elvira never knows of her friend's "sacrifice."

Freeman's women maintain rivalries over other matters as well, including money, clothing, and children. All do so primarily from prideful motives, yet Freeman consistently shows us how paltry and, in the long run, ridiculous their efforts are. In "The Winning Lady" (1909), fashionable Mrs. Adeline Wyatt is proud of her "superior" and righteous appearance; she "regarded many of the other ladies [at her card party] with a somewhat pharisaical feeling." However, to her own horror, she one day cheats at the game and for a cheap prize at that. "When she had entered Mrs. Lennox's house that afternoon," she afterwards recalls in despair, "she had been a good, handsome, happy, self-satisfied, within-the-limits-of-virtue woman. She would leave it a fool and a sinner; that she was becomingly clad in prune-color would make not a whit of difference."[2]

Selma Woodsum in "The Liar" (1918), one of Freeman's several patriotic war stories, is embarrassed because her son is one of the few young men in the neighborhood who has not enlisted. She therefore steals an ink-stained uniform; hanging it on her line, she allows her neighbors to think her son has not only fought but has even earned a "red badge." Selma's evasive answers to her women friends' queries are so convincing that soon the entire neighborhood is "under the firm impression that poor, gallant Leon Woodsum had returned wounded from the front, and had lost the sight of one eye, if not both."[3]

The brief summaries above indicate that many of Freeman's plots involving women rivals turn on themes of cheating, lying, or theft, as a woman breaks from her tightly held moral convictions (and thereby faces the threat of damnation, a very real concern in Freeman's world) in order to gain her women friends' admiration. Though she does not condone the action, Freeman's disapprobation for these women is never sharp. Rather, she clearly understands their powerful inner need for security or approval from their peers. These women seek above all to maintain the appearance of a "good"—or smart, or fashionable— woman and often thereby succeed in deceiving their friends. However, Freeman shows us these women's overweening pride or vanity merely masks the fearful and guilty goadings of their consciences. Other stories with this theme include "Her Christmas" (1909), "The Fighting McLeans" (1910), and "The Gospel According to Joan" (1927).

Freeman's women compete intensely with each other; their daily lives are often consumed with worry over others' opinions of them and with attempts to "save face" in the absence of material or emotional security. Perhaps the most disturbing in Freeman's stories of women's relationships with each other are those in which a domineering woman keeps a weaker woman, with whom she often lives, in fear either of her physical power or her emotional scorn. In these stories, the weaker or more childlike woman has often received a marriage proposal; in intense jealousy, the stronger woman forbids her to marry. Eventually, however, the dominating woman relents. For example, in "Julia—Her Thanksgiving" (1909), Elsie, a clinging and dependent woman, imitates stronger Julia in all ways, even to the point of dressing like her. "I don't believe Elsie White ever set her feet outside Julia Benham's tracks in her life," the garrulous first-person narrator informs her audience. Elsie unhesitatingly lends Julia all of her money at Julia's request, and Julia, through imprudent investments, loses the majority of it. Only when the two are reduced to poverty does Julia allow Elsie to marry the beau she has been forced, by Julia's envy, to refuse years before.

In the murder mystery "The Long Arm" (1895), a story written in conjunction with Joseph Edgar Chamberlin, which won both authors a substantial monetary prize in the 1895 Bacheller Syndicate Short Story Contest, Phoebe Dole's jealousy leads her to murder a neighbor because she suspects her companion, Maria Woods, has become romantically involved with him. Ostensibly based on the Lizzie Borden slayings of 1892, more evidence suggests Freeman took her subject from the equally sensational Alice Mitchell case of the same year, in which a mentally disturbed Tennessee woman murdered her lesbian lover to "make it sure that no one else could get her."[4]

It should be noted that several other Freeman women characters evince signs of lesbianism, although the author never develops the particular relationship fully enough to make its full import clear. Both *The Portion of Labor* (1901) and *The Shoulders of Atlas* (1908) present similar ambiguously rendered female liaisons. The latter work is especially interesting in its portrayal of several intense female-female relationships, including a particularly volatile "quasi-lesbian, quasi-mother-daughter relationship" between an older woman and her much younger ward (Donovan, 128). The relationship between the characters Eunice Fairweather and Ada Harris in the short story "A Moral Exigency" has also been read as one evincing signs of "buried homosexuality" (Glasser, "Mary E. Wilkins Freeman," 333). Clark briefly notes two other tales with possible lesbian overtones, "The Love of Parson Lord" (1900) and "The Tree of Knowledge" (1900), speculating finally on the possibility of a latent homosexuality in Freeman herself. "Certainly the people closest to her were always women," Clark concludes. "And certainly, the women in her early stories and some of the later ones have passionate feelings for each other" (185).

It is impossible to know whether or not Mary Freeman experienced discord with Mary John Wales over the possibility of Freeman's marrying. As mentioned, Freeman's extant letters tell us little about her relationship with Wales; we do know, however, that after 1897, when Mary Wales's father died, Freeman, as does Elsie in "Julia—Her Thanksgiving," supported her friend financially, even lending her at one point all of the royalties from one of her novels (Foster, 141). In that same year, 1897, Mary Wilkins became engaged to Charles Freeman but continued to delay her wedding some five more years. When Mary and Charles finally did marry, Mary Wales was witness to the wedding. After moving with her husband to New Jersey, Freeman continued to help Mary Wales financially; each year she also returned to Randolph to visit. When Wales fell seriously ill in the spring of 1916, Freeman wrote poignantly to fellow author Florence Morse Kingsley: "My husband and I expect to go to Randolph, Mass., next Monday. That is where I made my home with friends after my own family died. My life long friend there is dying" (Kendrick, 353). Though she and Charles may have indeed made the trip to Randolph at this time, Freeman apparently did not return in August for Wales's funeral (Foster, 183).

These, then, are the few known facts about Freeman's friendship with Mary John Wales. While we can glean little from them, Freeman's tales concerning the rivalry between adult women friends (and between sisters as well) indicate Freeman knew her subject firsthand. Mary Freeman may well have delayed her marriage because of some emotional pressure—Mary Wales's jealousy, perhaps, or Freeman's own guilt at leaving the Wales family when they apparently badly needed her financial help. Whatever the source of these stories' themes, they expose a dark side of women's relationships with each other which, far from a "sisterhood" or "community" of shared values, indicate Freeman depended on, yet may also have feared, strong, maternal—and perhaps, ultimately vindictive—women.

As friends and rivals, women in Freeman's stories form close emotional ties with one another. But the strongest and most tenacious bond in Freeman's New England, the most intimate relationship this author portrays, is that between adult sisters. Historically, this relationship has been little studied. Smith-Rosenberg's research on nineteenth-century women notes the extreme centrality of close-kin relationships, especially sister relationships, in women's lives during that century. Unlike most other female-female friendships, she concludes, "sisterly bonds continued across a lifetime" (62).

Toni McNaron's *The Sister Bond: A Feminist View of a Timeless Connection* explores some of the intricacies of famous sister dyads over time, such as that of Christina and Maria Rossetti and that of Emily and Lavinia Dickinson. In her introduction, McNaron speaks of the ambiguous nature of her relationship with her own sibling, one which is common to many sisters. "I feel closer to her on some psychic level than to any friends or lovers," she writes. "I yearn for a kind of exchange that is not possible without our becoming the same person" (3). Yet despite such a desire for intimacy, she adds further, adult sisters are often acting out a pattern of competitive behavior ingrained from earliest childhood: "Either one sister encourages the other to play out some complementary self that she does not or cannot become, or forces around them are such that complementarity becomes the pattern within which both act out their adult lives. It is as though unconsciously the pairs . . . evolve a system in which they develop only certain parts of themselves. in order to cut down on or avoid altogether the powerful pulls toward competition found within virtually any family" (4).

Many of the sister pairs that McNaron's work examines created and evolved such role patterns for each other in order to establish separate identities within the family, often as a preventive measure for dealing with jealousy over or competition for parental attention. Each sister may thus come to define the other as her opposite or as a version of her expanded self. Moreover, twin sisters "must work unusually hard to learn to take individual responsibility for their own personalities" (7).

Freeman's many stories involving sisters point to personal experience with the kind of ambiguity and intricacy McNaron's research has uncovered in these relationships. Foster tells us that in their youth Mary's only sister, Anna, was considered more talented, witty, and likeable than Mary, especially among the young people of Brattleboro (32). At the time of her death in her middle teens, Anna was not only engaged to be married but had already won considerable public acclaim in town for her musical ability: she was organist at the Congregational church and pianist for the Brattleboro Choral Union. Her obituary in the *Vermont Phoenix* sadly stated, "With this talent so brilliantly manifesting itself, coupled as it was with a worthy ambition and an untiring energy, to no young person in Brattleboro did the future open with brighter promise" (Kendrick, 43).

Although Freeman's letters reveal little about her relationship with her sister, one can surmise her feelings at Anna's death. Born in 1859, soon after the death of the Wilkinses' infant son, Anna was the beloved baby of the family, seven years younger and with a personality markedly different from Mary's. Whereas Mary was quiet, shy, and retiring, Anna was outgoing, lively, and cheerful. Both young women were musically inclined; to the end of her life, Freeman played the piano beautifully. Whereas Anna continued her early training in music, Mary turned briefly to painting and then later to writing, publishing her first verses not long after Anna's death. To some extent, Mary and Anna seem to have unconsciously evolved for themselves the kind of "complementarity" McNaron speaks of in sister relationships; each developed a part of herself to be different from that of her sister, perhaps in order to avoid the potential threat of competition in the family.

Several of Freeman's stories concerning sister pairs indicate that she may have felt some jealousy of her "baby" sister's talents, popularity, and in particular her forthcoming marriage. Evidence from her stories further suggests that, at Anna's death, Freeman experienced the grief of losing an intimate friend, the fear of evolving a separate identity away from that of her sister, and the guilty apprehension of being the remaining child in the family, the one who must now "make up" to her parents all they had lost. In various ways, each of the following stories reveals Freeman's inner turmoil over her complex relationship with her sister, turmoil that apparently lasted throughout her adult life.

Freeman's most poignant statement concerning the closeness and even necessity of the sister bond is expressed in a skillfully executed short story in which, ironically, the presence of a sister is merely illusory. "Sister Liddy" (1891) is set in the village poorhouse. With disconcerting realism, Freeman sketches portraits of its poverty-stricken or mentally imbalanced inhabitants, persons she may have recalled from her days in Brattleboro while living adjacent to the town poorhouse. One woman has "overworked" on her farm; she "sat in a rocking-chair and leaned her head back . . . she kept her mouth parted miserably, and there were ghastly white streaks around it and her nostrils." Another woman violently pulls her bed to pieces the moment the matron has made it up. Still others crouch silently in corners as orphaned children play ball across the floor of the barren room.

The more vociferous of the older women spend their days bickering about who had once possessed the finest clothing, household goods, or other such evidence of wealth. Only Polly Moss, who "had been always deformed and poor and friendless," is unable to join in the rivalry. Searching for some memory to make her these women's equal, yet finding none, she "invents" the best possession of all: a sister. "You'd orter have seen my sister Liddy," she blurts out to the stunned group:

> My sister Liddy was jest as handsome as a pictur' . . . she could sing the best of anybody anywheres around. . . . She used to sing in the meetin'-house, she did, an' all the folks used to sit up an' look at her when she begun. She used to wear a black silk dress to meetin', an' a white cashmire shawl, an' a bunnit with a pink wreath around the face,

an' she had white kid gloves. . . . [S]he married a real rich fellar from Bostown . . . an' she had a great big house with a parlor an' settin'- room, an' a room to eat in besides the kitchen. . . . An' her furnitur' was all stuffed, an' kivered with red velvet, an' she had a pianner. . . . She was allers dretful lovin', an' had a good disposition.

Polly's story develops over time: "[she] was questioned and cross- examined concerning her sister Liddy and the glories of her sister were increased daily." Only on her deathbed does a conscience-stricken Polly confess her deception. "I s'pose I've been dretful wicked," she mourns, "but I ain't never had nothin' in my whole life. I—s'pose the Lord orter have been enough, but it's dretful hard sometimes to keep holt of him, an' not look anywheres else, when you see other folks a-clawin' an' gettin' other things, an' actin' as if they was wuth havin'. . . . I—s'pose I—was dretful wicked . . . but—I never had any sister Liddy."

"Sister Liddy" is a revealing story, coming from a woman whose sister had died fifteen years earlier. Polly's beautiful, talented, but imaginary sister represents for her all she is not, the fulfillment of her frustrated, limited self. Polly develops her story through the process of storytelling and embellishment; she has found that, by postulating herself as sister to a woman who is charming, talented, and wealthy, she is able to gain the admiration and respect of her women friends and to rest secure in a new-found identity. In using Polly's point of view, and having Polly create the literary persona of Liddy, Freeman may have been playing out in fantasy her own relationship with her dead sister Anna. Like Polly, she creates here an ideal "other," a sub- stitution for the role she ultimately could not play in real life—that of her sister. This ideal sister in "Sister Liddy," however, is not dupli- cated elsewhere in Freeman's fiction; rather, her many other stories involving sister pairs are sharply realistic as she explores the ramifica- tions of this inseparable tie.

The extreme, even cloying closeness of the sister bond and, often, the inner chaos that results when one sister is left alone is expressed in a number of tales. Several of these show two adult women who, having lived together for years, are nearly merged into one identity; each sister has become for the other an extension of self. In "A Gala Dress" (1891), sisters Elizabeth and Emily Babcock, poor yet proud elderly women of a once genteel family, own between them only one good black silk dress, that staple of a nineteenth-century woman's wardrobe. Over the years, therefore, as they "starved daintily," they have carefully evolved a plan of sharing the dress while assiduously avoiding the suspicions of their nosy friend, Matilda Jennings; each sister retrims the dress, one with lace and one with velvet, when it is her turn to appear at a social function.

In "A Far-Away Melody" (1887), an early story that possibly reveals Freeman's lingering emotional distress over Anna's death, an extremely close relationship between elderly twins is wrenched apart by one of the sister's dying. The remaining woman's grief at being left behind is coupled with guilt that she may have spoken sharply to her sister hours before she died. "I was cross with her this afternoon," she sobs. "I was cross, an' spoke up sharp to her, because I loved her, but I don't think she knew." "This sister-love was all she had ever felt, besides her love of God, in any strong degree," the narrator explains; "all the passion of devotion of which this homely, commonplace woman was capable was centered in that, and the unsatisfied strength of it was killing her."[5]

Finally, in a very short, odd tale titled "The Three Old Sisters and the Old Beau" (1900), three elderly maiden sisters, who have over time become virtually indistinguishable from one another, have for years been courted by the same man. When two of the sisters die, Camilla, the remaining sister, finally assents to marrying the "old beau," but her lifelong identification with her sisters has been so complete that "no one ever knew, whether she wore her own or her sister's wedding-gown, or had wedded her own or her sister's old Beau." Commenting on the ominous tone of the conclusion to the story, Susan Allen Toth states that "as a final form of death-in-life, this strange wedding denies the three sisters even their individual identities"; the story, for Toth, sums up many of Freeman's themes of "unfulfillment" and "wasted life" ("Parable," 566).

Close friendships between sisters also involve outbreaks of jealous anger over the most trivial of concerns as each sister strives to establish some small token of individual identity to distinguish her from her sibling. In "Billy and Susy" (1909), two elderly sisters who have been given similar kittens quarrel bitterly over which kitten is hers. In "Life

Everlastin'" (1891), Mrs. Ansel rails angrily against her sister's "improper" habits, which, she feels, reflect negatively on herself: "It
seems to me sometimes if Luella would jest have a pretty new bonnet,
an' go to meetin' Sabbath-days like other folks, I wouldn't ask for
anything else," she confides to a friend. In a humorous scene from
"Something on Her Mind" (1912), three sisters, attempting to discover the reason behind their young niece's depression, become miffed
when each contends *she*—and not her sister—has experienced the
greatest trials in life:

> "We must talk to [our niece] . . . each by herself," [Amelia suggests].
> "We must tell her, if necessary, things about our own lives which we
> have survived. . . ."
> "If you think it will do her good, I have lived through troubles like
> most people, and I can tell her about them, although I have never
> spoken of them to any living soul and never expected to," said [Julia].
> She spoke with an air of delicate importance.
> Amelia eyed her sharply. "I would like to know, Julia Spencer, what
> dreadful troubles you have lived through that we don't know about,"
> said she, "when you've been right here with us in this house all your
> life and had everything you wanted."

Rivalry among sisters can also have a sharper edge. In at least seven
of her short stories, Freeman portrays a situation in which a woman,
in one manner or another, deprives her sister of a lover. These include
"The Scent of the Roses" (1891); "A Pot of Gold" (1891); "Amanda
and Love" (1891); "The Tree of Knowledge" (1900); "The Gift of
Love" (1906); "Dear Annie" (1914); and "Sarah Edgewater" (1918).
Several of these concern an "older but wiser" sister who, injured herself, seeks to "save" her younger sibling from the perils of falling in
love. In "The Tree of Knowledge," for example, middle-aged Cornelia
finally confesses that it is she who has been sending "uplifting" letters
to her much younger sister Annie and signing them with a man's
name. Cornelia explains, "I had in my youth a bitter experience . . .
I discovered the treachery and wickedness of man. I threw my heart
away upon one who was unworthy, and I wanted to save my sister
from a like fate. I wanted to fill her mind with such a pure ideal that
there could be no danger."
In "Amanda and Love," a story filled with suppressed tension

and violence, an older sister's envy erupts when her younger sister is visited by a man. Old enough to be Love's mother, Amanda is fiercely protective of her younger sister. She scorns Love's suitor, Willis, considering him unworthy of her sister's affections. Love resents Amanda's chastisement; once she even turns on her "with a look as if she were feeling for the claws which nature had denied her." A clinging and weak woman, however, Love suppresses her resentment while yet managing to continue her affair with young Willis.

Love's courtship eventually forces Amanda to confront her own deepest fears. Less attractive and accomplished than Love, Amanda has long lived vicariously through Love's beauty and talents, depending on her sister as a source for her own pride and identity. When that identity is threatened by the intrusion of a rival, Amanda at first employs a "subtle psychological warfare" (Crowley, 59) to drive Willis away and retain Love's affection; she consistently embarrasses the young man when he visits and afterward pampers Love with affection. However, when Willis deserts Love and the young girl falls gravely ill, Amanda, out of fear for her sister's life, chooses to overcome her selfish envy and humiliates herself by going to the young man to plead that he renew his courtship. Willis visits Love that evening; leaving the two alone in the sitting room and retiring to the kitchen, Amanda sat alone by the window and "wept patiently."

In these tales of one sister's jealous emotional control of another, Freeman seems to empathize with the older and more dominant woman. As in the two stories described above, this older sister slowly comes to realize that her selfish manipulation is driving her younger sibling's affection farther and farther from her, the very opposite effect she has wished her caretaking efforts to have. Her final, self-abasing surrender of power, however, comes only after much inner conflict. Freeman portrays such a woman as valiant in her struggle to release the pride, fear, and guilt that have long bound her in an unhealthy relationship to her sister.

We cannot know, ultimately, if Freeman herself experienced the same complexity of emotion with her sister Anna or even with her sisterlike friend Mary Wales. Her many tales of intimate and yet competitive sister relationships, however, allow us to conclude that the inherent intricacy and ambiguity of this dyad fascinated Freeman throughout her life as she explored myriad situations for and postulated several conclusions to its emotional dilemmas.

In speaking of her women characters' competitive "friendships," it is important to consider Freeman's narrative and thematic use of gossip, an element of her fiction having much to do with the formation and development of such relationships. "In the background of Freeman's stories the village gossips are always scurrying, waiting to carry news," one critic has accurately stated. "These stories are filled with the sounds of eager footsteps entering rooms unannounced; doors flung open into dining rooms, parlors, and even bedrooms; low voices exchanging confidences about someone who has just crossed the threshold" (Toth, "Defiant Light," 88). Freeman's women gossip incessantly and unabashedly; gossip forms, establishes, and determines the quality and duration of women's relationships with each other.

One way that we can read and interpret Freeman's fiction concerning women's lives is to regard the gossip she employs in narration as a form of discourse primarily concerned with the intricacies—the forming, developing, and maintaining—of relationship. In fiction, the artistic and narrative uses of gossip are many. A writer may use gossip to orient readers socially, conferring on them a privileged "insider" status while simultaneously reassuring them that they—as listeners only—are not guilty of wrongdoing in acquiring such covert information. "The narrator establishes with the reader an alliance based on the superior knowingness of both," Patricia Meyer Spacks states in her study of the subject, Gossip: "Utterly free of moral culpability . . . we enjoy the pleasure of knowing and thinking about people's bad behavior" (216–17).

In using gossip as a narrative device, Freeman aligns her readers with the social world of the story while at the same time assuming—though disguised through her gossipers—normative control and power over this world. Thus, gossip in Freeman's stories serves to bind author, readers, and characters together in a comforting alliance based on shared values—or so it would initially seem. Yet Freeman soon reverses our expectations. As the story continues, we readers who have initially felt privileged to be "insiders" to the gossiper's superior insight begin to realize that the gossiper herself along with the community she represents, and not necessarily the object of her scorn, is guilty of a self-centered and petty parochialism. Freeman carefully manipulates our responses so that our sympathies shift from the gossiper's norm of "proper" social behavior to an acceptance and approval of the person whom gossip has isolated and ostracized.

Reading Freeman's tales employing gossip in this light can serve to guide our responses to this "female"-oriented fiction. With its homey familiarity, promises of intrigue to follow, and initial assurances of a comforting alliance between women, Freeman's gossip allows us to enter quickly into her characters' lives and their relationships: after reading a page or two, we feel as though we have known these people all our lives. However, as we begin to understand the (usually selfish) motives of the gossiper, and as we increasingly question her judgment, we begin to see the odd or ostracized woman as, in reality, heroic in her courage, fortitude, and convictions. Freeman skillfully uses this mode of traditionally "female" discourse to lead us gently to the one theme implicit in much of her fiction: a rejected, lonely, or otherwise socially misfitted individual is eventually revealed as, in actuality, the most generous, courageous, and laudable of all.

Thematically, gossip operates in Freeman's fiction to create and maintain social cohesion and community from isolated and introspective individuals. In their familiar talk of family, friends, and social events, Freeman's women evince their lively and ongoing concern with human ties, but gossip's negative side is also clearly manifest in these stories. Gossip easily becomes a means of subversive power—a weapon—for those who have no other form of social control. Women's gossip in these stories often revolves around the weaknesses and follies of men, but even more importantly, gossip establishes a kind of social or pecking order among women themselves, distinguishing the "haves" from the "have-nots," the "insiders" from the "outsiders." Gossip's social function in these stories is inherently ambiguous: on the one hand, it solidifies values and relationships by maintaining stable social bonds; on the other hand, maliciously used, it destroys the very human ties it seeks to build.

Skilled in the presentation of dialogue, Freeman based many of her stories and several of her novels on the garrulous reports of narrators who serve to carry news, tell tales, and eagerly interpret events for their willing audiences. Both *The People of Our Neighborhood* (1898), a collection of related short stories, and *The Jamesons* (1899), a short novel, are told in the first person through the eyes of female "insiders" who presume on their ability to speak for the feelings and opinions of the entire village.

Freeman's women gossip for a variety of reasons, but mostly to establish themselves as "insiders" and "proper" women vis-à-vis "outside" or "strange" women in their small communities. Gossip serves to identify and isolate the odd or eccentric woman who fails to conform to the gossiper's norm. A woman in Freeman's world may be ostracized for her unseemly clothing, bad temper, poor housekeeping, or general failure to adhere to the strictures of village etiquette. The narrator of "Lydia Wheelock: The Good Woman," a story in *The People of Our Neighborhood,* confides to the reader that Lydia's poverty disturbs her female neighbors to the point that "we felt that we ought to avoid looking at her poor bonnets in order not to hurt her feelings." In "The Boomerang" (1917), notorious gossip Emmeline prides herself on judging others' financial situations through observance of the state of their clothing. "If Emmeline had been here," one neighbor warns another, "all the neighbors would have known about your dresses." The entire Maddox family in "The Apple Tree" (1903) are considered social pariahs by their "furious housekeeper" neighbor because of their lackadaisical attitude toward work.

Far more scandalous in the community is the strong-willed woman who fights, against all propriety, to maintain her "odd" or "eccentric"—in the eyes of the village gossips, at least—way of life. Sophia Bagley in "The Pumpkin" (1900) decides to manage the farm alone after the death of her brother. She must initially deal with the town's incredulity: "'You ain't going to run the farm?' said [a] calling neighbor, who was a sort of scout of village gossip, having come in advance to spy out the land. 'Why not?' demanded Sophia . . . 'I enjoy good health, and I've got common-sense, and I ain't afraid to work.'"

Similarly, quick-witted and penurious Hannah in "About Hannah Stone" (1901) is condemned by village gossip for insisting on working her farm alone, "like a man." The first-person narrator, an old schoolmate of Hannah's, speaks freely of Hannah's peculiarities: "Everybody said that Hannah Stone was a strange woman. In the first place she lived all alone . . . [and] she goes right out in the field and works, ploughing and planting, wood-chopping, too." "I said to Caroline that it didn't seem right and according to the fitness of things," the narrator comments after confiding in her sister. "Caroline and I often used to talk about Hannah, and it wasn't any too complimentary what we said," she states truthfully.

Hannah is best known about town for driving a hard bargain. Though it is rumored that she is well-off, she is so shrewd and scrupulous in her business dealings that "nobody could overreach her and, maybe in consequence, it was said that she overreached other people." "The village rang" with stories about Hannah; the townsfolk vie with each other in attempting to outsmart her. When even the deacon seeks to cheat her by substituting the wrong cow for one she has bought from him, Hannah shames him in front of his churchgoers one Sunday morning by sitting resolutely on his front steps while the cow grazes on his lawn. Needless to say, she wins her argument and soon receives the cow she actually purchased. Yet though "that story got all over town, and though it didn't reflect to the credit of the Deacon, for some reason or other it did not seem to prepossess people in favor of Hannah," the narrator informs us, adding that "Sister Caroline and I, in talking it over one afternoon, agreed that sometimes it seemed as if people, especially men folks, liked women better that they *could* take in."

When Hannah insists that the minister pay for a Sunday school Christmas tree that had inadvertently been cut from her property, the woman narrator finally scolds her openly: "If I had known what a mean woman you would grow up to be, a woman mean enough to grudge one tree out of a whole grove for Christmas . . . I would never have sat next to you when we went to school," she tells Hannah. Hannah refuses to answer. To everyone's surprise, however, she appears a few days thereafter with a beautifully decorated tree loaded with presents for each member of the community, gifts she has obviously spent many months in making and wrapping. Astounded, the women quickly contrive to put together presents for Hannah, whom they had purposely not provided for earlier, and "when that great Christmas tree had been carried into the meeting-house, the women there most had hysterics," the narrator relates.

Humbled at Hannah's generosity, the narrator apologizes to her for her harsh speech. Hannah "looked at me with a curious kind of dignity," the narrator relates, "like one standing up for her principles . . . 'Givin' is givin', and sellin' is sellin',' said she," adding as she looked at her gifts with tears in her eyes and a "little-girl look in her face," "'I never had a Christmas present before in my life.'"

As she does in a number of her short stories, Freeman uses the gossiping narrative voice in "About Hannah Stone" to shift our sympathies toward the victim of the gossip. Though the subject for gossip in the village community for her "odd" ways, Hannah is slowly revealed to us as a sensitive and generous person despite her apparently haughty and tight-fisted demeanor. We learn early in the story, for example, that Hannah labors around the farm "like a man" primarily to aid the deaf-and-dumb hired man, an old family helper, who has recently contracted consumption. Still, it is not until Hannah shocks the village by delivering the Christmas tree that the gossiping narrator and the other townsfolk realize that Hannah has been unfairly judged and that gossip has served to perpetuate her ostracism. As is often the case with Freeman's isolated characters, Hannah's prideful dignity, her insistence on the proper distinction between "sellin'" and "givin'," has caused her to be misunderstood. The narrator confesses at the conclusion of the story that she has "learned a lesson," presumably about overly hasty judgment of others and the pernicious effects of gossip.

Freeman's women are equally ostracized and even feared for their more personal eccentricities. Several women are shunned because of their reputations as "witches": Jenny in "Christmas Jenny" (1891), for example, because she lives an isolated and lonely existence in the forest outside of town; and Mrs. King in "A Modern Dragon" (1887), who refuses to attend meeting and is rumored to be a "spiritualist." Even smaller "strange" habits may cause a woman to be scorned by other women in Freeman's close, homogeneous communities in which men and women alike were subjected to extreme pressure to conform. Esther Gay in "An Independent Thinker" (1887) is severely criticized and shunned by all for not attending Sunday meeting: "I ain't goin' to hev you goin' over to Esther Gay's, Sabbath day," a neighbor of Esther's warns her daughter. "She ain't no kind of a girl. . . . Stayin' home from meetin' an' knittin'. I ain't goin' to hev you over thar, Laviny." The female protagonist in "Amanda Todd: The Friend of Cats" (1898) is also looked at askance because "she does not go to meeting" and because she "never wears a bonnet, and she keeps [too many] cats." She is likewise criticized for her bad temper, a reprehensible failing in the eyes of women in Freeman's New England. Other women who also incur an "unfortunate name" in town because of ill temper are Hetty Fifield in "A Church Mouse" (1891) and Jane White in "The Christmas Ghost" (1900). In the latter story, such gossip— along with that concerning her "dingy" looking laundry on the line— eventually loses Jane a prospective husband.

Freeman, then, often makes use of the device of gossip, both technically and thematically in her short stories, to establish a dynamic between the gossiper, the seemingly "correct" worldly wise woman; the reader, who feels immediately invited into this "homey" world of women's talk; and the woman gossiped about, the "outside" woman whose oddity in the community, though laughed at initially by others, soon begins to command the reader's admiration. The Lydia Wheelocks, the Hannah Stones, the Christmas Jennys, the Esther Gays— these humble and plain, but hardworking, honest, and independently minded women—are those whom Freeman generally advances as her ideal. Women's gossip in these stories allows the author to guide her readers to accept, finally, the type of woman that Freeman often felt herself to be: the woman "outside the pale" of "normal" women's experience.

The facts behind Freeman's own friendships with other women, as well as with her sister Anna, remain sketchy at best. However, from her many perceptive tales exploring the intricate patterns of closeness and envy in women's relationships with other women, it is probable that Freeman experienced relationships with other women as both intimate and problematic. Needing others' affection and approval, she nevertheless appears to have been painfully cognizant of the emotional damage one woman could inflict on another through emotional cruelty or tyranny, perhaps, or through gossip. Freeman rarely wrote of women's friendships as relationships based on mutual affection or support. Rather, both her women friends and sister pairs play out roles involving patterns of dependence and domination, of power and weakness. In such careful probing of the tacit and often hidden elements in the complex relationship between adult women friends and adult sisters, Freeman again shows herself above all an extremely perceptive analyst of women's psychology.

CHAPTER 6

Women Alone

"I Hadn't Orter Feel This Way"

In her later years, Freeman began and never completed a startling story that, more than any other of her works, conveys the inner struggle of a woman who finds herself alone in life. Longing to maintain her integrity and independence of mind, she nevertheless longs also to fit into the course of a "normal" woman's life, forming close and intimate relational bonds with other human beings. Finding ultimately that it is impossible to meld these desires, she rebels against a society seemingly intent on keeping her "outside the pale" of life and a "Providence" that, despite her good behavior, refuses to provide for her inner needs. Revealing as it is of Freeman's mind and art, this passage may serve as a paradigm for her stories about women who are not involved in relationships with others; for this reason it is quoted here at length: [1]

> I am a rebel and what is worse a rebel against the Overgovernment of all creation. . . . I even dare to think that, infinitesimal as I am, . . . I, through my rebellion, have power. All negation has power. I, Jane Lennox, spinster, as they would have designated me a century ago, living quietly, and apparently harmlessly in the old Lennox homestead in Baywater, am a power.

I do not understand in what manner I am a power against the Whole, perhaps only through my antagonism toward the part. I do not imagine, I know, that my antagonism toward the little works definite harm. That I have proved.

My life-long friend and next-door neighbor Julia Esterbrook . . . has just run across the lawn after borrowing vanilla to flavor the cake for the Friday bridge party which meets at her house this week. Julia has never returned the last vanilla which she borrowed, or the vanilla before that, and before that. Julia owes me an endless chain of vanilla, but what of it? It rather pleases me. I like to have a definite charge of either carelessness or dishonesty against her. It raises me in my own esteem. I have never seemed able to rise on stepping stones of my dead self to higher things for the excellent reason that my real self has as many lives as a cat.

But I can rise on the faults of my friends if I do not call them to account. This morning I rather have a sensation of being seated on a little throne of vanilla bottles. . . . Another thing which pleases me, gratifies my pride in my astuteness is that Julia, without knowing it, never borrows very good vanilla. I keep my own vanilla in a separate bottle. Julia's is in a bottle by itself containing a cheaper vanilla, much diluted. . . .

I often wonder if I might not have been very decent, very decent indeed, if I had laid hold on the life so many of my friends lead. If I had only had a real home of my own with a husband and children in it. That was my birthright, but I was deprived of it, with neither trade nor barter.

And another thing which was my birthright: the character of the usual woman. I am a graft on the tree of human womanhood. I am a hybrid. Sometimes I think I am a monster, and the worst of it is, I certainly take pleasure in it.

No mortal can exist without a certain satisfaction in herself. Satisfaction in myself I certainly have, or perhaps satisfaction may not be the right word. Perhaps pride is better, pride which intoxicates like forbidden stimulants. . . .

I sometimes wonder what would have been the state of the world, had it not been for the Tables of Stone. Once made they could not be broken. They were broken. They are broken now. Could the Devil have existed, even in the imagination of men, had it not been for those terrible and sacred Tables of the Law? Did he exist in the fullest sense before?

It is a pity that those tables could have been broken, that the will and strength of mortal man should have been sufficient to break them.

Here am I, a woman, rather delicately built, of rather delicate tastes, perfectly able to break those commandments, to convert into dust every one of those Divine laws. I shudder before my own power, yet I glory because of it.

Several things strike us at once about this passage that combines much of Freeman's probing of the heart and sensibility of the single woman who, alone, lives an intense life in her own mind. The first-person, self-reflective speaker, unusual in Freeman's canon, begins by identifying herself as both "spinster" and "rebel"; indeed, the two terms are synonymous in her mind. She attributes her "abnormality" among women to the fact that she has somehow "failed" through circumstance or perhaps even through choice to marry; failed, as she terms it, to "lay hold on the life so many of my friends lead." Moreover and most importantly, she ascribes this failure not to her own fault but to that of God—of "Providence." "I was deprived of my birthright," she tells us, "with neither trade nor barter."

As a result of the injustice of this deprivation, the speaker has resolved to make full use of her "monstrosity"; she declares revolt against God himself, "the Overgovernment of all creation." Written from the heart, this passage from Freeman's unfinished work records the agony and frustration of a woman who, having striven to be "upright" and "proper" all of her life, feels God has nevertheless failed to ratify his end of the bargain in neglecting to provide her the means to a "normal" female life—a husband and a family. As a result, her lack of connection to others has left her with a sense of self fundamentally incomplete; she is "a graft on the tree," "a hybrid."

Therefore, this woman will assert what she does have, her own free will, her choice to rebel. Although she knows fully well how laughably paltry this enterprise is in the face of a God whose existence and almighty power she never for a moment doubts, her desire to revenge herself for the constant, humiliating mockery she feels this God has subjected her to consumes her. Her power in asserting her will against that of the Creator both amazes and frightens her; she can if she chooses "convert into dust every one of those Divine Laws."[2]

The woman's revolt remains largely interior, however, manifesting itself outwardly in only a seemingly trivial matter. The necessity of maintaining proper and decorous behavior in order to be accepted by others overrides any desire she might have to display her defiance. In secretly outwitting her neighbor over the bottle of vanilla and also scorning that woman's ignorance of the matter, the speaker stages a quiet yet insidious rebellion not so much against her friend as against God himself. She consciously revels in her own wit, pride, and ability to manipulate her material goods in order to keep the best for herself while at the same time retaining the outer appearance of a "good" and "harmless" woman.

This passage from the incomplete work "I Am a Rebel" contains many of the themes present in Freeman's other works concerning the single woman who lives alone. Put quite simply, Freeman's women who are alone and uninvolved in a relationship with either a man or another woman become rebels in a manner similar to that described in this aborted short story. Cut off either voluntarily or through circumstance from ties to other human beings, Freeman's women search for meaning and purpose in their lives. Usually, they do this through a guilty assertion of their own will against a God (or often, his earthly representative, the minister) they feel has reneged on his promise of reward for their ardent striving to live a righteous life.

Freeman often depicts women who feel thus "condemned" to lives alone as inwardly torn by rage, frustration, envy, and defiance. Feeling mocked by God, they bristle against the constricting stereotypes of "spinster" and "old maid" which their society imposes on them. They often feel useless and superannuated; in Freeman's rural New England, little sympathy exists for a woman, especially an older one, who cannot contribute materially to society. Like the woman in the passage quoted above, these women may seek some small form of compensation or comfort that they feel is "due" them since Providence has denied them a family and means of social identity. Clinging, therefore, to some small definition of themselves, a possession or talent, they react fiercely when it is threatened and rage internally against the God that will not allow them to retain even *that* measure of comfort.

Both young and old women stage "strikes" or rebellions against Providence in this manner; yet in doing so, they are haunted—and sometimes even guiltily pleased—by the knowledge that, no matter how gentle and good they appear to their neighbors, they are in reality "bad" women, women who seem to themselves to be "monstrous." It is this knowledge that their outer selves so skillfully belie their inner beings that often comes to provide these women, in the end, with the sense of individuality and identity denied them by others. Knowing little of others' private lives, they conclude they alone are "odd," and they therefore create a self that magnifies and even glories in that oddity.

This fragmented piece is more than a passing mood of Freeman's; its significance to her life and her thought on women and their concerns is great. On the one hand, Freeman was evidently morally conscientious and scrupulous to an extreme; her self-professed "New England conscience" exacted a compliance from her which manifested itself in a desire to appear at all times generous, kind, and pleasing to others. "I will tell you frankly, I *hate* being written up as [much as] I would having a nerve laid bare and all that ever reconciles me to it is the consideration that it may help somebody," she once wrote to an editor who had begged her for a rare personal interview, adding, "I never mean to hurt anybody, but I get awfully tired, and there are so many people not to hurt" (Kendrick, 134–35). A similar tone of conciliation and compliance marks much of her personal correspondence.

Yet her many stories about the secret torments of conscience experienced by women who are alone reveal another side of Freeman quite apart from her outward display of decorum and graciousness. Speaking of a publicity photograph she had just made for *Ladies' Home Journal,* Freeman wrote to Kate Upson Clark at the height of her career, "I have tried very hard to look cheerful, but I should have enjoyed 'making a face' much more. You think I am modest, but I am not. I am vicious" (Kendrick, 141). This inward "viciousness" often marks her protagonists. One theme she returns to time and again in her fiction is that of the guilty, tortured consciences of persons who in one manner or another feel themselves impostors or hypocrites. The plots of at least six of her fourteen novels turn on this theme: *Jane Field* (1893); *The Debtor* (1905); *By the Light of the Soul* (1907); *"Doc" Gordon* (1906); *The Butterfly House* (1912); and *An Alabaster Box* (1917). Moreover, Freeman's short stories about the hidden discrepancy between the inner and outer lives of women are among her strongest and best developed, clearly evincing intense personal identification with her subject.

Freeman remained single until the age of forty-nine, and as we have seen, doubted the value or efficacy of marrying at all. Her personal letters, characteristically laconic, allow us mere glimpses into her feelings about being for so many years one of the New England "spinsters" that she was famous in her own lifetime for depicting. In several letters written after her marriage, she makes light of the term. Shortly after her marriage in 1902, for example, she wrote to Clark, "I have almost forgotten that I ever was an old maid, I am getting so used to 'Mrs.' It is queer how soon the new seems old!" (Kendrick, 286).

What Freeman felt about her single state in the years before her marriage is primarily discernible, as is often the case, through her fiction. In at least one of her novels and in a number of her short stories, Freeman reveals the bitterness and rebellion she seems to have experienced not so much as a result of being single as of being expected to act the part of a New England spinster. As a single woman, she apparently strove inwardly against the "hard Providence" that had assigned her a role in life that was inherently anomalous and lonely in its continual status as "outsider."[3]

The novel By the Light of the Soul (1907) may serve as a prelude to the short stories in which Freeman reveals ambiguity over her long-unmarried state. Published five years after her marriage, when Freeman was fifty-five, this lengthy work chronicles the growth in sensibility of protagonist Maria Edgham, an intelligent, beautiful, yet humorless young woman who is tortured by an overly scrupulous conscience. An indifferent Fate, which Maria comes to believe "overran individuals in its way, like Juggernaut" deprives her of her mother at a young age, substitutes for that mother a cold and spiteful stepmother, strips Maria's beloved father of his health, and subjects Maria to an unconsummated "marriage" to a schoolboy. This last event—improbably and even preposterously developed—severs Maria from close human contact all her life; believing that the "vows" she has taken are binding (they clearly are not), she never again allows herself either to love or to accept another's love.

In a further complication, Maria finds that her half-sister, Evelyn, has fallen in love with Maria's own "husband"; in a self-renunciatory act, Maria decides to stage her own death in order to free Evelyn to marry him. Fleeing to another part of the world, she is "adopted" by a dwarf woman whom she meets on the train. "You are also outside the pale in some way," the woman tells her upon meeting her. "I always know such people when I meet them. . . . [T]he moment I saw you I said to myself: she also is outside the pale, she also has escaped from the garden of life."

Despite its improbable plot, *By the Light of the Soul* contains some similarities to Freeman's own life. Foster considers the novel to be the author's "spiritual autobiography" (170). Like Mary Freeman, Maria Edgham is pretty, intelligent, proud, and willful yet, at the same time, emotionally insecure to an extreme. She prefers her weaker and sensitive father to her dominating mother yet, upon the death of both, feels "lost" without parental protection. Her self-esteem comes largely from her career, from her excellence at teaching. In her personal life, she keeps aloof from both men and women; she longs for close friends but is unable to reveal herself to them because of her acute sensitivity.

Similar in some external details to Freeman's own life, this novel also allows us insight into her inner conflict. Though outwardly Maria "was quiet and obedient, and very unobtrusive," her inner spirit in reality, Freeman tells us, was "full of rebellion." Throughout the un-folding consequences of her unfortunate "marriage," Maria increasingly seethes inwardly against a persecuting Calvinistic God who, though she redoubles her attempts to be "good," appears only to mock her efforts: "She thought of the half-absurd, half-tragic secret [her marriage] which underlay her life, and she could not honestly think herself very much to blame for that. . . . Maria realized that she was full of self-righteousness, but she was also honest. . . . She thought of the doctrine which she had heard, that children were wholly evil from their birth, and it did not seem to her true. She could *say* that she had been wholly evil from her birth, but she felt that she should, if she did say so, tell a lie to God and herself."

Maria's later conversion to belief in a loving God comes about sud-denly through a mystical experience; however, this newfound belief merely allows her to retreat even further from a world that she has found increasingly hostile and inexplicable. Her final identification

with the dwarf woman—a freak, she believes, like herself—is her ultimate act of self-abnegation. Both desiring, yet loathing and fearing
the life of a "normal" married woman, a life Freeman here equates
with weakness, pettiness, and submission, Maria finally relinquishes
all of her ambitious ideals in silent protest against a society that has
consistently made her feel an outcast. In the end, she embraces her
"deformity" and, in doing so, establishes finally an identity of her
own—one as "outsider."

A number of Freeman's short stories also express the fierce inner
rebellion of the single woman who feels cheated by and ostracized
from life by the workings of a coldly malevolent Fate or, as it is vari-
ously known, Providence. As is the case of Maria in *By the Light of the
Soul,* such women often find a similar satisfaction in taking refuge in
their "perversity." It has been observed that this retreat into witchlike
deformity or perversity is a continual theme in women's local-color
fiction, and Freeman's portraits of women alone fit this pattern.[4] Their
rebellions, moreover, usually take the form of a seemingly small or
insignificant act of defiance, for Freeman's rebels are more often than
not "quiet" rebels. In "For the Love of One's Self" (1905), for example, factory worker Amanda Dearborn despises the prettier yet
weaker girls around her who, unlike herself, attract the attention of
the young men. Though outwardly a steady, quiet, and reliable em-
ployee, "her thoughts were anarchistic, even blasphemous. . . . [S]he
realized with a subtle defiance and rebellion that she was not, in a
spiritual sense, a good woman." Defying an unloving Providence, she
"rebels" by refusing one holiday season to send her customary token
gifts to distant relatives. Rather, she guiltily decides to assert what she
sees as her great "selfishness" by indulging in a gift for herself.[5]

"The Parrot" (1901) is an interesting psychological study of a
woman whose inner existence is one of continual warfare between
differing factions of her own personality. Martha, a minister's spinster
daughter, is torn between "the influence of a stern training" and "a
rampant force of individuality." Full of inner conflict, she strives to
contain and control her fearful aggression by maintaining an outward
appearance of unrelentingly proper compliance and uniformity. She
dresses in uncompromising black; her house, too, is "sharply angled"
with a "clean, repellent glare of windows" and a yard of "evenly
slanted" grass.

This outer exactitude, however, merely masks Martha's perpetual inner "vague and unreasoning sense of immorality." Her only relief from the self-torment that such spiritual division produces comes through her sole worldly indulgence, a brightly colored pet parrot. With its shrieking outbreaks of profanity, the parrot is a constant source of humiliation for Martha; nevertheless, she insists on keeping it, sensing that in some ineffable way it reflects her deepest desires.

Once, we are told, Martha has an "adventure" : she falls in love with a young minister, who, after courting her briefly, suddenly reveals that he has long had a fiancée back in the city. In the following weeks, though maintaining perfect outer decorum, Martha feels as if "she would have gone mad." When the minister and his new bride return to pay the customary wedding call, Martha greets them calmly; inwardly, however, "her very soul stormed and protested." Suddenly, the parrot, escaping from its cage, swoops down on and attacks the bride's bonnet, shredding its ribbons and bows. Amid the young man's shouts and the bride's tears, Martha suddenly realizes the bird is the one means available to her of expressing her "improper" and even sacrilegious thoughts. She "recognized in the fierce bird a comradeship and an equality, for it had given vent to an emotion of her own nature, and she knew forevermore that the parrot had a soul."

Perhaps Freeman's strongest statement of the inner rebellion of the "spinster" and her secret scorn of weaker, more conventional women is contained in her chapter entitled "The Old-Maid Aunt" in the corporately written novel *The Whole Family* (1908). An ambitious project originally proposed by Howells which subsequently turned into a disaster for all involved, this novel brought together twelve prominent authors of the day, including William Dean Howells, Elizabeth Jordan, Henry James, Elizabeth Stuart Phelps, Alice Brown, and Mary Wilkins Freeman.[6] Each writer was assigned a chapter in the continuing soap-opera-like saga of a "typical" American family. Freeman, already famous for her portrayal of New England spinsters in such stories as "A New England Nun" and "A Village Singer," was asked to follow Howells's initial chapter, "The Father," with the narrative of the young maiden aunt, Elizabeth Talbert.

Howells's chapter commenced a simple, as yet undeveloped plot and set a homey, comfortable, "realistic" tone; a pleasantly garrulous father at work in his backyard discusses with a neighbor his daughter

Peggy's recent wedding engagement. Although he imposed no explicit guidelines, Howells obviously wished the eleven other authors to build on his plot and, especially, to maintain his tone. To his consternation, Mary Freeman completely reversed these expectations. Apparently somewhat peeved at Howells's conventional representation of the spinster aunt in his chapter ("we gathered that Miss Talbert was not without the disappointment which endears maiden ladies to the imagination," Howells had written), Freeman decided to base her chapter on the "shattering" revelation that Peggy's fiancé, young Harry Goward, was actually in love with the maiden aunt herself, who at thirty-five was a full fifteen years older than he. This rewriting of Howells's text seems almost gleeful on the part of Freeman; once again, as she does later in the fragment "I Am a Rebel," Freeman assumes the role of transgressor, one who breaks the Tablets and revises "sacred" truths.

Needless to say, Howells felt that Freeman's scandalous chapter had ruined the novel. However, Elizabeth Jordan, the editor of the collection and herself a middle-aged single woman, overrode Howells and accepted Freeman's chapter for inclusion in the novel; she later referred to its reception as "the explosion of a bomb-shell on our literary hearthstone" (Bendixen, "Introduction," xxiii). From there on, the novel did indeed become disastrous as other writers tried to work out the complexities of the plot introduced by Freeman. Far from Howells's original conception of the quiet and happy extended family group, the plot, as it evolved through each subsequent writer, focused increasingly on family rivalry and misunderstanding.

Freeman's letters to Jordan at the time reveal the basis of her decision to "make the novel hers" by thoroughly modernizing the maiden aunt. She confesses that at first the prospect somewhat daunted her:

> To tell the truth such an innovation in the shape of a maiden aunt rather frightened me, but the old conception of her was so hackneyed. . . . Mr. Howells evidently clings to the old conception of her. You and I know that in these days of voluntary celibacy on the part of women an old maid only fifteen years older than a young girl is a sheer impossibility, if she is an educated woman with a fair amount of brains. Moreover, a young man is really more apt to fall in love with her. . . . Why, the whole plot of the novel must be relegated back to Miss Aus-

tin, and *Godey's Lady's Book,* and all that sort of thing, if the old conception holds. . . . I don't think Mr. Howells realizes this. He is thinking of the time when women of thirty put on caps, and renounced the world. . . . I do think the whole freshness and novelty of the book depends upon my conception of that part [Kendrick, 313].

And what about the "spinster" aunt, Elizabeth Talbert? After Howells's stodgy introduction, Freeman's chapter is refreshing in its assumption of a witty, ironic stance. "Here I am the old-maid aunt," Elizabeth begins; "Not a day, not an hour, not a minute, when I am with other people, passes that I do not see myself in their estimation playing that role as plainly as if I saw myself in a looking-glass." The "old-maid aunt," however, is in reality a beautiful, educated, and cultured woman. She delights in shocking family and neighbors alike by such unconventional actions as wearing bright pink gowns and colorful ribbons in her hair instead of dignified black silk and a cap.

Elizabeth especially revels in the secret that young Harry is madly in love with her and not with his fiancée. No one, she realizes, would ever remotely consider that an unmarried woman of thirty-five could possibly be attractive to a younger man or—worse—could possibly have sexual feelings herself. "Possibly living in a brainless house has affected the mental outlook of my relatives," she notes with scorn. "They do not know that today an old-maid aunt is as much of an anomaly as a spinning wheel, that she has ceased to exist, that she is prehistoric."

Elizabeth also feels, however, the sharp, daily stings her "anomalous" status affords her in the family and in society as a whole. Although one of Freeman's more forthright woman protagonists, her rebellions are covert and repressed. She is lonely; she belongs nowhere and does not feel free to participate in the lives of her married peers. Other women are suspicious, accusing her of trying to steal their husbands: "If you can't get a husband for yourself," a neighbor woman warns her on one occasion, "you might at least let other women's husbands alone!" Elizabeth seeks comfort, therefore, in what she terms the "minor sweets" of life: travel, pretty clothes, theater. Yet she admits to herself in a candid moment, "I have everything except—well, except everything. That I must do without. But I will do without it gracefully, with never a whimper, or I don't know myself."

"There must be a queer streak in me. Funny Jane Austin, New England spinster type isn't it?" Freeman remarked to a friend with self-deprecating humor in 1908 (Kendrick, 331). Though she was willing to joke about it occasionally with friends, long after her marriage Freeman clearly recalled her rancor at the "old-maid" stigma imposed on her for much of her adult life. She continued to discuss in her fiction the inner fears, turmoil, and, especially, sense of rebellion against God and society which she no doubt experienced to some degree as an unmarried woman. With great intensity, she explores the restless sense of inner division which does not allow her female protagonists to rest content in any state of life. Her stories about single women reflect both her lifelong desire to lead a "normal" woman's life as a married woman and her equally strong disdain for such a role as a complacent and potentially stifling one.

Like the "old-maid" aunt Elizabeth Talbert, Freeman certainly cherished at times the freedom inherent in her single state; unlike her married friends, she could unencumberedly enjoy the finer things of life and take pride in the intellectual and cultural advantages she possessed. At the same time, she was quite aware that her society was unrelenting in the narrow role it had assigned to the spinster. Freeman's stories show us the intense inner conflict and covert rebellion of women like herself who felt themselves, because of their singleness, continually "outside the pale" of everyday human life.

Like her younger unmarried women who rage internally at both Providence's and society's injustice in deeming them "spinsters," Freeman's older solitary women also experience intense inner rebellion. In "The Balsam Fir" (1903), old Martha Elder, a "tall, fair, gentle woman," who outwardly seemed to all "perfectly contented and happy," was in reality, "very different . . . from what people thought. Nobody dreamed of the fierce tension of her nerves as she sat at her window sewing through the long summer afternoons, drawing her monotonous thread in and out of dainty seams; nobody dreamed what revolt that little cottage roof, when it was covered with wintry snows, sometimes sheltered. . . . [H]er own tracks, which were apparently those of peace, [were] in reality those of a caged panther." "If you want to see the loneliest thing in all creation, look at a woman all alone in the world," Martha remarks to her only confidante, a stone-deaf neighbor woman.

Alone and lonely, older women face an added threat to their sense of security and self-esteem: poverty. Fears of the ultimate humiliation, the poorhouse, dominate their vision. Moreover, an acute feeling of having nothing in life—no husband, no family, no close or intimate friends, no material goods—instills in these older women a fierce need to defy God himself, often along with God's representative on earth, the village minister. Such women cling to any and all marks, however small or petty, of their own individuality: a carefully treasured possession, perhaps, or even a natural or assumed talent. Freeman's many stories of older women alone are remarkable in their perceptive, sympathetic identification with the sensibility of the elderly poor, especially so when considering that many of them were written when Freeman was still a young woman. From the beginning of her career to the end, she exhibited a marked degree of empathy for the poor, no doubt based on her own experience of poverty as a young woman. "No body knows how some of these country women, with large families, and small purses do work," she wrote in 1885. "O they are the ones I would help, if I were rich. Nothing, hardly, touches me so much" (Kendrick, 62).

In "An Object of Love" (1887), old Ann Millet lives an impoverished and lonely life with only a beloved cat, Willy, for companionship. She struggles daily with a humiliating sense of deprivation. "I'd orter be thankful," she tries to convince herself. "I've got my Bible an' Willy, an' a roof over my head. . . . An' p'rhaps some other woman ain't lonesome because I am. . . . I never orter complain."

When her cat disappears, Ann immediately blames the workings of the mysterious Providence with which she has long tried to reconcile herself. In rebellion, she stubbornly refuses to attend Sunday worship. Neighbors chide her for placing such affection in a mere animal, but "I ain't never hed anything like other women," Ann responds. "I ain't hed no folks of my own sence I kin remember. I've worked hard all my life, an' hed nothin' at all to love." Her neighbors remind her that she ought to be looking to the Lord alone for earthly comfort, but Ann angrily retorts, "I'm *here*, an' I ain't *thar;* an' I've got hands, an'

I want somethin' I kin touch." Ann's minister, as is usually the case with the clergymen Freeman describes, is completely ineffectual in attempting to soothe the seething fire of her spirit. "It was a case entirely out of his experience," the narrator tells us, "and he did not know how to deal with it."

Ann's cat is soon found—she discovers to her chagrin that she has inadvertently locked it in the basement—and guilty over her wickedness, she sheepishly returns to church. Freeman's emphasis in this story lies, of course, not in the scanty action of the plot but in the important spiritual crisis of the woman protagonist. After years of being suppressed, Ann's festering sense of being wronged or cheated by God out of the comfort and security of human love finally erupts. Her blame of and defiance against Providence over her missing cat is, finally, as important and frightening a step for her as the heretical statements of a theological dissident would be.

Other poverty-stricken Freeman protagonists stage similar rebellious "strikes" against an unloving and impractical Providence. In "The Strike of Hannah" (1906), Hannah, a poor woman raising several children alone, steals her rich employer's Thanksgiving dinner to "set the law of equals right." When asked by one of her frightened children whom the banquet is for, she answers scornfully, "Providence." In "A Tardy Thanksgiving" (1887), poor and lonely Mrs. Munzy adamantly refuses one year to celebrate the holiday; she has, she maintains, absolutely nothing to be thankful for. Instead of attending meeting, therefore, she insists she will "celebrate" the day by staying home and doing her autumn "pig work," the dirtiest and most oppressive job she knows. Far more than a minor scandal in the eyes of her neighbors, Mrs. Munzy's revolt, she knows, is "an outright rebellion against the will of the Lord." Refusing to pay homage to what she perceives as an ungenerous God, she finds that she is more "honest in being unthankful" than feigning a thanksgiving she cannot feel.

This latter quotation is taken from yet another story with a similar theme, "Thanksgiving Crossroads" (1917). All three represent good examples of Freeman's frequent holiday writings, which were requested of her by such magazines as *Collier's*, *Woman's Home Companion*, and *Ladies' Home Journal*. Because of the holiday nature of the assignments, each story ends in a sentimentalized manner: Hannah

and her children in "The Strike of Hannah" are finally taken in
and supported by her wealthy employer; Mrs. Munzy in "A Tardy
Thanksgiving" repents when she injures herself while doing her work
and believes God has issued her a warning; and Amelia Armstrong and
Phoebe May in "Thanksgiving Crossroads," complaining at their hard
lot, learn to be thankful for the little they have when they discover a
starving family in their neighborhood. These endings, however, do
not do justice to the intense inner struggles of the women protagonists
portrayed in the stories.

In a July 1906 letter to Hayden Carruth, fiction editor of *Woman's
Home Companion,* Freeman reveals one of the techniques she used to
generate such commissioned stories; the "germ" originally formed a
picture in her mind and she composed her tale around it. She also
records the high fees that such work commanded:

> Yes, Five hundred dollars for a Thanksgiving story to be delivered for
> the first of August. . . . It will be a New England story. . . . I think I
> can give you already a title (although I may change the name of the
> woman) The Strike of Hannah Jennings. I will suggest, although I may
> be exceeding my province, for a first illustration a well dressed, pros-
> perous family, grandparents, parents, aunt with beau, little girls, and
> boy, standing with bewildered and ag[h]ast faces, at an entirely empty
> table, in a well furnished dining-room; for a second illustration the
> same people with hastily adjusted wraps standing before a miserable
> little shanty, in the open door of which stands defiantly a tall, angular,
> strong-faced, poor woman. In the background, a miserable interior
> swarming with children, and a table loaded with a Thanksgiving din-
> ner. If an artist cares, or you think advisable for him to follow out these
> suggestions, I will suit the story to the pictures. If you wish for fewer
> figures, I will write for them. I have not the story fully in mind, but
> shall have soon. It gives me pleasure to write it for you, and I shall
> endeavor to make it suitable for your Magazine (Kendrick, 309–10).

In many of her stories, Freeman records not only the inner turmoil
of a solitary woman who must come to terms with her conception of
God or Providence but also the outer strife of an older woman's battle
to maintain self-respect in a community whose religiosity, as exempli-
fied by the village minister, does not exceed a token Sunday morning
charity. In these stories, Freeman strongly indicts the hypocrisy, inef-

fectuality, and, ultimately, inhumanity of a Christianity that emphasizes outward rituals of worship over inner spirituality.

Freeman apparently saw such false religious belief as especially damaging to women who, in a patriarchal society, were expected—by
other women as well as men—to submit unequivocally to the dictates
of minister and church governing board alike. Not to do so was seen
as an affront to God himself. Not only do these women realize that,
in asserting their own convictions, they are isolating themselves socially—for gossip soon spreads the rumor of their apostasy—but they
also fully expect to have warranted God's imminent wrath and, hence,
eternal damnation. As does the woman in "I Am a Rebel," these
women both "shudder before [their] own power, yet . . . glory because of it."

Yet ultimately, Freeman shows us, such rebellious women triumph
in their stubborn retention of principle. An innate sense of justice,
righteousness, and human love impels them to a defiance that, in the
long run, evinces a Christianity far greater than that espoused by the
minister and his complacent church-going congregation. Born of extreme loneliness and fed by the misunderstanding and even hostility
of others, the deep inner strength and moral conviction of these
women sustain them spiritually, despite their isolation from the community. Out of utter necessity, they have come to believe in and rely
on the inner light of their own consciences.

The story "An Independent Thinker" (1887) is one of Freeman's
earliest tales concerning an older woman who refuses to conform to
others' beliefs or to be hypocritical for the sake of human acceptance.
Because she is quite deaf, Esther Gay sees no point in attending
church; she cannot understand a word the minister says. Yet despite
her logical excuse, her neighbors subject her to gossip and ostracism.
Esther stands firm; she spends her Sundays defiantly rocking by the
front window, nodding ostentatiously to the church-goers who pass by
and knitting with a vengeance. Only later is it learned that the money
she earns by her handiwork is given to help her poorer acquaintances,
the very people who have shunned her for her lack of conventional
piety. "I ain't goin' to give up my principles," she insists all the while:
"I s'pose you think it would be better for an old woman that's stone
deaf, an' can't hear a word of the preachin', to go to meetin' an' set

there, doin' nothin' two hours, instead of stayin' to home an' knittin', to airn a leetle money to give to the Lord. All I've got to say is, you kin think so, then. I'm a-goin' to do what's right, no matter what happens."

Luella Norcross in "Life Everlastin'" (1891), also refuses to go to church service, and she is possibly the only Freeman character who candidly admits to being an unbeliever.[7] Like Esther's in the story above, her active service on behalf of the poor is, for her, more evincing of sound moral principles than mere attendance at Sunday meeting. "I'm not a believer, an' I won't be a hypocrite," she asserts to her minister when he comes to warn her about the state of her soul. "I ain't never worried much about my soul's salvation. I've had too many other souls to think about. An' it seems to me I'd be dreadful piggish to make goin' to heaven any reason for believin' a thing that ain't reasonable."

Yet Luella comes to a point in this story where, alone and confused, she finally accepts Christianity and the gospel message of atonement because of an experience that convinces her of mankind's ultimate helplessness in the face of tragedy. Delivering some handiwork to a neighboring couple one day, she finds to her horror that they have been murdered in their own home. Furthermore, she is quite sure she knows their killer: the hired man, John Gleason, whom she has fed out of compassion many times. Luella must wrestle with her conscience in deciding whether or not to turn the man in. For the first time, she falls on her knees in prayer: "O God . . . have I got to give him up—have I? Have I got to give him up to be hung? What's goin' to become of him then? Where'll he go to when he's been so awful wicked? Oh, what shall I do? Here he is a-takin' my vittles, an' comin' to my house, an' a-trustin' me!" Finally, after much inner struggle, she calls the authorities to apprehend the man. To her neighbors' surprise, she appears in church the following Sunday. "I've made up my mind that I'm goin' to believe in Jesus Christ," she tells them. "I ain't never, but I'm goin' to now, for . . . *I don't see any other way out of it for John Gleason!*"

Freeman also depicts the older woman who is alone as striving, sometimes fiercely, to retain her self-respect by defending a precious token of security or identity. In several of Freeman's best stories, a woman's job, reputation, or position in the community is threatened by community members who have ceased to regard the older woman as a human being with inherent rights to dignity and respect. Rather, she has become superannuated in the village; her strength and ability gone, she is now perceived as merely a burden that others must carry. Freeman's powerful statement of abhorrence for a society that discards as "useless" the woman spinster or the woman alone is most evident in these poignant stories of an elderly woman's fight for recognition of her own autonomous being.

No one cares to take in "sharp tongued" old Hetty Fifield in "A Church Mouse" (1891); moreover, the town has not yet gotten around to building a poorhouse. Hetty has come to the point in life at which, literally, she is homeless. Insisting on her right to support from a self-confessed "Christian" community, Hetty strategically moves herself into the church meetinghouse, determined to be its sexton, and the town fathers grudgingly allow her to remain. Although the worshippers tolerate for a time her lace and embroidery embellishments of the usually austere edifice—Hetty is an accomplished fancy-worker—they object openly when she takes to cooking cabbage and turnips for her Saturday night meal; the lingering smell upsets their pristine Sabbath morning devotion. A delegation of men is subsequently sent to evict her. Hetty, the "church mouse,"· fights for her position "like a little animal driven from its cover, for whom there is nothing left but desperate warfare and death."

Like their husbands, the majority of the women in the small village initially refuse to help Hetty in her plight. No one invites her to live with them, making excuses instead for their lack of charity. "Everybody's havin' company; I never seen anything like it," Hetty comments scornfully. It is the wife of one of the two deacons of the church who informs her husband of the unacceptable smell in the meetinghouse—the men have not noticed it—but ultimately it is through the efforts of a single forceful woman, wife of the other deacon, that Hetty gains her right to remain in the meetinghouse and under even better conditions than she had hoped for. Mrs. Caleb Gale rallies to Hetty's defense. After admitting to their helplessness in dealing with Hetty, the men allow Caleb to bring his wife into the situation: "mother'll know how to manage her," Caleb assures them. "Stout and handsome

and full of vigor," Mrs. Gale is impatient with the men's efforts to
evict Hetty, who by now has bolted herself inside the church building.
"They are a parcel of fools," she remarks to another woman as a crowd
begins to gather. "I ain't goin' to have father draggin' her [out] . . .
by the hair of her head," but her instructions to Caleb were at first
"drowned out . . . by a masculine clamor."

Cornered and desperate, Hetty cries out to the crowd from a window. "Jest let me say one word," she pleads: "Can't I stay here, no-
how? . . . I've had to fight to keep a footin' on the earth, an' now I'm
gittin' too old for't. If I can jest stay here in the meetin'-house, I won't
ask for nothin' any better. I sha'n't need much to keep me, I wa'n't
never a hefty eater. . . . Won't you let me stay? I ain't complainin',
but I've always had a dretful hard time; seems as if now I might take a
little comfort the last of it, if I could stay here."

Touched by her words, "Mrs. Gale's voice rang out clear and strong
and irrepressible. 'Of course you can stay in the meetin'-house,' said
she; 'I should laugh if you couldn't. Don't you worry another mite
about it. . . . [Y]ou've kept the meetin'-house enough sight cleaner
than I've ever seen it.'" Taking their cue from the "majestic" and
"defiant" Mrs. Gale, other women now speak up for Hetty, suggesting
she be given a little antechamber in the church for her own. As the
crowd disperses, Mrs. Gale remains, making sure that Hetty is left in
peace. Once established in her small room, Hetty is supremely happy;
all she has asked for all along is a bit of space and peace and quiet.
Though alone and unwanted, she has triumphed, proving to the town
that even an elderly, poor woman has the right to such basic human
needs.

In two stories also collected in 1891, "A Village Singer" and "A
Poetess," elderly women do not fare as well as Hetty; their skill and
resourcefulness fail to alter the conventional opinions of "old maids"
held by both the village minister and the congregation. Like Hetty,
however, both women in these stories struggle to transcend the dead
rituals of the community's hypocritical religiosity to attain a deeper
truth based on a common humanity. Both are artists, and in their art
is the deepest expression of their identity. When that art is subjected
to harsh criticism from those in authority, most notably the town
minister, these women literally die, so complete has been their self-

identification with their creative expression. In Freeman's stark portrayal of these life and death situations, the basic conflict is not so much that between the woman and her minister as it is the artist and a God who has inexplicably given her natural talent, bid her develop that talent, and then denied her the means for its expression. The injustice of the situation appalls; it ultimately kills.

"A Poetess" is a central story in Freeman's canon for its exploration of the close bonds that tie a woman's self-esteem to her sense of usefulness to others in the community. More importantly, this story explores fundamental religious and ethical questions as a woman strives to come to terms with an apparently unloving and indifferent Providence. Fifty-year-old Betsey Dole, unmarried and living in extreme poverty, relies on her verse writing, not only to provide herself with a purpose for living, but also with a means of solidarity with others. A lover of beauty—she grows flowers in her garden when vegetables would certainly have been more practical—Betsey expends every ounce of her energy on writing poetry, even forgetting in her intense absorption to eat her meals and to take her rest.

That Betsey's poetry is apparently conventional sentimental verse ("Flowers rhymed sweetly with vernal bowers, home with beyond the tomb, and heaven with even," the narrator informs us) is beside the point here. What matters is that in writing Betsey is able to exercise an empathy with others that not only expands her own limited circumstances and enlarges her soul but also consoles and uplifts her friends and neighbors. When a woman who has recently lost a child asks Betsey to write a eulogy and yet suggests that Betsey, as an "old maid," is unable to comprehend a mother's grief, Betsey defies the charge. "I guess I can enter into her feelin's considerable," she concludes to herself, and she soon shows herself more than capable of doing so. So complete is her power of sympathetic identification with others, that even as she speaks to Mrs. Caxton about her dead son, "her face took on unconsciously lines of grief so like the other woman's that she looked like her for the minute." Moreover, the young mother is well-satisfied with Betsey's verse once it is completed. The satisfaction is mutual; her praise was to Betsey "as if her poem had been approved and accepted by one of the great magazines."

Betsey's satisfaction is short lived, however. The young village minister, who has published a verse or two in a magazine, carelessly remarks to a woman villager that Betsey's eulogy was in ridiculously bad taste. Through gossip, the news inevitably gets back third-hand to Betsey, and Freeman records carefully her reaction to the minister's judgment. Alone, in an outburst of passion that at first seems uncharacteristic, she turns violently on the unjust God who has given her the desire to write in the first place: " 'I'd like to know if it's fair,' said she. 'I'd like to know if you think it's fair. Had I ought to have been born with the wantin' to write poetry if I couldn't write it—had I? Had I ought to have been let to write all my life, an' not know before there wa'n't any use in it? Would it be fair if that canary-bird there, that ain't never done anything but sing, should turn out not to be singin'? Would it, I'd like to know? S'pose them sweet-peas shouldn't be smellin' the right way? I ain't been dealt with as fair as they have, I'd like to know if I have.' " Receiving, of course, no answer to her bitter cry, Betsey swiftly reaches into her neat cupboard and without hesitation burns each one of her carefully preserved poems in the kitchen fire. "Other women might have burned their lovers' letters in agony of heart," the narrator points out. "Betsey had never had any lover, but she was burning all the love-letters that had passed between her and life."

Weakened, her passion and energy "purged" by the burning of her life's work, Betsey soon falls deathly ill. Visited in her final days by the very minister who has condemned her writing, Betsey makes two requests. She asks that he bury her with the ashes of her poetry, which she has carefully preserved in a sugar bowl; and she asks that he write some verses about her once she is gone. Abashed and bewildered, the minister complies, and in his compliance Betsey achieves a measure of victory although clearly a Pyrrhic one. Never doubting for a moment that the minister's judgments are correct—he is, after all, a male and a figure of authority—Betsey consciously calls forth from the minister the very empathy he lacks, as evinced earlier in his callous and unthinking gossip. As Betsey has striven to "enter into the feelings" of those that have requested poetry of her, so she ensures that the minister must likewise strive for sympathetic identification with the very subject and commissioner of this new work: herself. Though the price is no less than her death, she thus teaches the young, untried man a lesson about the human virtue of empathy.

A skillfully executed story throughout in its terse dialogue and sharply rendered series of dramatic confrontations, "A Village Singer" achieves near-perfection in the multiple layers of meaning and the irony of its brief conclusion. Elderly Candace Whitcomb is simply "replaced" in her forty-year position as lead singer at church services by a younger woman, Alma Way; she is told only that her voice is becoming "cracked." She revenges herself by singing as loudly as possible from her home across from the church each Sunday, timing herself carefully so that she succeeds in drowning out the solos performed by Alma. Scorning the token photograph album she is given by the community to appease their obvious guilt over her dismissal (she uses it as a footstool—"An' I ain't been particular to get the dust off my shoes before I used it neither," she remarks), outspoken Candace angrily confronts her minister when he comes to reprove her: "My voice is as good an' high to-day as it was twenty year ago; an' if it wa'n't, I'd like to know where the Christianity comes in. I'd like to know if it wouldn't be more to the credit of folks in a church to keep an old singer an' old minister, if they didn't sing an' hold forth quite so smart as they used to, ruther than turn 'em off an' hurt their feelin's. I guess it would be full as much to the glory of God."

He, however is completely helpless in the face of a situation that requires concrete and creative decision. "Like a block of granite," he is "incapable of understanding a woman like this . . . he could not account for such violence, such extremes, except in a loss of reason." Abdicating his responsibility in deciding Candace's case, he suggests that they kneel to "ask the guidance of the Lord." Furious, Candace retorts, "I don't see any use prayin' about it . . . I don't think the Lord's got much to do with it, anyhow."

Despite her words, however, Candace's quarrel, like Betsey Dole's, is very much with "the Lord." It is, after all, "the Lord" who has made her a woman and given her a lovely voice, one the author assures us has not "cracked" despite the congregation's claim. It is "the Lord" who has placed her in a community in which an aging woman is not valued. Older men such as "the old bachelor tenor," William Emmons, and the minister himself continue to be acceptable and vital community members, but older women are expected to recede more and more into the background. It is thus "the Lord" whose apparent injustice Candace inwardly rails against as she struggles toward some understanding of her life and the meaning of her work which is based on values far more profound than those of a superficial and hypocritical community. Most tragically, like all of Freeman's women questers, she must struggle alone to answer the deepest and most basic of human questions.

Art thrives on the artist's passion and an environment that fosters creative freedom, qualities that were effectively stifled in Freeman's New England village. Rollin Hartt's description of the cultural life of such villages as mythical "Sweet Auburn" precisely expresses the plight of any person who may have had aspirations toward artistic expression: "[U]nder normal conditions, a gifted personality matured in isolation is the kind that will come to greatness when it meets an adequate opportunity. But the conditions of life in Sweet Auburn are not normal. . . . [T]he curse has fallen upon our aesthetic life. . . . [V]ersatile minds [are] put to petty and unworthy uses, a native art instinct bowing down before vulgar mediocrity, a musical sense unconsciously outraged. . . . Sweet Auburn, as it stands today, is a great though a neglected opportunity" (717–18).

Lack of opportunity for expression on a wider scale beyond the constricted cultural life of the village is a major factor limiting Freeman's artists, but the fact that they are women artists limits them much further. Passion is considered unwomanly; rebellion from the norm, forwardness. After the minister pays his visit to Candace, her passion and rebellion in the face of such a repressive atmosphere give her entire system a mortal shock. Physically and emotionally weakened, she prepares to creep into her bed; but before doing so, she passively observes a rampant forest fire from her back door. She herself "was in the roar of an intenser fire," the narrator tells us; "the growths of all her springs and the delicate wontedness of her whole life were going down in it."

This inner fire has the effect of purging Candace of the guilt and agony she has experienced in her defiance; it is a "transfiguring fire," but it exacts from Candace both the passion that has been the source of her art and her very life itself. In the same sentence, we are told that the fire that "transfigures" also destroys. Soon after her confrontation with the minister, Candace falls ill; she "gave up at the first" and relinquishes her remaining energy through a series of reconciliations, each carefully considered. She first requests that her sister "brush up" the photograph album a bit, thus making peace with the community that has so perfunctorily rejected her. Next, she asks the minister's forgiveness: "I—hadn't ought to—spoke so," she confesses to him. "I hope the Lord will—forgive me." Finally, she makes peace with her rival, Alma Way, and her nephew, Wilson Ford, Alma's fiancé. She had earlier cut Wilson Ford out of her will; now she reverses that decision. Additionally, she bequeaths to Alma all of her possessions, making Alma her heir and thus, in a symbolic way, also recognizing her as her successor. In a final gesture of apparent humility, she asks her rival to sing for her, and Alma graciously obliges the dying woman.

It should be noted that Candace has specified the song she wishes to hear as perhaps her last on earth: "Jesus, Lover of My Soul." It is reasonable to postulate that she means the lyrics, familiar ones to a Freeman audience, to communicate things she cannot or will not say to Alma and Wilson. The verses of this old hymn give us a clue to the desperate cry of Candace's inner being, one seeking refuge in the midst of "the storm of life." Defenseless against its enemies, the soul pleads with God for response: "Wilt Thou not regard my call, Wilt Thou not accept my prayer? Lo, I sink, I faint, I fall." Receiving only silence in return, the speaker finally, "hoping against hope," can only put trust in God, concluding that "dying . . . behold, I live." It is thus the centuries-old Christian paradox of "life-in-death" that on the surface appears to console the dying Candace.

The text of this Charles Wesley hymn is based on a biblical passage that also merits exploration. Freeman's audience would merely have to glance at the top of their hymnal page to check the reference, and many of them would have been able to recite the text from memory. Isaiah 32 is no less than a harsh indictment of a corrupt society and a powerful vision of a kingdom of justice to come:

> Behold, a King shall reign in righteousness, and princes shall rule in judgement. . . . And the eyes of them that see shall not be dim, and the ears of them that hear shall hearken. The heart also of the rash shall understand knowledge, and the tongue of the stammerers shall be ready to speak plainly. The vile person shall be no more called liberal,

nor the churl said to be bountiful. For the vile person will speak villainy, and his heart will work iniquity, to practice hypocrisy. . . . [H]e deviseth wicked devices to destroy the poor with lying words, even when the needy speaketh right.

Moreover, the text then turns to address the women of Jerusalem in particular: "Rise up, ye women that are at ease; hear my voice, ye careless daughters; give ear unto my speech. Many days and years shall ye be troubled, ye careless women: for the vintage shall fail, the gathering shall not come. Tremble, ye women that are at ease; be troubled, ye careless ones" (Isaiah 32:1–11, AV)

Given such multiple layers of text, it is now possible to interpret fully the magnitude of Candace's ironic final statement to Alma Way. Like Betsey Dole in "A Poetess," Candace chooses her rival as her successor and attempts thereby to impart to that successor a final lesson. As Betsey teaches the minister to empathize with one apparently out of his range of experience, so the elderly, impoverished, spinster-woman Candace passes down a lesson of a woman's lot in an unjust society. Through the text of Isaiah she alerts the conventional, already aging Alma of the dangers of complacency and overconfidence, warning her of the ultimate failure of art for a woman in such a stifling, patriarchal atmosphere: "the vintage shall fail, the gathering shall not come." As Freeman's well-versed audience would certainly also recall, Jesus referred to this Old Testament passage when bidding the women mourning his crucifixion to "weep not for me, but weep for yourselves and for your children" (Luke 23:28, AV). In thus warning Alma Way, Candace mourns a subsequent generation whose lack of basic human values will only repeat that of her own.

The name "Alma Way" is significant: "the soul's way." Having accepted Alma as her successor, Candace completes her lesson to her one-time rival by a deft final statement that culminates the layers of irony already present in the conclusion of this story. Once more, Candace points this "soul" on a better, truer way. As Alma finishes the song, Candace remarks, "You flatted a little on—soul." She simultaneously reminds the younger woman that she, Candace, is the more accomplished artist and confirms her authority as teacher. She also reminds Alma that Alma will no doubt reach the point where her singing is deemed unacceptable or "flat" by the congregation. Finally, she covertly admonishes Alma that Alma, too, has been guilty of conforming too closely to the conventions of a community that refuses to recognize human dignity in an aging woman. Like the rest of the congregation, Alma also has "flatted"—constricted or hardened—her "soul." Candace's quiet plea is rather for that soul's enlargement and growth in fundamental human compassion.

Like that of Betsey Dole and Candace Whitcomb, Freeman's art was her life. Though initially turning to writing as a means of gainful employment, she continued to adhere to a strict daily writing schedule and worried greatly about her ability to meet it even long after achieving financial independence. Her writing continued to be of prime importance to her, taking precedence over social and familial duties. "My work is, at present, of such a very urgent nature, that I am obliged to deny myself nearly every social recreation that comes in my way and keep close at home, with pen in hand," she wrote in 1895 (Kendrick, 182). In a number of letters, she mentions her tendency to overwork; in fact, her exhausting routine appears to have contributed to some of her lifelong ailments—fatigue, headaches, and insomnia. "I have been really very ill from overwork alone," she wrote in 1901. "I might have died, I think" (Kendrick, 255).

Freeman's success came as a result of her disciplined writing habits. For much of her life, her daily routine provided her with a structure and a purpose that otherwise might have been lacking in the life of a woman who did not have the daily duty of caring for a family, one who disliked the typical leisured occupations of card parties and visiting. Her writing brought her friends and professional colleagues; like that of Betsey Dole in "A Poetess," it also afforded her the means of empathizing with those people her reticence and shyness often would not allow her to approach in everyday life—young girls, middle-aged housewives, poor and lonely women. Her art, too, provided her with a sense of stability when friends failed and relationships fell apart. She simply could not conceive of life without it. Two years before her death, her marriage having ended in bitterness and her career itself jeopardized by the changing times, she still looked to her writing as having provided her not only with great satisfaction but with ultimate purpose in life. "I feel [my writing] is all I came into the world for," she wrote, "and [that I] have failed dismally if it is not a success" (Kendrick, 424).

Some of Freeman's most poignant stories are those involving women who are alone and who struggle to come to terms with their solitude. A deep-thinking and spiritual person (Henry Alden once called her "an infant sphinx"), Freeman never took life lightly; as a single woman, she apparently struggled for years to determine and to accept the roles and responsibilities her society designated for the unmarried woman. Wishing to retain her independence and often scorning conventional marriage, she nevertheless found her status as "old maid" at once anomalous and constricting; a sense of profound inner division and intense internal conflict thus mark her works dealing with this subject matter. In the end, no matter what the magnitude of their outer or inner rebellion, Freeman's solitary women nearly always echo the despairing—and guilty—cry of the woman protagonist in "An Object of Love" as she struggles both to assert and repress her fierce inner conviction of injustice and deprivation: "I hadn't orter feel this way."

CONCLUSION

This study of Mary Wilkins Freeman's short stories has focused on the struggles, defeats, and triumphs of her many women protagonists in the ordinary, everyday circumstances of their lives. As they strive to form and maintain relationships with parents, men, other women, and with their God, Freeman's female protagonists attempt to come to terms with the roles and responsibilities prescribed for women in their time and place, the preindustrial turn-of-the-century New England village. Through their affiliations with others, they learn to define, accept, or compromise themselves; in their relationships, therefore, lie the seeds of their identities as both women and as human beings.

As recent studies in the sociology and psychology of gender have pointed out, women tend to achieve identity through an intricate and carefully maintained web of relationship. These studies indicate that women, more so than men, have evolved, perhaps because of their own mothering by a woman, what has been called an "ethic of care" (Gilligan, 74), one that places attachment to and intimacy with others at the center of their moral, emotional, and even physical well-being. Freeman's writings of nearly a century ago concur with this modern-day conclusion. As a woman author writing to a primarily though not exclusively female audience about women's concerns, Freeman wrote tale after tale of women struggling in and with relationships. An acute observer of women's lives and an accurate student of women's psychology, Freeman strove to "tell the truth," writing of what she knew first-hand or from the lives of those around her. Her immense popularity in her day testifies to her ability to touch the heart and emotions of a generation of readers.

Freeman wrote of women in relationships; paradoxically, her women remain fundamentally alone. Their lifelong search for connection and intimacy is more often than not frustrated; they find it ultimately impossible to achieve fulfillment or realize their dreams in a society that has defined the role of women—and therefore the extent and magnitude of their relationships to others—in a narrow and constricting manner. Arthur Machen has captured the essence of their resulting isolation in *Hieroglyphics*:

> So this is my plea for Miss Wilkins. . . . she has painted a society, indeed, but a society in which each . . . stands apart, responsible only for himself and to himself, conscious only of himself and his God. You will note this, if you read her carefully, you will see how this doctrine of awful, individual loneliness prevails so far that it is carried into the necessary and ordinary transactions of social life. . . . I call it a witness to the everlasting truth that, at last, each . . . must stand or fall alone, and . . . must, to a certain extent, live alone with his own soul [Machen, 159–60].

Family relationships in Freeman's world are cold and distant. A young woman's relationship with her mother is especially problematic, strained by the expectation that she marry well; a fortunate marriage confers prestige and material security on parent and child alike. Little hope exists in a Freeman village for the financial or social success of the unmarried woman, but a young woman's choices among available suitors are severely limited; the few eligible men in the villages are all too often undesirable. Practical and level-headed, a Freeman protagonist often chooses to compromise part of herself in marrying; she enters marriage with her eyes open, yet continuing to hope for a degree of happiness she has not witnessed in her mother's life.

Whether she marries or remains single, a Freeman woman's adult friendships with other women are often based on a rivalry or power struggle that excludes the possibility of a deep or satisfying relationship. Should a woman remain unmarried, she often finds herself internally divided between a desire for the "normal" life of other women, one which she feels is "due" her from Providence, and an equally strong disdain for such a life as one necessarily full of compromise and submission. Especially as she ages, her tenacious hold on a token of identity—a talent, a possession—becomes critical. After years of silent repression, such a woman often comes to a breaking point when that means of identity is threatened. "The sudden revolt of a spirit that will endure no more from circumstances" forms the dramatic action of some of Freeman's most powerful works (Matthiessen, 408).

As Freeman saw it, a woman's role in the New England village at the turn of the century was one fraught with tension and ambiguity. Writing at a time and in a place marked by transition from an older, more stable, and more uniform world to one in which lifestyles and gender roles were changing, Freeman was aware that she was recording an era that was, even as she wrote, already receding. "I have . . . a fancy that my characters belong to a present that is rapidly becoming *past*, and that a few generations will cause them to disappear," she wrote (Kendrick, 84). The overriding concern of her short fiction was to explore the ambiguities of womanhood in this time and place as she experienced them. Torn between submission and rebellion, between duty and freedom, between dependence and independence, Freeman's many differing women characters can be seen as constituting a composite portrait of Freeman herself. An unusual woman who led a full and varied life alternating between poverty and wealth, between obscurity and fame, between the life of a single artist and the life of a "normal" woman in marriage, Freeman spent her writing career translating these feelings and experiences into her art. "I suppose it seems to you as it does to me that everything you have heard, seen, or done, since you opened your eyes on the world, is coming back to you sooner or later, to go into stories," she once remarked to Sarah Orne Jewett (Kendrick, 99). Though her personal correspondence gives us some valuable, yet limited insight into her personality, the reiterated concerns and complications of her nearly 250 short stories provide us with our best clue to the mind and heart of this author.

Little "happens" of an overt nature in a Freeman story, but great adventures are undertaken and great discoveries made; Freeman's women live intense, vibrant—and often fearful—interior lives as they seek in their loneliness to form human and spiritual bonds. Though Freeman's rebel figures such as Sarah Penn and Candace Whitcomb are outstanding characters in her canon, our rediscovery of Freeman should not stop there. Her strength as an artist lies in her ability to draw pictures through language of the unspoken aspirations, desires, fears, sorrows, and joys that make up many aspects of women's lives, whether they are rebellious in their undertakings or not. Freeman thus warrants reevaluation as an artist who will endure not only for her pioneering work in the techniques of realism but also because her women's themes make her work of universal appeal. Full of a "riveting authenticity," they still have the power to compel nearly a century after they were written. As British critic Sylvia Warner remarked in 1966, "if I had had the courage of my convictions downstairs, when everyone was talking about Joyce and Pound and melting pots, I would have said, 'Why don't you think more of Mary Wilkins?'" (134). It is encouraging to see that we *are* thinking more of Mary Wilkins these days.

APPENDIX

Bibliography of Mary Wilkins Freeman's Works

SHORT FICTION

This complete listing of Freeman's adult short fiction is presented here for the first time. Arranged alphabetically, it includes several short sketches such as "After the Rain" and "Pastels in Prose" which cannot properly be considered short stories; it likewise includes unfinished manuscripts. Publishing information given is for the collection if collected before 1930 (the year of Freeman's death) and for original publishing dates if not collected before this date.

"About Hannah Stone," *Everybody's* 4 (Jan. 1901): 25–33.

"After the Rain," *Century* 45 (Dec. 1892): 271.

"Amanda and Love," *A New England Nun and Other Stories* (New York: Harper and Brothers, 1891), 288–304.

"Amanda Todd: The Friend of Cats," *The People of Our Neighborhood* (Philadelphia: Curtis Publishing Company, 1898), 75–90.

"Amarina's Roses," *The Fair Lavinia and Others* (New York: Harper and Brothers, 1907), 43–83.

"The Amethyst Comb," *The Copy-Cat and Other Stories* (New York: Harper and Brothers, 1914), 211–36.

"The Apple-Tree," *Six Trees* (New York: Harper and Brothers, 1903), 169–207.

"Arethusa," *Understudies* (New York: Harper and Brothers, 1901), 147–69.

"The Auction," *Woman's Home Companion* 36 (Oct. 1909): 7–8, 93.

"Away from Sunflower Ranch," *Boston Evening Transcript: The Holiday Transcript*, Dec. 1890, p. 4.

"The Balking of Christopher," *The Copy-Cat and Other Stories* (New York: Harper and Brothers, 1914), 267–91.

"The Balsam Fir," *Six Trees* (New York: Harper and Brothers, 1903), 101–27.

"The Bar Light-House," *A Humble Romance and Other Stories* (New York: Harper and Brothers, 1887), 180–91.

"Betsey Somerset," *Harper's Bazar* 26 (18 Mar. 1893): 205–7.

"Big Sister Solly," *The Copy-Cat and Other Stories* (New York: Harper and Brothers, 1914), 107–35.

"Billy and Susy," *The Winning Lady and Others* (New York: Harper and Brothers, 1909), 103–22.

"The Blue Butterfly," *Woman's Home Companion* 40 (Jan. 1913): 3–4, 44.

"The Boomerang," *Pictorial Review* 18 (Mar. 1917): 22–24, 44.

"Both Cheeks," *Edgewater People* (New York: Harper and Brothers, 1918), 215–31.

"Bouncing Bet," *Understudies* (New York: Harper and Brothers, 1901), 99–119.

"Brakes and White Vi'lets," *A Humble Romance and Other Stories* (New York: Harper and Brothers, 1887), 107–17.

"The Bright Side," *Harper's Monthly* 146 (Apr. 1923): 630–44.

"The Brother," MS (c. 1927). (Cited in Foster, 213.)

"A Brotherhood of Three," *Harper's Weekly* 41 (18 Dec. 1897): 1248–50; also in *Illustrated London News* 111 (18 Dec. 1897): 879–81.

"The Buckley Lady," *Silence and Other Stories* (New York: Harper and Brothers, 1898), 55–110.

"The Butterfly," *The Givers* (New York: Harper and Brothers, 1904), 229–65.

"Calla-Lilies and Hannah," *A New England Nun and Other Stories* (New York: Harper and Brothers, 1891), 99–120.

"The Cat," *Understudies* (New York: Harper and Brothers, 1901), 3–16.

"Catherine Carr," *The Love of Parson Lord and Other Stories* (New York: Harper and Brothers, 1900), 143–81.

"The Cautious King, and the All-Round Wise Woman," *Harper's Weekly* 53 (26 June 1909): 22–24.

"The Chance of Araminta," *The Givers* (New York: Harper and Brothers, 1904), 192–228.

"The Christmas Ghost," *Everybody's* 3 (Dec. 1900): 512–20.

"Christmas Jenny," *A New England Nun and Other Stories* (New York: Harper and Brothers, 1891), 160–77.

"A Christmas Lady," *Ladies' Home Journal* 27 (Dec. 1909): 17–18.

"A Christmas Pastel/In Prose," *Boston Evening Transcript*, 19 Dec. 1891, p. 20.

"The Christmas Sing in Our Village," *The People of Our Neighborhood* (Philadelphia: Curtis Publishing Company, 1898), 149–61.

"A Church Mouse," *A New England Nun and Other Stories* (New York: Harper and Brothers, 1891), 407–26.

"Cinnamon Roses," *A Humble Romance and Other Stories* (New York: Harper and Brothers, 1887), 164–79.

"The Cloak Also," *Harper's Monthly* 134 (Mar. 1917): 545–55.

"The Cock of the Walk," *The Copy-Cat and Other Stories* (New York: Harper and Brothers, 1914), 33–54.

"A Conflict Ended," *A Humble Romance and Other Stories* (New York: Harper and Brothers, 1887), 382–98.

"A Conquest of Humility," *A Humble Romance and Other Stories* (New York: Harper and Brothers, 1887), 415–36.

"The Copy-Cat," *The Copy-Cat and Other Stories* (New York: Harper and Brothers, 1914), 1–31.

"Coronation" (previously titled "The Door Mat"). *The Copy-Cat and Other Stories* (New York: Harper and Brothers, 1914), 183–209.

"Criss-Cross," *Harper's Monthly* 129 (Aug. 1914): 360–72.

"Cyrus Emmett: The Unlucky Man," *The People of Our Neighborhood* (Philadelphia: Curtis Publishing Company, 1898), 41–57.

"D. J.: A Christmas Story," *Mail and Express Illustrated Saturday Magazine* (New York) (5 Dec. 1903): 14–15, 22, 30; also in *Advance* 46 (17 Dec. 1903): 766–69.

"Daniel and Little Dan'l," *The Copy-Cat and Other Stories* (New York: Harper and Brothers, 1914), 83–106.

"Dear Annie," *The Copy-Cat and Other Stories* (New York: Harper and Brothers, 1914), 293–351.

"A Devotee of Art," *Harper's Bazar* 27 (27 Jan. 1894): 69–71.

"A Discovered Pearl," *A New England Nun and Other Stories* (New York: Harper and Brothers, 1891), 253–67.

"The Doctor's Horse," *Understudies* (New York: Harper and Brothers, 1901), 85–96.

"The Doll Lady," *Harper's Monthly* 124 (Jan. 1912): 279–90.

"Down the Road to the Emersons," *Romance* 12 (Nov. 1893): 3–24.

"An Easter-Card," *Everybody's* 4 (Apr. 1901), 372–77.

"Eglantina," *The Givers* (New York: Harper and Brothers, 1904), 93–131. Republished in *The Fair Lavinia and Others* (New York: Harper and Brothers, 1907), 87–108.

"Eliza Sam," *The Winning Lady and Others* (New York: Harper and Brothers, 1909), 281–303.

"The Elm-Tree," *Six Trees* (New York: Harper and Brothers, 1903), 1–40.

"Emancipation," *Harper's Monthly* 132 (Dec. 1915), 27–35.

"Emmy," *Century*, 41 (Feb. 1891), 499–506.

"Eunice and the Doll," *Boston Evening Transcript* 13 Dec. 1897, p. 8; 14 Dec. 1897, p. 10; also in *Pocket Magazine* 5 (Mar. 1898): 1–41; also in *Best Things from American Literature*, ed. Irving Bacheller (New York: The Christian Herald, 1899), 369–82.

"Evelina's Garden," *Silence and Other Stories* (New York: Harper and Brothers, 1898), 111–183.

"The Fair Lavinia," *The Fair Lavinia and Others* (New York: Harper and Brothers, 1907), 3–39.

"Far Away Job," *Woman's Home Companion* 36 (Dec. 1909): 6–7, 72–75.

"A Far-Away Melody," *A Humble Romance and Other Stories* (New York: Harper and Brothers, 1887), 208–18.

"The Fighting McLeans," *The Delineator* 75 (Feb. 1910): 113–14, 150–52.

"The Fire at Elm Grove," *Good Cheer* 4 (June, 1884): 5–6.

"Flora and Hannah," *The Winning Lady and Others* (New York: Harper and Brothers, 1909), 307–17.

"The Flowering Bush," *Edgewater People* (New York: Harper and Brothers, 1918), 101–27.

"For the Love of One's Self," *Harper's Monthly* 110 (Jan. 1905): 303–16.

"Friend of My Heart," *Good Housekeeping* 57 (Dec. 1913): 733–40.

"A Gala Dress," *A New England Nun and Other Stories* (New York: Harper and Brothers, 1891), 37–53.

"A Gatherer of Simples," *A Humble Romance and Other Stories* (New York: Harper and Brothers, 1887), 280–95.

"General: A Christmas Story," *10 Story Book* 1 (Jan. 1902): 10–15.

"Gentian," *A Humble Romance and Other Stories* (New York: Harper and Brothers, 1887), 250–265.

"A Gentle Ghost," *A New England Nun and Other Stories* (New York: Harper and Brothers, 1891), 234–52.

"The Gift of Love," *Woman's Home Companion* 33 (Dec. 1906): 21, 22, 73.

"The Givers" (previously entitled "The Revolt of Sophia Lane"), *The Givers* (New York: Harper and Brothers, 1904), 3–50.

"The Gold," *The Fair Lavinia and Others* (New York: Harper and Brothers, 1907), 231–54.

"The Gospel According to Joan," *The Best Stories of Mary E. Wilkins*, ed. Henry Wysham Lanier (New York: Harper and Brothers, 1927), 441–65.

"The Great Pine," *Six Trees* (New York: Harper and Brothers, 1903), 67–99.

"A Guest in Sodom," *Century* 83 (Jan. 1912): 343–51.

"The Hall Bedroom," *Collier's* 30 (28 Mar. 1903): 19, 22–23; also in *Short Story Classics (American)*, ed. William Patten (New York: P. F. Collier and Son, 1905), 4: 1231–57.

"The Happy Day," *McClure's* 21 (May 1903): 89–94.

"Her Christmas," *The Winning Lady and Others* (New York: Harper and Brothers, 1909), 209–40.

"The Home-Coming of Jessica," first printed in *Woman's Home Companion* (unlocated). Reprinted in *The Home-Coming of Jessica* (by Mary E. Wilkins); *An Idyl of Central Park* (by Brander Matthews); *The Romance of a Soul* (by Robert Grant) (New York: Crowell and Kirkpatrick, 1901), 3–17.

"An Honest Soul," *A Humble Romance and Other Stories* (New York: Harper and Brothers, 1887), 78–91.

"Honorable Tommy," *Woman's Home Companion* 43 (Dec. 1916): 15–16, 68.

"The Horn of Plenty," *Collier's* 48 (18 Nov. 1911): 22–23, 30, 32, 34, 36.

"How Charlotte Ellen Went Visiting," *Boston Evening Transcript*, 1 Nov. 1897, p. 10; 2 Nov. 1897, p. 8; also in *New York Ledger* 54 (14 May, 21 May 1898): 17–18 each issue.

"Humble Pie," *Independent* 57 (1 Sept. 1904): 477–84.

"A Humble Romance," *A Humble Romance and Other Stories* (New York: Harper and Brothers, 1887), 1–24.

"Hyacinthus," *Harper's Monthly* 109 (Aug. 1904): 447–58; also in *Quaint Courtships*, ed. William Dean Howells and Henry Mills Alden (London: Harper and Brothers, 1906), 75–107.

"I Am a Rebel," undated MS, privately owned. (Cited in Foster, 142–43.)

"In Butterfly Time," *A Humble Romance and Other Stories* (New York: Harper and Brothers, 1887), 315–29.

"An Independent Thinker," *A Humble Romance and Other Stories* (New York: Harper and Brothers, 1887), 296–314.

"An Innocent Gamester," *A New England Nun and Other Stories* (New York: Harper and Brothers, 1891), 363–83.

"The Jade Bracelet," *Forum* 59 (Apr. 1918): 429–40.

"The Jester," *The Golden Book* 7 (June 1928): 821–28.

"Johnny-In-The-Woods," *The Copy-Cat and Other Stories* (New York: Harper and Brothers, 1914), 55–82.

"Josiah's First Christmas," *Collier's* 44 (11 Dec. 1909): 9–10.

"Joy," *The Givers* (New York: Harper and Brothers, 1904), 132–55.

"The Joy of Youth," *The Winning Lady and Others* (New York: Harper and Brothers, 1909), 71–100.

"Julia—Her Thanksgiving," *Harper's Bazar* 43 (Nov. 1909): 1079–82.

"Juliza," *Two Tales* 1 (12 Mar. 1892): 1–14; also in *Romance* 10 (July 1893): 352–70.

"A Kitchen Colonel," *A New England Nun and Other Stories* (New York: Harper and Brothers, 1891), 427–47.

"The Last Gift," *The Givers* (New York: Harper and Brothers, 1918), 266–96.

"The Liar," *Edgewater People* (New York: Harper and Brothers, 1918), 153–85.

"Life Everlastin'," *A New England Nun and Other Stories* (New York: Harper and Brothers, 1891), 338–62.

"Little-Girl-Afraid-Of-a-Dog," *The Winning Lady and Others* (New York: Harper and Brothers, 1909), 35–68.

"The Little Green Door," *New York Times* 13–15 Apr. 1896, p. 9 each day; also in *Pocket Magazine* 3 (July 1896): 56–90; and in *New York Ledger* 52 (25 Apr. 1898): 16–17.

"Little Lucy Rose," *The Copy-Cat and Other Stories* (New York: Harper and Brothers, 1914), 137–62.

"The Little Maid at the Door," *Silence and Other Stories* (New York: Harper and Brothers, 1898), 225–54.

"Little Margaret Snell: The Village Runaway," *The People of Our Neighborhood* (Philadelphia: Curtis Publishing Company, 1898), 23–38.

"The Lombardy Poplar," *Six Trees* (New York: Harper and Brothers, 1903), 129–67.

"The Long Arm" (by Mary E. Wilkins and J. Edgar Chamberlin), *Pocket Magazine* 1 (Dec. 1895): 1–76; also in *The Long Arm and Other Detective Stories* (London: Chapman and Hall Limited, 1895), 1–66.

"The Lost Book," *Book Culture* 1 (Sept. 1899): 136.

"The Lost Dog," *Understudies* (New York: Harper and Brothers, 1901), 53–61. "The Lost Ghost," *The Wind in the Rose-Bush and Other Stories of the Supernatural* (New York: Doubleday, Page and Co., 1903), 201–37.

"Louisa," *A New England Nun and Other Stories* (New York: Harper and Brothers, 1891), 384–406.

"The Love of Parson Lord," *The Love of Parson Lord and Other Stories* (New York: Harper and Brothers, 1900), 3–81.

"A Lover of Flowers," *A Humble Romance and Other Stories* (New York: Harper and Brothers, 1887), 192–207.

"Lucy," *The Givers* (New York: Harper and Brothers, 1904), 51–92.

"Luella Miller," *The Wind in the Rose-Bush and Other Stories of the Supernatural* (New York: Doubleday, Page and Co., 1903), 75–104.

"Lydia Hersey, of East Bridgewater," *Silence and Other Stories* (New York: Harper and Brothers, 1898), 255–80.

"Lydia Wheelock: The Good Woman," *The People of Our Neighborhood* (Philadelphia: Curtis Publishing Company, 1898), 91–109.

"A Mistaken Charity," *A Humble Romance and Other Stories* (New York: Harper and Brothers, 1887), 234–49.

"A Modern Dragon," *A Humble Romance and Other Stories* (New York: Harper and Brothers, 1887), 60–77.

"The Monkey," *Understudies* (New York: Harper and Brothers, 1901), 19–36.

"A Moral Exigency," *A Humble Romance and Other Stories* (New York: Harper and Brothers, 1887), 219–33.

"Morning-Glory," *Understudies* (New York: Harper and Brothers, 1901), 217–30.

"Mother-Wings," *Harper's Monthly* 144 (Dec. 1921): 90–103.

"Mountain-Laurel," *Understudies* (New York: Harper and Brothers, 1901), 173–90.

"Mrs. Sackett's Easter Bonnet," *Woman's Home Companion* 34 (Apr. 1907): 5–7.

"The Mystery of Miss Amidon," *Boston Evening Transcript*, 22 Dec. 1900, p. 18.

"Nanny and Martha Pepperill," *Harper's Bazar* 28 (14 Dec. 1895): 1021–23.

"A Narrow Escape/How Santa Claus Baffled the Mounted Police," *Detroit Sunday News*, 25 Dec. 1892, p. 12.

"A New England Nun," *A New England Nun and Other Stories* (New York: Harper and Brothers, 1891), 1–17.

"A New England Prophet," *Silence and Other Stories* (New York: Harper and Brothers, 1898), 184–224.

"A New-Year's Resolution," *The Winning Lady and Others* (New York: Harper and Brothers, 1909), 321–28.

"Noblesse," *The Copy-Cat and Other Stories* (New York: Harper and Brothers, 1914), 163–81.

"An Object of Love," *A Humble Romance and Other Stories* (New York: Harper and Brothers, 1887), 266–79.

"An Old Arithmetician," *A Humble Romance and Other Stories* (New York: Harper and Brothers, 1887), 368–81.

"Old Lady Pingree," *A Humble Romance and Other Stories* (New York: Harper and Brothers, 1887), 148–63.

"The Old Man of the Field," *Edgewater People* (New York: Harper and Brothers, 1918), 26–50.

"An Old Valentine," *The Home-Maker* 8 (Feb. 1890): 367–74; also in *Romance* 9 (Feb. 1893): 50–64.

"Old Woman Magoun," *The Winning Lady and Others* (New York: Harper and Brothers, 1909), 243–77.

"One," MS (c. 1928). (Cited in Foster, 213.)

"One Good Time," *The Love of Parson Lord and Other Stories* (New York: Harper and Brothers, 1900), 195–233.

"On the Walpole Road," *A Humble Romance and Other Stories* (New York: Harper and Brothers, 1887), 134–47.

"Other People's Cake," *Collier's* 42 (21 Nov. 1908): 14–15, 32, 34, 36–37.

"The Other Side," *Harper's Bazar* 24 (26 Dec. 1891): 993–95.

"The Outside of the House," *Edgewater People* (New York: Harper and Brothers, 1918), 128–52.

"The Parrot," *Understudies* (New York: Harper and Brothers, 1901), 65–81.

"Pastels in Prose," *Harper's* 86 (Dec. 1892): 147–48.

"A Patient Waiter," *A Humble Romance and Other Stories* (New York: Harper and Brothers, 1887), 399–414.

"Peony," *Understudies* (New York: Harper and Brothers, 1901), 193–213.

"Phebe Ann Little: The Neat Woman," *The People of Our Neighborhood* (Philadelphia: Curtis Publishing Company, 1898), 59–73.

"The Pink Shawls," *The Fair Lavinia and Others* (New York: Harper and Brothers, 1907), 111–42.

"A Poetess," *A New England Nun and Other Stories* (New York: Harper and Brothers, 1891), 140–59.

"The Poor Lady," *Woman's Home Companion* 38 (Oct. 1911): 7–8, 84–86; 38 (Nov. 1911): 17–18, 75–77; 38 (Dec. 1911): 23–24, 70; 39 (Jan. 1912): 25–26, 56; 39 (Feb. 1912): 23–24, 62–63; 39 (Mar. 1912): 20, 93–96; 39 (Apr. 1912): 23–24.

"A Pot of Gold," *A New England Nun and Other Stories* (New York: Harper and Brothers, 1891), 178–97.

"The Price She Paid," *Harper's Bazar* 21 (10 Mar. 1888): 158–59.

"Prince's-Feather," *Understudies* (New York: Harper and Brothers, 1901), 123–43.

"The Prism," *Century* 62 (July 1901): 469–74.

"The Prop," *Saturday Evening Post* 190 (5 Jan. 1918): 12–13, 109–10.

"A Protracted Meeting," *The Housewife* 6 (Feb. 1891): 6; 6 (Mar. 1891): 6.

"The Proud Lucinda," *Harper's Bazar* 24 (7 Feb. 1891): 101–3.

"The Pumpkin," *Harper's Bazar* 33 (24 Nov. 1900): 1863–71.

"A Quilting Bee in Our Village," *The People of Our Neighborhood* (Philadelphia: Curtis Publishing Company, 1898), 111–28.

"The Reign of the Doll," *The Givers* (New York: Harper and Brothers, 1904), 156–91.

"'A Retreat to the Goal,'" *Edgewater People* (New York: Harper and Brothers, 1918), 285–315.

"The Return," *Woman's Home Companion* 48 (Aug. 1921): 21–22, 83.

"The Revolt of 'Mother,'" *A New England Nun and Other Stories* (New York: Harper and Brothers, 1891), 448–68.

"The Ring with the Green Stone," *Edgewater People* (New York: Harper and Brothers, 1918), 261–84.

"Robins and Hammers," *A Humble Romance and Other Stories* (New York: Harper and Brothers, 1887), 118–33.

"The Rocket," undated MS; also entitled "One Old Lady." Manuscript and Archives Division, New York Public Library.

"Rosemary Marsh," *Harper's Bazar* 30 (11 Dec. 1897): 1026.

"A Rustic Comedy," *Ladies' Home Journal* 8 (Mar. 1891): 7–8.

"Santa Claus: Two Jack-Knives," *Springfield* (Mass.) *Sunday Republican*, 15 Dec. 1901, p. 24.

"Sarah Edgewater," *Edgewater People* (New York: Harper and Brothers, 1918), 3–25.

"The Saving of Hiram Sessions," *Pictorial Review* 16 (May 1915): 20–21, 70–72.

"The Scent of the Roses," *A New England Nun and Other Stories* (New York: Harper and Brothers, 1891), 198–214.

"The School-Teacher," *Harper's Bazar* 28 (6 Apr. 1895): 262.

"The School-Teacher's Story," *Romance* 13 (Feb. 1894): 5–18.

"The Secret," *The Fair Lavinia and Others* (New York: Harper and Brothers, 1907), 187–228.

"The Selfishness of Amelia Lamkin," *The Winning Lady and Others* (New York: Harper and Brothers, 1909), 125–72.

"Serena Ann: Her First Christmas Keeping," *Hartford Daily Courant*, 15 Dec. 1894, p. 10.

"Serena Ann's First Valentine," *Boston Evening Transcript*, 5 Feb. 1897, p. 9; also in *New York Ledger* 53 (13 Feb. 1897): 6–7; also in *The English Illustrated* 17 (June 1897): 235–42.

"The Shadow Family," *The Boston Sunday Budget*, 1 Jan. 1882 (unlocated).

"The Shadows on the Wall," *The Wind in the Rose-Bush and Other Stories of the Supernatural* (New York: Doubleday, Page and Company, 1903), 41–72.

"She Who Adorns Her Sister Adorns Herself," *Harper's Bazar* 38 (May 1904): 456–60.

"Silence," *Silence and Other Stories* (New York: Harper and Brothers, 1898), 1–54.

"Sister Liddy," *A New England Nun and Other Stories* (New York: Harper and Brothers, 1891), 81–98.

"A Slayer of Serpents," *Collier's* 44 (19 Mar. 1910): 16–17, 19, 36, 38.

"The Slip of the Leash," *Harper's Monthly* 109 (Oct. 1904): 668–75.

"The Soldier Man," *Edgewater People* (New York: Harper and Brothers, 1918), 232–60.

"A Solitary," *A New England Nun and Other Stories* (New York: Harper and Brothers, 1891), 215–33.

"Something on Her Mind," *Harper's Bazar* 46 (Dec. 1912): 607–8.

"Sonny," *Lippincott's* 47 (June 1891): 776–85; also in *Romance* 8 (Nov. 1892): 13–27.

"Sour Sweetings," *Edgewater People* (New York: Harper and Brothers, 1918), 186–214.

"The Southwest Chamber," *The Wind in the Rose-Bush and Other Stories of the Supernatural* (New York: Doubleday, Page and Company, 1903), 107–64.

"A Souvenir," *A Humble Romance and Other Stories* (New York: Harper and Brothers, 1887), 350–67.

"A Sparrow's Nest," *Good Cheer* 6 (Aug. 1887): 3–4.

"The Squirrel," *Understudies* (New York: Harper and Brothers, 1901), 39–50.

"Starlight," *Woman's Home Companion* 35 (Dec. 1908): 19–20, 74.

"The Steeple," *Hampton-Columbian* 27 (Oct. 1911): 412–20.

"The Stockwells' Apple-Paring Bee," *The People of Our Neighborhood* (Philadelphia: Curtis Publishing Company, 1898), 129–47.

"A Stolen Christmas," *A New England Nun and Other Stories* (New York: Harper and Brothers, 1891), 321–37.

"The Story of Little Mary Whitlow," *Lippincott's* 21 (May 1883): 500–504.

"A Stress of Conscience," *Harper's Bazar* 25 (25 June 1892): 518–19; also in *Illustrated London News* 100 (25 June 1892): 785–87.

"The Strike of Hannah," *Woman's Home Companion* 33 (Nov. 1906): 9–10, 50–52.

"A Study in China," *Harper's Bazar* 20 (5 Nov. 1887): 766–67.

"Susan: Her Neighbor's Story," *Harper's Bazar* 32 (23 Sept. 1899): 801, 804.

"Susan Jane's Valentine," *Harper's Bazar* 33 (17 Feb. 1900): 132–33.

"Sweet-Flowering Perennial," *Harper's Monthly* 131 (July 1915): 287–97.

"Sweet-Williams," *Harper's Bazar* 28 (25 May 1895): 418.

"A Symphony in Lavender," *A Humble Romance and Other Stories* (New York: Harper and Brothers, 1887), 37–48.

"Tall Jane," *St. Louis Republic* 25 Oct. 1891, p. 5; also in *Detroit Sunday News*, 25 Oct. 1891, p. 12.

"A Tardy Thanksgiving," *A Humble Romance and Other Stories* (New York: Harper and Brothers, 1887), 49–59.

"A Taste of Honey," *A Humble Romance and Other Stories* (New York: Harper and Brothers, 1887), 92–106.

"Thanksgiving Crossroads," *Woman's Home Companion* 44 (Nov. 1917): 13, 58, 60.

"A Thanksgiving Thief," *Ladies' Home Journal* 9 (Nov. 1892): 1–2.

"The Third Miss Merryweather," *Good Cheer* 3 (Sept. 1884): 7.

"The Three Old Sisters and the Old Beau," *The Love of Parson Lord and Other Stories* (New York: Harper and Brothers, 1900), 185–92.

"Timothy Sampson: The Wise Man," *The People of Our Neighborhood* (Philadelphia: Curtis Publishing Company, 1898), 1–21.

"A Tragedy from the Trivial," *Frank Leslie's Popular Monthly* 50 (Aug. 1900): 334–49; also in *Cornhill* 83, n.s. 10 (Jan. 1901): 63–79.

"The Travelling Sister," *The Winning Lady and Others* (New York: Harper and Brothers, 1909), 175–206.

"The Tree of Knowledge," *The Love of Parson Lord and Other Stories* (New York: Harper and Brothers, 1900), 85–140.

"The Twelfth Guest," *A New England Nun and Other Stories* (New York: Harper and Brothers, 1891), 54–80.

"Two for Peace," *Lippincott's* 68 (July 1901): 51–70.

"Two Friends," *Harper's Bazar* 20 (25 June 1887): 450–51.

"Two Old Lovers," *A Humble Romance and Other Stories* (New York: Harper and Brothers, 1887), 25–36.

"The Umbrella Man," *The Copy-Cat and Other Stories* (New York: Harper and Brothers, 1914), 237–66.

"Uncle Davy," *Detroit Sunday News*, 10 Jan. 1892, p. 10.

"The Underling," *The Fair Lavinia and Others* (New York: Harper and Brothers, 1907), 257–308.

"An Unlucky Christmas," *Harper's Bazar* 29 (12 Dec. 1896): 1037–39.

"An Unwilling Guest," *A Humble Romance and Other Stories* (New York: Harper and Brothers, 1887), 330–49.

"Up Primrose Hill," *A New England Nun and Other Stories* (New York: Harper and Brothers, 1891), 305–20.

"The Vacant Lot," *The Wind in the Rose-Bush and Other Stories of the Supernatural* (New York: Doubleday, Page and Company, 1903), 167–98.

"Value Received," *Edgewater People* (New York: Harper and Brothers, 1918), 74–100.

"A Village Lear," *A New England Nun and Other Stories* (New York: Harper and Brothers, 1891), 268–87.

"A Village Singer," *A New England Nun and Other Stories* (New York: Harper and Brothers, 1891), 18–36.

"The Voice of the Clock," *Edgewater People* (New York: Harper and Brothers, 1918), 51–73.

"A Wandering Samaritan," *Cosmopolitan* 2 (Sept. 1886): 28–33.

"A War-Time Dress," *Cosmopolitan* 25 (Aug. 1898): 403–16.

"A Wayfaring Couple," *A New England Nun and Other Stories* (New York: Harper and Brothers, 1891), 121–39.

"The Whist Players," *Century* 44 (Oct. 1892): 817.

"The White Birch," *Six Trees* (New York: Harper and Brothers, 1903), 41–65.

"The White Shawl," undated MS. Manuscript and Archives Division, New York Public Library.

"The Willow-Ware," *The Fair Lavinia and Others* (New York: Harper and Brothers, 1907), 145–83.

"The Wind in the Rose-Bush," *The Wind in the Rose-Bush and Other Stories of the Supernatural* (New York: Doubleday, Page and Company, 1903), 3–37.

"The Winning Lady," *The Winning Lady and Others* (New York: Harper and Brothers, 1909), 3–32.

"The Witch's Daughter," *Harper's Weekly* 54 (10 Dec. 1910): 17, 32.

"Wrong Side Out," *10 Story Book* 1 (July 1901): 10–16.

Novels, Collections, Plays, Films

This list does not include recent collections of Freeman's works.

An Alabaster Box, [by Mary Wilkins Freeman and Florence Morse Kingsley]. New York: D. Appleton and Company, 1917.

An Alabaster Box. Directed by Chester Withey. Vitagraph Company of America motion picture production, 1917.

The Best Stories of Mary E. Wilkins, ed. Henry Wysham Lanier. New York: Harper and Brothers, 1927.

The Butterfly House. New York: Dodd, Mead and Company, 1912.

By the Light of the Soul. New York: Harper and Brothers, 1907.

The Copy-Cat and Other Stories. New York: Harper and Brothers, 1914.

The Debtor. New York: Harper and Brothers, 1905.

"Doc" Gordon. New York: Authors and Newspapers Association, 1906.

Edgewater People. New York: Harper and Brothers, 1918.

Eglantina: A Romantic Parlor Play. *Ladies' Home Journal* 27 (July 1910): 13–14, 38.

The Fair Lavinia and Others. New York: Harper and Brothers, 1907.

False Evidence (based on *Madelon*). Metro motion picture production, 1919.

Giles Corey, Yeoman: A Play. New York: Harper and Brothers, 1893.

The Givers. New York: Harper and Brothers, 1904.

The Heart's Highway, A Romance of Virginia in the Seventeenth Century. New York: Doubleday, Page and Company, 1900.

A Humble Romance and Other Stories. New York: Harper and Brothers, 1887.

The Jamesons. New York: Doubleday and McClure Company, 1899.

Jane Field. New York: Harper and Brothers, 1893.

Jerome, a Poor Man. New York: Harper and Brothers, 1897.

The Love of Parson Lord and Other Stories. New York: Harper and Brothers, 1900.

Madelon. New York: Harper and Brothers, 1896.

A New England Nun and Other Stories. New York: Harper and Brothers, 1891.

Pembroke. New York: Harper and Brothers, 1894.

The People of Our Neighborhood. Philadelphia: Curtis Publishing Company, 1898.

The Pilgrim's Progress. Adapted to a motion picture play by Mary E. Wilkins and William Dinwiddie. New York, 1915.

The Portion of Labor. New York: Harper and Brothers, 1901.

Red Robin, A New England Drama. Copyrighted in 1892 and 1893 but unlocated. (Cited in Kendrick, 455 n. 1.)

The Shoulders of Atlas. New York: Harper and Brothers, 1908.

Silence and Other Stories. New York: Harper and Brothers, 1898.

Six Trees. New York: Harper and Brothers, 1903.

Understudies. New York: Harper and Brothers, 1901.

The Whole Family: A Novel by Twelve Authors. Mary W. Freeman, William D. Howells, Henry James, et al. New York: Harper and Brothers, 1908.

The Wind in the Rose-Bush and Other Stories of the Supernatural. New York: Doubleday, Page and Company, 1903.

The Winning Lady and Others. New York: Harper and Brothers, 1909.

The Yates Pride: A Romance. New York: Harper and Brothers, 1912.

NONFICTION

"Emily Bronte and *Wuthering Heights.*" In *The World's Great Woman Novelists,* edited by T. M. Parrott, 85–93. (Philadelphia: The Booklovers Library, 1901).

"The Girl Who Wants to Write: Things to Do and to Avoid," *Harper's Bazar* 47 (June 1913): 272.

"Good Wits, Pen and Paper." In *What Women Can Earn: Occupations of Women and Their Compensation,* edited by G. H. Dodge et al., 28–29. (New York: Frederick A. Stokes Co., 1899).

"He Does Not Want a Fool," *The Delineator* 72 (July 1908): 80, 135.

"How I Write My Novels: Twelve of America's Most Popular Authors Reveal the Secrets of Their Art," *New York Times,* 25 Oct. 1908, mag. sec., 3–4.

"If They Had a Million Dollars: What Nine Famous Women Would Do If a Fortune Were Theirs," *Ladies' Home Journal* 20 (Sept. 1903): 10.

"Introductory Sketch" in "Biographical Edition" of *Pembroke* (New York: Harper and Brothers, 1899).

"Mary E. Wilkins." In *My Maiden Effort: Being the Personal Confessions of Well-Known American Authors as to Their Literary Beginnings*, 265–67. (Garden City, N.Y.: Doubleday, Page and Company, 1921).

"Mary E. Wilkins Freeman: An Autobiography" in "Who's Who—and Why: Serious and Frivolous Facts About the Great and the Near Great." *The Saturday Evening Post* 190 (8 Dec. 1917): 25, 75.

"New England, 'Mother of America,'" *Country Life in America* 22 (July 1912): 27–32, 64–67.

"We Are With France." In *For France*, edited by Charles H. Towne, 336. (Garden City, N.Y.: Doubleday, Page and Company, 1917).

"A Woman's Tribute to Mr. Howells," *The Literary Digest* 44 (9 Mar. 1912): 485.

NOTES

Introduction

1. Mary E. Wilkins (Freeman), "The Revolt of 'Mother,'" in *A New England Nun and Other Stories* (New York: Harper and Brothers, 1891), 451–52. Unless otherwise noted, all stories cited hereafter are by Freeman; the dates given for each represent the date of the collection it appeared in, if appropriate, or the date of its original publication if not collected in Freeman's lifetime. Complete information on publication of individual works can be found in the Appendix.

2. Freeman uses this expression several times to describe Maria Edgham, the protagonist in her quasi-autobiographical novel *By the Light of the Soul* (1907).

3. Not counted in this total of separate volumes are those volumes published in Freeman's lifetime which merely duplicate under different titles previously collected Freeman stories; for example, *A Far-Away Melody and Other Stories* (1890) is not included because it is a reprinting of fourteen of the twenty-eight stories appearing previously in *A Humble Romance and Other Stories* (1887). Also not counted are volumes in which one Freeman story appears along with works by other authors: for example, "The Long Arm," which appeared in *The Long Arm and Other Detective Stories* (1895).

4. See Mary R. Reichardt, ed. *Uncollected Stories of Mary Wilkins Freeman* (Jackson: University Press of Mississippi, 1992).

Chapter 1

1. It should be noted that Freeman contradicted herself several years later in a letter to Henry Wysham Lanier, editor of the final collection of short stories issued in her lifetime, *The Best Stories of Mary E. Wilkins*. To Lanier, Freeman wrote with typical self-deprecation that "The Shadow Family" was "a poor imitation of Dickens" (Kendrick, 410).

CHAPTER 2

1. "It is never from anything but a sense of duty that I commence to write," she wrote to Edward Everett Hale in 1875 (Kendrick, 58).

2. See Josephine Donovan, *New England Local Color Literature: A Women's Tradition* (New York: Frederick Ungar, 1983).

3. Many of the local-colorists never married (Alice Brown, Sarah Orne Jewett, and Mary Murfree), were widowed early or were separated from their husbands (Kate Chopin and Celia Thaxter), or married extremely late (Rose Terry Cooke and Freeman).

4. See Ann Douglas's *The Feminization of American Culture* (New York: Alfred A. Knopf, 1977).

CHAPTER 3

1. I am indebted to Alice Glarden Brand for the phrase used in the subtitle of this chapter. It so accurately describes the feeling of near-suffocation many of Freeman's adult children experience while still living at home. She uses it in "Mary Wilkins Freeman: Misanthropy as Propaganda," 83, n. 2.

2. The following novels also contain significant examples of mother-daughter relationships: *Jane Field* (1893) in which a daughter elopes against her mother's will; *Pembroke* (1894) in which a mother discovers her unwed daughter pregnant; *"Doc" Gordon* (1906) in which a daughter feels rivalry with her mother over suitors; and *By the Light of the Soul* (1907) in which after her mother's death a young girl must learn to live with a "cold" stepmother.

3. A full discussion of the dramatic "stages" of the story can be found in Joseph R. McElrath's "The Artistry of Mary E. Wilkins Freeman's 'The Revolt.'"

4. Only a handful of Freeman's stories for adults describe a happy childhood ("The Joy of Youth" [1909], for example) or a contented motherhood ("A Gatherer of Simples" [1887], "Christmas Jenny" [1891], and "The Pumpkin" [1900], for example). In this latter category, a single woman has often adopted the child.

5. Such characterizations of the mother-figure have been studied in the works of other female writers; I mention a few useful sources here. Gilbert and Gubar's *The Madwoman in the Attic* discusses the "monster mother" in Emily Dickinson, the "absent mother" in Jane Austen, and the "witch mother" in Charlotte Bronte. Davidson and Broner's *The Lost Tradition: Mothers and Daughters in Literature* discusses how mothers have been portrayed in both male and female writing throughout history. Its bibliography, in which several Freeman stories are cited, is particularly useful. Smith-

Rosenberg's *Disorderly Conduct* documents the changing values leading to a redefinition of "mother" in the late nineteenth century in two chapters: "The Female World of Love and Ritual: Relations Between Women in Nineteenth-Century America" and "The New Woman as Androgyne: Social Disorder and Gender Crisis, 1870–1936."

6. It should be noted that several of Freeman's mothers are also cruel to their sons over the question of marriage. In "A Wandering Samaritan" (1886), a mother locks her disobedient son in the cellar to prevent him from marrying, and in "The Soldier Man" (1918), a vampirelike mother saps her son's physical energy when he attempts to marry against her will.

CHAPTER 4

1. The subtitle for this chapter is a paraphrase of Sarah Penn's advice to her daughter in "The Revolt of 'Mother.'"

2. The proper clothing for the occasion is extremely important to many of Freeman's female protagonists. Often, it serves as a woman's sole means of self-respect. Odd clothing ostracizes a woman from others and provokes neighborhood gossip (for example, "A Modern Dragon" [1887] and "A War-Time Dress" [1898]); poor clothing shames and humiliates the wearer as well ("A Gala Dress" [1891], for example).

3. Freeman, incidently, was quite fond of animals all of her life. Her letters often go on at length about her various pets, and her experiences with animals figure prominently in such short stories as "An Object of Love" (1887); "Amanda Todd, The Friend of Cats" (1898); "The Cat" and "The Lost Dog," as well as other animal stories in *Understudies* (1901); and "Billy and Susy" (1909).

4. Besides Hamlin Garland's comment on visiting Freeman, see, for example, "A New England Recluse" by Albert Doyle and "A New England Nun" by Willis Boyd Allen. Allen writes about Freeman, "Always unassuming and modest in the exercise of her special gift of ability to record the emotions and aspirations of the 'common people,' herself throughout most of her career a veritable 'New England nun,' she shunned the glare of publicity." Though Freeman remained shy and retiring throughout her life, and though she insisted on turning down many invitations in order to fulfill her demanding work schedule, she was far from being as reclusive as Louisa Ellis in "A New England Nun." Freeman's dislike of being equated with her protagonist may be evinced from a letter written to Florence Morse Kingsley around 1916: "The worst of it [is that] people always expect me to walk out of my own stories and there is an inevitable shock. . . . One of my publishers seemed really a bit indignant because he did not find me attired in my best

black silk and living in New Jersey in these latter days in a little white New England cottage" (Kendrick, 349).

CHAPTER 5

1. Always highly sensitive about her appearance, Freeman was disturbed at the prospect of aging and expresses this anxiety not only in "Sweet-Flowering Perennial" but also in such works as "A Patient Waiter" (1891), "The Three Old Sisters and the Old Beau" (1900), "The Travelling Sister" (1909), and "The Amethyst Comb" (1914). All of these stories involve women protagonists who seek, even desperately, to retain the beauty and vitality of youth. Yet Freeman also acknowledges the folly of such enterprise. "When a man or woman holds fast to youth, even if successfully," her narrator comments in "The Amethyst Comb," "there is something of the pitiful and the tragic involved."

2. Freeman's "society novel," *The Butterfly House* (1912), though largely devoid of plot, is interesting in its satire of such "ladies' clubs." Here, women's relationships are presented in the worst possible light; grasping, petty, and envious, these women compete intensely for social adulation. Evidently, Freeman used Metuchen, New Jersey, the town to which she moved once she had married, as the model for "Fairbridge" and the Quiet Hour club, to which she belonged, as the model for the "Zenith Club."

3. An ardent patriot, Freeman wrote several other stories set in wartime: "The Prop" (1918), "Both Cheeks" (1918), and "The Return" (1921).

4. For a fuller discussion of the possible origin of this story, see Faderman, 292–93.

5. As mentioned earlier, of interest too in considering the effect of Anna Wilkins's death on the Wilkins family is the story "A Gentle Ghost," in which a mother and her surviving daughter are haunted by a dead daughter's spirit (see pages 53–54).

CHAPTER 6

1. This untitled and undated manuscript, Edward Foster indicates, was given him by Mrs. A. B. Mann of Randolph, Massachusetts (206, n. 8). I quote this passage verbatim from Foster's *Mary E. Wilkins Freeman*, 142–43.

2. Of note are similar lines Freeman used in a 1915 letter to Hayden Carruth, editor of *Woman's Home Companion*. Speaking of a photograph of herself which Carruth had admired, Freeman stated, "I have never had a photograph which did not misrepresent me morally as well as physically. . . . I sometimes wonder if I am really in any sense a fixed quantity, rather [I appear] a sort of transparency. There has always been something a little uncanny

about it. . . . I have a frightful conviction that I look capable of nothing except afternoon teas or breaking all the Commandments and sulking because there are no more. My photographs have always looked to me as representing me in one or the other phase" (Kendrick, 347).

3. Although Freeman generally depicts such women as "outsiders," according to the 1885 Randolph, Mass., census single women between the ages of twenty and seventy-nine accounted for nearly one third of the total female population: 329 single women out of a total of 1053 women. In 1885, Freeman was thirty-three years old.

4. See Ann Douglas Wood, "The Literature of Impoverishment: The Women Local Colorists in America, 1865–1914," *Women's Studies* 1 (1972): 25.

5. Freeman's many stories about gift giving and receiving (one of her collections of stories is entitled *The Givers*) are noteworthy, reflecting Carol Gilligan's conclusion in *In a Different Voice* that "the cardinal sin in the ladder of feminine virtue" is that of selfishness (129). If, as Gilligan has stated, a woman's sense of morality (and thus identity as a "good" person) depends on her ability to form and maintain relationships, gift-giving becomes all important as a means of defining and solidifying a woman's affiliations. In Freeman's world, the women most culpable of moral wrongdoing are those who persist in giving the *wrong* gifts; that is, those who do not consider the needs of the person to whom they are giving and rather give only to fulfill their own needs. Stories that develop this theme include "An Unwilling Guest" (1887), "A Mistaken Charity" (1887), "The Revolt of Sophia Lane" (1903), "The Pink Shawls" (1907), and "The Selfishness of Amelia Larkin" (1909).

6. For a full account of the writing of this corporate novel, see Alfred A. Bendixen's "Introduction" to *The Whole Family*.

7. Although neither story involves a solitary woman per se, both "The Bar Light-House" (1887) and "The Balking of Christopher" (1914), two stories that span Freeman's writing career, contain further interesting examples of Freeman's religious views. In the former story, Sarah Reed, a married woman whose father and brother have both been killed at sea, lives a life continually questioning the idea of a loving God. "I ain't never had any evidence, so to speak," she curtly informs the young minister when he calls. "I ain't never had a prayer answered in my life. . . . Ef you call it answerin' a prayer to give one thing when you ask for another, I don't." "The Balking of Christopher," one of Freeman's few stories with a male protagonist, revolves around Christopher's revolt against God. An older married man, he one day simply decides to "give up" life's struggles. "Why did I have to come

into the world without any choice?" he demands of his minister. "I am no free agent. . . . I'm a slave—a slave of life." When not receiving a satisfactory reply, he revolts by isolating himself from friends and family on a mountainside, hoping "to get once, on this earth, my fill of the bread of life." For a sensitive reading of this latter story, see Beth Wynne Fisken, "'Unusual' People in a 'Usual Place': 'The Balking of Christopher' by Mary Wilkins Freeman."

WORKS CITED

Allen, Willis Boyd. "A New England Nun." *Boston Evening Transcript*, 20 Mar. 1930, sec. 2: 3.

"American Academy Honors Two Women." *New York Times*, 24 Apr. 1926, sec. 1: 7.

Auerbach, Nina. *Communities of Women: An Idea in Fiction.* Cambridge, Mass.: Harvard University Press, 1978.

Bachelard, Gaston. *The Poetics of Space.* Boston: Beacon Press, 1969.

Baym, Nina. *Woman's Fiction: A Guide to Novels by and About Women in America, 1820–1870.* Ithaca, N.Y.: Cornell University Press, 1978.

Bendixen, Alfred. "Afterword" to Mary Wilkins Freeman, *The Wind in the Rose-Bush and Other Stories of the Supernatural,* 239–58. Chicago: Academy Chicago, 1986.

———. "Introduction" to Mary Wilkins Freeman et al, *The Whole Family: A Novel by Twelve Authors,* xi–li. New York: Ungar Press, 1987.

Brand, Alice Glarden. "Mary Wilkins Freeman: Misanthropy as Propaganda." *New England Quarterly* 50 (Mar. 1977): 83–100.

Brooks, Van Wyck. *New England: Indian Summer, 1865–1915.* New York: E. P. Dutton, 1940.

———. *Three Essays on America.* New York: E. P. Dutton, 1934.

Brownmiller, Susan. *Femininity.* New York: Simon and Schuster, 1984.

Chamberlin, Joseph Edgar. "Authors at Home: Miss Mary E. Wilkins at Randolph, Mass." *The Critic* 32 (5 Mar. 1898): 155–57.

Chodorow, Nancy. *The Reproduction of Mothering: Psychoanalysis and the Sociology of Gender.* Berkeley: University of California Press, 1978.

Clark, Michele. "Afterword" to Mary Wilkins Freeman, *"The Revolt of 'Mother' " and Other Stories,* 165–201. New York: Feminist Press, 1974.

Courtney, William L. "Miss Mary Wilkins." In *The Feminine Note in Fiction,* 199–224. London: Chapman and Hall, 1904.

Cowley, Malcolm, ed. *After the Genteel Tradition: American Writers Since 1910*. New York: W. W. Norton, 1937.

Crowley, John W. "Freeman's Yankee Tragedy: 'Amanda and Love.'" *Markham Review* 5 (Spring 1976): 58–60.

Davidson, Cathy N., and E. M. Broner, eds. *The Lost Tradition: Mothers and Daughters in Literature*. New York: Frederick Ungar, 1980.

Donovan, Josephine. *New England Local Color Literature: A Women's Tradition*. New York: Frederick Ungar, 1983.

Douglas, Ann. *The Feminization of American Culture*. New York: Alfred A. Knopf, 1977.

Doyle, Albert. "A New England Recluse." *Donahoe's Magazine* 35 (Mar. 1896): 286–89.

DuPlessis, Rachel Blau. *Writing Beyond the Ending: Narrative Strategies of Twentieth-Century Women Writers*. Bloomington: Indiana University Press, 1985.

Faderman, Lillian. *Surpassing the Love of Men: Romantic Friendship and Love Between Women from the Renaissance to the Present*. New York: William Morrow and Co., 1981.

Fischer, Lucy Rose. *Linked Lives: Adult Daughters and Their Mothers*. New York: Harper and Row, 1986.

Fisken, Beth Wynne. "'Unusual' People in a 'Usual Place': 'The Balking of Christopher' by Mary Wilkins Freeman." *Colby Library Quarterly* 21 (June 1985): 99–103.

Foster, Edward. *Mary E. Wilkins Freeman*. New York: Hendricks House, 1956.

Gallagher, Edward J. "Freeman's 'The Revolt of 'Mother.'" *The Explicator* 27 (Mar. 1969): 1–2.

Gardiner, Judith Kegan. "On Female Identity and Writing by Women." In *Writing and Sexual Difference*, edited by Elizabeth Abel, 177–91. University of Chicago Press, 1982.

Garland, Hamlin. *Hamlin Garland's Diaries*. Edited by Donald Pizer. San Marino, Cal.: Huntington Library, 1968.

———. *Roadside Meetings*. New York: Macmillan, 1930.

Gilbert, Sandra M., and Susan Gubar. *The Madwoman in the Attic: The Woman Writer and the Nineteenth-Century Literary Imagination*. New Haven, Conn.: Yale University Press, 1979.

Gilligan, Carol. *In a Different Voice: Psychological Theory and Women's Development*. Cambridge, Mass.: Harvard University Press, 1982.

Glasser, Leah Blatt. "Mary E. Wilkins Freeman; The Stranger in the Mirror." *Massachusetts Review* 25 (Summer 1984): 323–39.

———. "'She Is the One You Call Sister': Discovering Mary Wilkins Freeman." In *Between Women: Biographers, Novelists, Critics, Teachers, and Artists Write About Their Work on Women*, edited by Carol Ascher et al., 186–211. Boston: Beacon Press, 1984.

Hamblen, Abigail Ann. *The New England Art of Mary E. Wilkins Freeman*. Amherst, Mass.: Green Knight Press, 1966.

Hartt, Rollin Lynde. "A New England Hill Town." *Atlantic Monthly* 83 (Apr. 1899): 561–74; (May 1899): 712–20.

Hawthorne, Nathaniel. "Ethan Brand." In *The Celestial Railroad and Other Stories*, 271–87. New York: Signet, 1963.

Hirsch, David H. "Subdued Meaning in 'A New England Nun.'" *Studies in Short Fiction* 2 (Spring 1965): 124–36.

Howells, William Dean. *Criticism and Fiction*. New York: Harper and Brothers, 1891.

———. "Editor's Study." *Harper's New Monthly* 75 (Sept. 1887): 638–42.

Kendrick, Brent L., ed. *The Infant Sphinx: Collected Letters of Mary E. Wilkins Freeman*. Metuchen, N.J.: Scarecrow Press, 1985.

Machen, Arthur. *Hieroglyphics: A Note Upon Ecstasy in Literature*. New York: Alfred A. Knopf, 1923.

McClave, Heather. *Women Writers of the Short Story*. Englewood Cliffs, N.J.: Prentice Hall, 1980.

McElrath, Joseph R. "The Artistry of Mary E. Wilkins Freeman's 'The Revolt.'" *Studies in Short Fiction* 17 (Summer 1980): 255–61.

McNaron, Toni A. H., ed. *The Sister Bond: A Feminist View of a Timeless Connection*. New York: Pergamon Press, 1985.

Macy, John. "The Passing of the Yankee." *The Bookman* (New York) 73 (August 1931): 616–21.

"Mary E. Wilkins." *The Bookman* (London) 1 (1 Dec. 1891): 102–3.

Matthiessen, F. O. "New England Stories." In *American Writers on American Literature*, edited by John Macy, 399–413. New York: Horace Liveright, Inc., 1931.

More, Paul Elmer. "Hawthorne: Looking Before and After." In *Shelburne Essays*, 2nd series, 173–87. Boston: Houghton Mifflin, 1905.

Norris, Frank. *The Responsibilities of the Novelist and Other Literary Essays*. New York: Doubleday, Page, and Co., 1903.

"Notes." *The Critic* 14 (23 Aug. 1890): 101.

Overton, Grant. "Mary E. Wilkins Freeman." In *The Women Who Make Our Novels*, 198–203. New York: Moffat, Yard, and Co., 1919.

Pattee, Fred Lewis. "On the Terminal Moraine of New England Puritanism." In *Sidelights on American Literature*, 175–209. New York: D. Appleton-Century, 1922.

Preston, George. "Concerning Good English." *The Bookman* (New York) 3 (1896): 358–62.

Pryse, Marjorie. "Afterword" to *Selected Stories of Mary E. Wilkins Freeman*, 315–42. New York: W. W. Norton, 1983.

———. "An Uncloistered 'New England Nun.'" *Studies in Short Fiction* 20 (Fall 1983): 289–95.

Reichardt, Mary R., ed. *Uncollected Short Stories of Mary Wilkins Freeman*. Jackson: University Press of Mississippi, 1992.

Scudder, Horace. "New England in the Short Story." *Atlantic Monthly* 67 (June 1891): 845–50.

Smith, Minna C. "Mary Wilkins at Home." *Boston Evening Transcript,* 12 June 1890, p. 4.

Smith-Rosenberg, Carroll. *Disorderly Conduct: Visions of Gender in Victorian America.* New York: Alfred A. Knopf, 1985.

Spacks, Patricia Meyer. *Gossip.* University of Chicago Press, 1986.

Thompson, Charles Miner. "Miss Wilkins: An Idealist in Masquerade." *Atlantic Monthly* 83 (May 1899): 665–75.

Toth, Susan Allen. "Defiant Light: A Positive View of Mary Wilkins Freeman." *New England Quarterly* 46 (Mar. 1973): 82–93.

———. "Mary Wilkins Freeman's Parable of Wasted Life." *American Literature* 42 (Jan. 1971): 564–67.

Tutwiler, Julia R. "Two New England Writers—In Relation to Their Art and to Each Other." *Gunton's Magazine* 25 (Nov. 1903): 419–25.

Wardwell, Mary E. "About Miss Wilkins." *The Citizen* 4 (Apr. 1898): 27–28.

Warner, Sylvia Townsend. "Item, One Empty House." *New Yorker* 42 (26 Mar. 1966): 131–38.

Westbrook, Perry D. *Acres of Flint: Writers of Rural New England, 1870–1900.* Washington, D.C.: Scarecrow Press, 1951.

Williams, Blanche C. "Mary Wilkins Freeman." In *Our Short Story Writers*, 160–81. New York: Moffat, Yard, and Co., 1920.

Wood, Ann Douglas. "The Literature of Impoverishment: The Women Local Colorists in America 1865–1914." *Women's Studies* 1 (1972): 3–40.

INDEX

Alcott, Louisa May, 44
Alden, Henry Mills, 10, 13, 46, 151
Auerbach, Nina, 44, 69, 86
American Academy of Arts and Letters, 15, 16
"American Academy Honors Two Women," 11
Atlantic Monthly, 20, 21, 56
Austen, Jane, 69, 86, 134–35, 136

Bacheller Syndicate, 109
Baym, Nina, 22
Bendixen, Alfred, 59, 134
Bookman, 16
Booth, Mary Louise, 10, 13, 18, 19, 46, 76, 93, 105, 106
"Boston marriage," 104
Boston Sunday Budget, 10
Brand, Alice Glarden, 57, 75
Brattleboro Retreat, 8
Brattleboro, Vermont, 7, 8, 9, 11, 12, 16, 26, 46, 76, 105, 112, 113
Brooks, Van Wyck, 33, 40
Brown, Alice, 23, 133
Brownmiller, Susan, 6

Carruth, Hayden, 139
Cary, Alice, 23
Century Magazine (Scribner's Monthly), 12, 21
Chamberlin, Joseph Edgar, 35, 109
Chodorow, Nancy, 62, 103

Chopin, Kate, 21
Clark, Kate Upson, 13, 105, 129, 130
Clark, Michele, 77, 78, 102, 110
Clemens, Samuel (Mark Twain), 21, 24, 26, 27
Collier's Magazine, 138
Cooke, Rose Terry, 21, 23, 24, 26, 29, 32
Courtney, William L., 29
Cowley, Malcolm, 40
Crane, Stephen, 40
Crowley, John W., 117

Davis, Rebecca Harding, 20
Deland, Margaret, 16
Detroit Free Press, 19
Dickens, Charles, 10, 35, 87
Donovan, Josephine, 62, 110
Douglas, Ann, 40. See also Wood, Ann Douglas
Dreiser, Theodore, 40
DuPlessis, Rachel Blau, 22

Evans, Augusta, 23
Everybody's, 99

Faderman, Lillian, 103
Fischer, Lucy Rose, 71
Foster, Edward, 4, 5, 8, 9, 10, 11, 14, 35, 45, 46, 76, 105, 110, 112, 131
Freeman, Charles Manning, 9, 10, 13–15, 35, 46–47, 77, 94, 97, 110